Inside Java™ 2
Platform Security

The Java™ Series

Lisa Friendly, Series Editor
Tim Lindholm, Technical Editor
Please see our web site (http://www.awl.com /cseng/javaseries) for more information on these titles.

Ken Arnold and James Gosling, *The Java™ Programming Language, Second Edition*
ISBN 0-201-31006-6

Mary Campione and Kathy Walrath, *The Java™ Tutorial, Second Edition: Object-Oriented Programming for the Internet* (Book/CD)
ISBN 0-201-31007-4

Mary Campione, Kathy Walrath, Alison Huml, and the Tutorial Team, *The Java™ Tutorial Continued: The Rest of the JDK™* (Book/CD)
ISBN 0-201-48558-3

Patrick Chan, *The Java™ Developers Almanac 1999*
ISBN 0-201-43298-6

Patrick Chan and Rosanna Lee, *The Java™ Class Libraries, Second Edition, Volume 2: java.applet, java.awt, java.beans*
ISBN 0-201-31003-1

Patrick Chan, Rosanna Lee, and Doug Kramer, *The Java™ Class Libraries, Second Edition, Volume 1: java.io, java.lang, java.math, java.net, java.text, java.util*
ISBN 0-201-31002-3

Patrick Chan, Rosanna Lee, and Doug Kramer, *The Java™ Class Libraries, Second Edition, Volume 1: Supplement for the Java™ 2 Platform, Standard Edition, v1.2*
ISBN 0-201-48552-4

Li Gong, *Inside the Java™ 2 Platform Security Architecture: Cryptography, APIs, and Implementation*
ISBN 0-201-31000-7

James Gosling, Bill Joy, and Guy Steele, *The Java™ Language Specification*
ISBN 0-201-63451-1

James Gosling, Frank Yellin, and The Java Team, *The Java™ Application Programming Interface, Volume 1: Core Packages*
ISBN 0-201-63453-8

James Gosling, Frank Yellin, and The Java Team, *The Java™ Application Programming Interface, Volume 2: Window Toolkit and Applets*
ISBN 0-201-63459-7

Jonni Kanerva, *The Java™ FAQ*
ISBN 0-201-63456-2

Doug Lea, *Concurrent Programming in Java™: Design Principles and Patterns*
ISBN 0-201-69581-2

Sheng Liang, *The Java™ Native Interface: Programmer's Guide and Specification*
ISBN 0-201-32577-2

Tim Lindholm and Frank Yellin, *The Java™ Virtual Machine Specification, Second Edition*
ISBN 0-201-43294-3

Henry Sowizral, Kevin Rushforth, and Michael Deering, *The Java™ 3D API Specification*
ISBN 0-201-32576-4

Kathy Walrath and Mary Campione, *The JFC Swing Tutorial: A Guide to Constructing GUIs*
ISBN 0-201-43321-4

Seth White, Maydene Fisher, Rick Cattell, Graham Hamilton, and Mark Hapner, *JDBC™ API Tutorial and Reference, Second Edition: Universal Data Access for the Java™ 2 Platform*
ISBN 0-201-43328-1

Inside Java™ 2
Platform Security

Architecture, API Design, and Implementation

Li Gong

ADDISON-WESLEY

An imprint of Addison Wesley Longman, Inc.

Reading, Massachusetts • Harlow, England • Menlo Park, California
Berkeley, California • Don Mills, Ontario • Sydney
Bonn • Amsterdam • Tokyo • Mexico City

The publisher offers discounts on this book when ordered in quantity for special sales. For more information, please contact: Corporate, Government and Special Sales; Addison Wesley Longman, Inc.; One Jacob Way; Reading, Massachusetts 01867.

ISBN: 0-201-31000-7
1 2 3 4 5 6 7 8 9-CRS-0302010099
First Printing, June 1999

Contents

Preface

Give me a lever and a fulcrum, and I can move the globe.
—Archimedes

Since Java technology's inception, and especially its public debut in the spring of 1995, strong and growing interest has developed regarding the security of the Java platform, as well as new security issues raised by the deployment of Java technology. This level of attention to security is a fairly new phenomenon in computing history. Most new computing technologies tend to ignore security considerations when they emerge initially, and most are never made more secure thereafter. Attempts made to do so typically are not very successful, as it is now well known that retrofitting security is usually very difficult, if not impossible, and often causes backward compatibility problems.

Thus it is extremely fortunate that when Java technology burst on the Internet scene, security was one of its primary design goals. Its initial security model, although very simplistic, served as a great starting place, an Archimedean fulcrum. The engineering talents and strong management team at JavaSoft are the lever; together they made Java's extensive security architecture a reality.

From a technology provider's point of view, security on the Java platform focuses on two aspects. The first is to provide the Java platform, primarily through the Java Development Kit, as a secure, platform on which to run Java-enabled applications in a secure fashion. The second is to provide security tools and services implemented in the Java programming language that enable a wider range of security-sensitive applications, for example, in the enterprise world.

I wrote this book with many purposes in mind. First, I wanted to equip the reader with a brief but clear understanding of the overall picture of systems and network security, especially in the context of the Internet environment within which Java technology plays a central role, and how various security technologies relate to each other.

Second, I wanted to provide a comprehensive description of the current security architecture on the Java platform. This includes language features, platform APIs, security policies, and their enforcement mechanisms. Whenever appropriate, I discuss not only how a feature functions, but also why it is designed in such a way and the alternative approaches that we—the Java security development team at Sun Microsystems—examined and rejected. When demonstrating the use of a class or its methods, I use real-world code examples whenever appropriate. Some of these examples are synthesized from the JDK 1.2 code source tree.

Third, I sought to tell the reader about security deployment issues, both how an individual or an enterprise manages security and how to customize, extend, and enrich the existing security architecture.

Finally, I wanted to help developers avoid programming errors by discussing a number of common mistakes and by providing tips for safe programming that can be immediately applied to ongoing projects.

How This Book Is Organized

This book is organized as follows.

Chapter 1. A general background on computer, network, and information security

Chapter 2. A review of the original Java security model, the *sandbox*

Chapter 3. An in-depth look at the new security architecture in JDK 1.2, which is policy-driven and capable of enforcing fine-grained access controls

Chapter 4. An explanation of how to deploy and utilize the new security features in JDK 1.2, including security policy management, digital certificates, and various security tools

Chapter 5. A demonstration of how to customize various aspects of the security architecture, including how to move legacy security code onto the JDK 1.2 platform

Chapter 6. A review of techniques to make objects secure and tips for safe programming

Chapter 7. An outline of the Java cryptography architecture along with usage examples

Chapter 8. A look ahead to future directions for Java security

This book is primarily for serious Java programmers and for security professionals who want to understand Java security issues both from a macro (architectural) point of view as well as from a micro (design and implementation) perspective. It is also suitable for nonexperts who are concerned about Internet security as a whole, as this book clears up a number of misconceptions around Java security.

Throughout this book, I assume that the reader is familiar with the fundamentals of the Java language. For those who want to learn more about that language, the book by Arnold and Gosling [2] is a good source.

This book is not a complete API specification. For such details, please refer to JDK 1.2 documentation.

Acknowledgments

It is a cliche to say that writing a book is not possible without the help of many others, but it is true. I am very grateful to Dick Neiss, my manager at JavaSoft, who encouraged me to write the book and regularly checked on my progress. Lisa Friendly, the Addison-Wesley Java series editor, helped by guiding me through the writing process while maintaining a constant but "friendly" pressure. The team at Addison-Wesley was tremendously helpful. I'd like particularly to thank Mike Hendrickson, Katherine Kwack, Marina Lang, Laura Michaels, Marty Rabinowitz, and Tracy Russ. They are always encouraging, kept faith in me, and rescued me whenever I encountered obstacles.

This book is centered around JDK 1.2 security development, a project that lasted fully two years, during which many people inside and outside of Sun Microsystems contributed in one way or another to the design, implementation, testing, and documentation of the final product. I would like to acknowledge Dirk Balfanz, Bob Blakley, Josh Bloch, David Bowen, Gilad Bracha, David Brownell, Eric Chu, David Connelly, Mary Dageforde, Drew Dean, Satya Dodda, Michal Geva, Gadi Guy, Graham Hamilton, Mimi Hills, Larry Koved, Charlie Lai, Sheng Liang, Tim Lindholm, Jan Luehe, Gary McGraw, Marianne Mueller, Tony Nadalin, Don Neal, Jeff Nisewanger, Yu-Ching Peng, Hemma Prafullchandra, Benjamin Renaud, Roger Riggs, Jim Roskind, Nakul Saraiya, Roland Schemers, Bill Shannon, Tom van Vleck, Dan Wallach, and Frank Yellin. I also appreciate the technical guidance from James Gosling and Jim Mitchell, as well as management support from Dick Neiss, Jon Kannegaard, and Alan Baratz. I have had the pleasure of chairing the Java Security Advisory Council, and I thank the external members, Ed Felten, Peter Neumann, Jerome Saltzer, Fred Schneider, and Michael Schroeder for their participation and superb insights into all matters that relate to computer security.

Isabel Cho, Lisa Friendly, Charlie Lai, Jan Luehe, Teresa Lunt, Laura Michaels, Stephen Northcutt, Peter Neumann, and a number of anonymous reviewers provided valuable comments on draft versions of this book.

G. H. Hardy once said that young men should prove theorems, while old men should write books. It is now time to prove some more theorems.

Li Gong
Los Altos, California
June 1999

CHAPTER 1

Computer and Network Security Fundamentals

The three golden rules to ensure computer security are: do not own a computer; do not power it on; and do not use it.
—Robert (Bob) T. Morris

Security is all about ensuring that bad things do not happen. This brief statement is deceptively simple. It can in fact have very complicated interpretations. Exploring these can help in understanding what security really means.

Certain "rule-of-thumb" principles apply to the concept of security in general. First, security is always related to utility. To ensure that bad things do not happen, you can simply do nothing. For example, a car stored in a garage cannot cause a traffic accident. But doing nothing with the car is clearly not what is intended. The real goal is to ensure that bad things do not happen while good things do get done.

Second, security is relative to the threat that one considers. For example, the effectiveness of your house's securely locked front door to prevent theft depends heavily on the types of thieves against which you are guarding. While the lock might deter a small-time thief, it might not pose a problem for a sophisticated one equipped with the right tools.

Third, security must be considered from an overall systems point of view. It is only as secure as the system's weakest point. That is, it is not enough to just secure the front door. A smart thief will try to enter the house from all potentially weak spots, and in particular those furthest away from where you have installed strong locks.

Fourth, security must be easy to accomplish. If it takes 30 minutes and great effort every time to unlock a complicated lock, you will tend to ignore the lock and leave the door open.

Fifth, security must be affordable and cost effective. For example, it clearly does not make sense to install a lock that is worth more than the contents it is guarding. This is made more complex by the fact that different people tend to value things differently.

Last but not least, security must be as simple as possible because, as experience indicates, the more complex a system is, the more error-prone it tends to be. It is better to have something that is simpler but more dependable.

Throughout this book, you will see that these "rule-of-thumb" principles apply equally well to computer security.

1.1   Cryptography versus Computer Security

Before moving on to specific topics, I want to clarify that *cryptography* and *computer security* are two distinct subjects. **Cryptography** is the art of encoding information in a secret format such that only the intended recipient can access the encoded information. The use of cryptography has progressed extensively over a long period of time, ranging from the ancient Caesar cipher, to cipher machines widely used in World War II, to modern cryptosystems implemented with computer hardware and software.

Computer security first became an issue only in the 1960s, when timesharing, multiuser computer (operating) systems were first built, such as Cambridge's early computing system [80] and MIT's Multics [69, newref 1]. After that, the field of computer security remained relatively obscure for years, apart from a brief active period in the mid-1970s [3, 32, 36, 75, newref 2, newref 3]. Security concerns then were based mostly on military requirements. Commercial security did not become fully mainstream until the Internet and electronic commerce (e-commerce), and Java technology in particular, took center stage in the 1990s.

Security mechanisms often can benefit from the use of cryptography, such as when running a network-based user login protocol. However, they do not necessarily depend on the use of cryptography, such as when implementing UNIX-style access control on files.

Yet cryptography does not exist in a vacuum. Cryptographic algorithms are usually implemented in software or hardware; thus their correct operation depends critically on whether there is an adequate level of system security. For example, if lack of access control means that an attacker can modify the software that implements the algorithm, then the lack of security directly impacts the utilization of cryptography.

1.2   Threats and Protection

In computer security literature, threats or attacks are usually classified into three categories.

1. **Secrecy attacks**. The attacker attempts to steal confidential information, such as passwords, medical records, electronic mail (e-mail) logs, and payroll data. The methods of attack vary, from bribing a security guard to exploiting a security hole in the system or a weakness in a cryptographic algorithm.

2. **Integrity attacks**. The attacker attempts to illegally alter parts of the system. For example, a bank employee modifies the deposit system to transfer customer money into his own account, thus compromising transaction integrity [61]. Or, a college student breaks into the college administration system to raise her examination scores, thus compromising data integrity. An attacker might also try to erase system logs in order to hide his footprint.

3. **Availability attacks**. The attacker attempts to disrupt the normal operation of a system. These are also commonly called *denial-of-service attacks*. For example, bombarding a machine with a large number of IP packets can effectively isolate the machine from the rest of the network. A cyber terrorist might attempt to bring down the national power grid or cause traffic accidents by compromising the computer-operated control systems.

These three categories of attacks are intricately related; that is, the techniques and results of attacks in one category can often be used to assist attacks in another. For example, by compromising secrecy an attacker could obtain passwords and thus compromise integrity by gaining access to and then modifying system resources, which in turn could lead to successful denial-of-service attacks. When a system failure occurs during an attack, most systems do not *fail safe*—that is, enter into a state that is deemed secure—because they are not designed to do so. For example, it has been shown that a system crash sometimes leads to a core dump in a publicly readable directory, where the core can contain sensitive information if the dump occurs at the right time.[1]

Similarly, protection mechanisms against these types of attacks in general are related. Roughly speaking, the mechanisms are for one or more of the following

---

[1] Of course, attacks can be viewed from other perspectives. For example, there is widespread public concern regarding the privacy of the unregulated and sometimes illegal collection and distribution of personal data, such as birth dates and U.S. Social Security Numbers.

purposes: attack prevention, detection, or recovery. Not all of these purposes can be fulfilled by the same mechanisms, as explained later in this chapter.

To protect data secrecy, you can store the data in an obscure place in the hope that attackers will not find it. Or you can install strict access control procedures to guard against unauthorized access. Or you can use encryption technology to encrypt the data such that attackers cannot access real data unless they can break the cryptosystem, which could be extremely hard, or they can steal the encryption key. Of course, multiple measures can be deployed at the same time. Note that, for secrecy, the most important technique is prevention. A loss of data is very hard to detect, and lost data are impossible to recover.

To protect data integrity, once again you can use any or all of the mechanisms mentioned previously. However, in this case, detection is easier and recovery is often possible. For example, for a file x, you could compute its hash value using a well-known one-way function $f()$ and store $f(x)$ separately. Now, if x is then modified to be x', $f(x)$ very likely will not be equal to $f(x')$, according to the properties of $f()$. Thus you can recompute the hash value and compare it with $f(x)$. A mismatch will indicate that integrity has been compromised.

Of course, if the corresponding $f(x)$ is also compromised, detection might not be possible. If the place to store $f(x)$ itself is not safe, you could use a keyed, one-way hash function and store $f(k, x)$ together with x. If k is kept secret, then it will still be difficult for attackers to modify x and the hash value in such a way as to avoid detection [22, 52].

To be able to restore the data to its original form after an integrity compromise, you can back up data and store the backup in a secure place [61]. Or you can use more-complicated distributed computing techniques to back up the data in an insecure network [34, 64, 73, 77].

Guarding against an availability attack is more complicated. This is because apart from applying the usual techniques of prevention and detection, surviving such attacks becomes critical. Here, computer security meets the field of fault-tolerant computing. Some interesting research results in this combined topic area, sometimes called *dependable systems*, are available. For further reading, consult the papers and their citations at [12, 24, 65, 73].

1.3   Perimeter Defense

Because of the multitude of potential weaknesses and the essentially unlimited number of attack scenarios, where each scenario can be a combination of various attack techniques, securing an entire system can be daunting, especially when the system includes multiple host machines connected via a network. Because a system is only as secure as its weakest link, the security coverage must be comprehensive. The task is further complicated by the fact that a system, for example the internal network deployed within a large enterprise, typically consists of machines of numerous different brands and types. These machines run different operating systems and different application software and are connected together with routers and other networking gears from various vendors offering different features and capabilities. In such a heterogeneous and evolving environment, examining the entire system and securing all of its components takes a long time if possible at all.

Faced with such a messy picture, it is no surprise that companies find it easier, both psychologically and physically, to simply divide the world into two camps, "Us" and "Them." Us includes all machines owned, operated, or in general trusted by the concerned enterprise, while Them includes all other machines, which are potentially hostile and cannot be trusted. Once the border is drawn, it is a matter of keeping Them out and Us in. Such a defensive posture is often called **perimeter defense**.

One approach to constructing a perimeter defense is simply not to connect Us with Them. Indeed, some military installations and commercial entities have internal networks that are entirely separated from the wider area network, the Internet. They might allow some isolated terminals or machines for outside connections, but these special machines are usually guarded to prevent their being connected to the internal network.

If the overall system contains machines scattered among different physical or geographical locations, leased lines or dedicated network connections can link the sites to form a private network.

If, however, the sites must communicate through the open network, then encryption can be deployed between every two communicating sites so that these sites form a virtual private network (VPN). This is depicted in the fictitious scenario in Figure 1.1, where, although all four campuses are connected to the Internet, three sites (MIT, UT Austin, and UCLA) form a VPN so that network traffic between them is automatically protected from eavesdropping from Stanford.

However, such total isolation from the outside does not always work well. For example, e-mail has become the "killer application" of the Internet as people increasingly demand the ability to communicate with the outside world via the Internet. The World Wide Web (Web) has made the Internet even more popular, and browsing the Web to locate information is important to productivity (if used judiciously, of course). These trends are driving previously closed enterprises to selectively open up their border control. Here is where firewalls play a critical role in constructing a more useful perimeter defense.

1.3.1   Firewalls

Firewalls come in different shapes and sizes [6]. Generally speaking, a **firewall** is a machine sitting between a private network and a public one. It functions as a filter for network traffic, with the responsibility of selectively allowing certain traffic through, in each direction, based on a security policy. A security policy can be very simple or quite complicated. This is because, often, filtering decisions are based on, for example, the source and destination of the traffic, the protocols used, and the applications involved, among others factors. The firewall also might redirect traffic, act as a proxy server, or even manipulate the traffic content before allowing it to pass through. It further might also encrypt traffic—indeed, encrypting firewalls can be used to form a VPN.

Perimeter defense as implemented by firewalls has been shown to be an effective security solution. A firewall provides a central point of control, where a corporate policy can be more easily implemented and updated. But it has certain problems. First of all, firewalls cannot filter or stop all network traffic. In fact, traffic for protocols such as HTTP is often deliberately let through firewalls. Generally, there is tension between the firewall and mobile code, because the former attempts to block or reduce incoming traffic, including that concerning what the latter is trying to achieve. A firewall can also be a bottleneck and a single point of communication failure for a large enterprise. Moreover, many applications on the desktop have to be rewritten to use the firewall as a proxy. This problem is less severe for new applications, which often have built-in proxy support.

1.3.2   Inadequacies of Perimeter Defense Alone

Perimeter defense alone is not sufficient, however, as a total security solution, for several reasons. Locating and securing all perimeter points are quite difficult. For example, in reported cases, direct telephone line-based connections are established (for example, for diagnostic purposes) that can effectively puncture the perimeter defense [61]. Further, when an enterprise supports allows its employees to work remotely and from home, inspecting and ensuring that those remote points of the internal network are adequately protected are impractical.

Even within an enterprise, controls are needed because not everything or everyone can be fully trusted. The most devastating attacks often occur from within. Such insider attacks usually incur comparatively large losses because insiders have a significant advantage over external hackers. For example, the accounting department must be protected so that only authorized employees may issue purchase orders, while the patent department must be isolated to prevent information leaks to competitors.

The remainder of this chapter reviews security models and techniques that are useful both within the perimeter and across organizational boundaries.

1.4   Access Control and Security Models

A **security model** is an abstraction of how one goes about controlling access to protected data. Like firewalls, security models come in various shapes and sizes because requirements can differ vastly for different applications and their environments. Multiple ways to classify security models are available, including the following:

♦ MAC and DAC models

♦ Data and information security models

♦ Static and dynamic models

1.4.1   MAC and DAC Models

One classification of security models centers on the concept of *mandatory access control*, or MAC. In a MAC security model, entities within a system are either subjects (roughly corresponding to the notions of users, processes, machines, and so on) or objects (roughly corresponding to the targets of control, such as files and data records). Each entity is assigned a sensitivity level. Such levels normally form a lattice over a "dominate" relationship so that, for example, if there are two levels, then either one dominates the other or the two are incompatible. For example, levels of "unclassified," "classified," "secret," and "top-secret" could have the dominate relationship shown in Figure 1.1.

MAC models meeting the requirements of multilevel security are exemplified by the work of Bell and LaPadula [3] in which is described a mathematical model for the security of the Multics system [69]. In the Bell-LaPadula model, a subject may have read access to an object if, and only if, its level dominates that of the object and may have write access to an object if, and only if, its level is dominated by that of the object. This is called informally *read-down* and *write-down,* or more precisely, no *read-up* and no *write-down.* Note that according to this model, two entities may communicate in both directions only when either they are at the same level or they do so via a trusted intermediary.

Non-MAC models are called *discretionary access control,* or DAC, models. The UNIX security model is similar to a DAC model in that the owner (user) of each file can determine who else can access it by setting the file's permission bits. Someone who can read a file can also make a copy of it and then let everyone read it. MAC models do not permit such discretionary decisions.

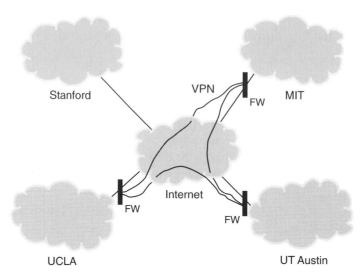

Figure 1.1   MAC security model.

1.4.2   Access to Data and Information

So far the discussion of access control has focused on models that specify explicit access to data, such as directly reading the content of a file stored on the file system. However, information can be transmitted implicitly, as experiences of human life can testify. In particular, cooperating parties can communicate through so-called *covert channels*, as compared to *overt channels*. For example, if two parties share the same disk partition and one party fills the disk to its full capacity, then the other party can notice this fact when a new file creation fails due to lack of space. By filling or not filling the disk, one party can transmit a "one" or a "zero" to the other party.

Investigation of this scenario began with Lampson's paper on the confinement problem [43]. In that paper, Lampson discussed the difficulty of restricting an application so that it cannot affect the outside world either directly or by transmitting information.

How critical this type of attack is hinges on the level of one's fear of infiltration by the enemy and on the perceived potential for severe damage that an insider can cause. The mode of insider attack has a long tradition. The fall of Troy eventually led to the term **Trojan horse**, which in the computer security field means any program that is planted on one's machine for the purpose of causing harm. (The premier computer security conference, the IEEE Symposium on Security and Privacy, has used a Trojan horse illustration on the cover of its proceedings.) Recent examples of such infiltrations are the several high-level U.S. government officials and employees convicted for leaking national secrets to foreign agents.

Early research into the confinement problem led to security models that are based on information flow instead of data access. In particular, the models put forward by Goguen and Meseguer served as the basis for extensive theory work in this area [18, 19]. Also, practical studies of covert-channel communication in real systems have been done. For example, a team at Digital Equipment Corporation constructed a case study in which two parties share the same disk. By placing files in strategic locations, one party can selectively read one file or another, which will cause a detectable delay when another party tries to read a third file. The delay is due to the speed of the disk-arm movement, and the two different delay values can be interpreted as 1 and 0. The value of such practical studies is mostly in determining the capacity, and therefore the usability and threat, of covert channels. For example, the disk-arm covert channel is usually a lot faster than the fill-up-disk-partition covert channel.

Note that the practical utility of covert channels is difficult to gauge. First, there is always the possibility of noise. For example, in the disk-arm case a third party independently accessing various files on the disk could significantly reduce the bandwidth of the covert channel. However, for very secret materials, such as cryptographic keys, a slow covert channel is adequate for leaking those secrets. Second, covert channels are exploitable only when one can plant Trojan horse programs. When such penetration occurs, other forms of communication that are easier to exploit are often possible.

Moreover, defense against covert channels is effective only "within the system." For example, a computer system that does not allow an insider to signal to the outside world cannot prevent the insider from memorizing the secrets and walking out with them. Nevertheless, some organizations, especially the U.S. government, take covert channels seriously. For example, researchers at the Naval Research Laboratory have been developing an extensive system called the "Pump" for the sole purpose of transmitting information with no or limited leakage of information through covert channels. The Java Development Kit (JDK) 1.2 does not comprehensively address the presence of covert channels.

1.4.3 Static versus Dynamic Models

At first glance, a security policy appears static. For example, an employee either can or cannot read file A. There is no third way, and that is that. In reality, security policies are dynamic—they can change over time. When that employee transfers into a different department in the organization, she might then be given access to a file to which she was previously denied access. In the MAC model, the sensitivity level of the data and the clearance level of people can also change. A datum can be upgraded or downgraded, or a person might gain or lose a particular level of security clearance.

Several notable security models exhibit this dynamism. One is the High-Watermark model [44], in which the sensitivity level of a datum keeps moving up according to the clearance level of the person who has had access to the data.

Another is the Chinese Wall model [8], which models the practice, especially in consulting firms and financial institutions, of enacting Chinese Wall to avoid conflicts of interest. For example, a consultant in the oil industry is available to consult with oil companies A or B, both of which are clients of the firm. Thus the consultant potentially can access materials related to either A or B. However, once the consultant accesses A's materials, access to B's will be denied due to conflict of interest. The Chinese Wall model attempts to represent such real-life policies.

Another dynamic model that has its root in the financial industry is the Clark-Wilson integrity model [11], which can be used to model the security requirements for performing financial transactions. For example, transactions over a certain monetary limit must be cosigned by two different people and in a particular order. This model was the first widely cited security model that clearly demonstrated the need for security models beyond those of interest to the military and to government agencies, which were primarily MAC security models.

1.4.4 Considerations Concerning the Use of Security Models

A model can be used, for example, to drive or analyze the design of a computer system or to form the basis of a system's operation. These practical uses of models resulted in a number of interesting issues that have been studied to various degrees.

First is *decidability*. That is, can you decide if a system is secure, when given a general security model of a real system and a particular requirement or condition of security (such as, an employee must not be allowed to access file A directly or indirectly). The answer to this question is no in the general case (see [32]). Later research to resolve this issue has primarily involved efforts to restrict the model's generality so that the issue becomes decidable. In most such models, the computational complexity to answer the security question is still NP-complete [72].

The second issue is that it often is impossible or infeasible to model, specify, or analyze an entire system as a whole because a practical system tends to be fairly large. This has led to work with *composability*. Here, a security model is constructed such that if various components satisfy some set of security properties and are connected in some particular ways, then the overall system automatically (via mathematical proof) satisfies another set of security properties [48, 57]. In practice, the ability to develop secure and composable systems is in the somewhat distant future.

Third, the need to retrofit security mechanisms into the so-called legacy systems, or at least to securely connect the systems together, means that the legacy systems must be securely interoperable. One definition of secure interoperability is that the security properties of each legacy system must be preserved under its original definition. However, in this case deciding if a particular interoperation is secure is often NP-complete [27] even under very simple models.

Finally, security does not mean only confidentiality. Modeling the integrity of a system is also critical. An early integrity model [Biba, 44] is the dual of the Bell-LaPadula confidentiality model. One can also view integrity as an aspect of dependability or correctness and thus can enlist the help of results from the field of fault tolerance.

1.5   Using Cryptography

While cryptography concerns the encoding and decoding of information, **cryptanalysis** is the reverse of cryptography and is the art of decoding, or "breaking," secretly encoded information without knowledge of the encryption keys. The term **cryptology** (or crypto, for short) refers to the whole subject field.

Security and cryptology are related but different fields—many people confuse them. They are orthogonal in the sense that each has its own utility without depending on the other, although technology from one can help the other. For example, all of the security models discussed so far do not need to use crypto at all. Crypto can be used to enhance confidentiality and integrity. It also is a field that can be studied in the abstract, without reference to computer security. However, modern crypto exists largely in the context of a computer and a communications system, in which features such as access control are useful in protecting the access to cryptographic keys. In fact, the easiest way to attack a crypto system is to try to compromise its key storage facility.

The most commonly used crypto concepts include these:

♦ one-way hash functions

♦ symmetric ciphers

♦ asymmetric ciphers

These are discussed in the following three subsections.

One final note about crypto in general is that all except one crypto system are theoretically insecure, according to theorems by Claude Shannon, in the sense that an enemy with sufficient knowledge and computing power can always break the crypto system. The only exception is a system called **one-time pad**, in which the secret key is as long as the plaintext itself and is never reused. A one-time pad system is practical only when the sender and recipient have a secure way to exchange the (potentially very large) key.

The most in-depth reference book currently available on this subject is *Handbook of Applied Cryptography* [51]. For readers who do not want to dive into deep background of cryptography and related research subjects, *Applied Cryptography* [74] is more suitable.

1.5.1 One-Way Hash Functions

A one-way hash function is an important building block to help achieve data integrity. Such functions are often used to protect data both in storage and in transit.

According to Knuth [38], the idea of hashing originated in 1953 with two groups of IBM researchers. The earliest reference I can find to the concept of one-way function was by Wilkes in 1968 [80], when he referred to the invention of one-way functions for the Cambridge Time-Sharing Computer System by Needham.[2]

The concept of one-way *hash* functions also dates back many years. A number of researchers such as Merkle [52], Naor and Yung [58], and Damgšard [13] have suggested definitions. Meyer and Schilling [54], Merkle [53], Rabin [64], Rivest [67], and others have presented practical designs for such functions.

Many different terms have been introduced relating to one way hash functions. Some of these are alternative names, and some are intended to emphasize differing assumptions. Examples are one-way (hash) function, collision-free (hash) function, fingerprinting function, modification detection code, and message authentication code.

Informally, a **one-way hash function** is a function that is easy to compute but difficult to reverse. Also, it is difficult to find two values with which the function would compute the same output value. Such properties allow the protection of integrity as follows. Suppose you store a file on the disk and you suspect that it might be tampered with. Using the file content as input, you can compute the hash function value, which can be a lot shorter than the file content itself. Later, you can take the current content of the file and feed it into the hash function. If the new hash value is identical to the old hash value, then it is highly likely that the file content has not been modified. In this case, the one-way hash function serves as an unforgeable link between the file content and its hash value. Figure 1.2 illustrates one way hash functions.

Designers often incorporate secret keys into the inputs of one-way hash functions such that the hash value cannot be correctly computed or predicted without

---

2   Roger Needham later remembered that the idea was first discussed in The Eagle public house in Cambridge in 1967. He also noted that it is a compliment to the hospitality of the public house that nobody remembers exactly who made the suggestion.

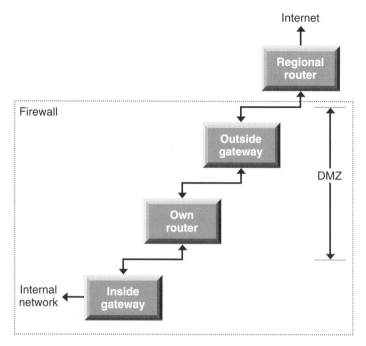

Figure 1.2   One way hash functions.

knowing the secret keys. In this case, such a keyed, one-way hash function serves as an unforgeable link, not only between the file content and its hash value, but also between the secret keys used (and thus the entities that possess the keys) and the hash value.

1.5.2   Symmetric Ciphers

A **symmetric cipher** is a transformation, operated under a secret key, that can translate its input, called *plaintext*, to its output, called *ciphertext*, in such a way that (excluding cryptoanalysis) only those entities possessing the secret key can recover the plaintext from the ciphertext (Figure 1.3).

Symmetric ciphers have a long history. Their first known use dates from the early Caesar system [39]. They since have been widely used; for example, the Data Encryption Standard (DES) [62], as well as the vast number of modern designs such as IDEA.

Symmetric ciphers are also called *secret-key ciphers* because the two communicating parties must share a secret key. This creates some difficulties in key management and key distribution. Moreover, because each pair of communicating

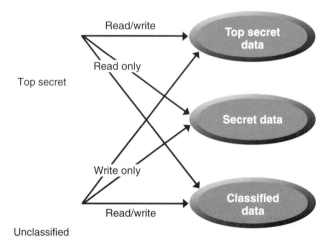

Figure 1.3   Symmetric cipher.

parties must share a distinct secret key, when a large group of parties talk to each other, in theory an exponential number of secret keys are needed.

Symmetric ciphers can be operated in different modes, such as various feedback modes. They can also be stacked to improve the crypto strength of the whole system, such as in the case of triple-DES.

1.5.3   Asymmetric Ciphers

An **asymmetric cipher** is similar to a symmetric cipher, except that it depends on a pair of keys (instead of just one key). One key of the pair is called the *public key* and is used to encrypt plaintext. Another key is called the *private key* and is used to decrypt ciphertext. See Figure 1.4. The keys are generated such that it is easy to deduce the public key, given the private key; the reverse, however, is very difficult. This property enables people to exchange their public keys over public channels and still conduct private communications. Compare this with symmetric cipher systems, in which people must arrange a shared secret key via a private channel. Notable asymmetric systems include Diffie-Hellman [14] and RSA [68]. Asymmetric systems are often used to encrypt and exchange keys for symmetric systems.

Another distinct property of some asymmetric systems is that the encryption and decryption are *reversible*. This means that one can apply the decryption operation with the private key to the plaintext, and one can recover the plaintext by applying the encryption operation with the public key to the ciphertext. In this case, since the public key is public, no confidentiality protection is provided. However, because only the holder of the private key can generate the ciphertext,

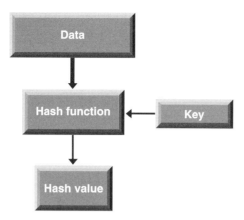

Figure 1.4   Asymmetric cipher.

the ciphertext can serve as a *digital signature* of the plaintext and anyone with the public key can verify the authenticity of the signature. RSA is perhaps the most widely used asymmetric system that can also be used to produce digital signatures. Another system, Digital Signature Algorithm (DSA), defined as a national standard by the U.S. government, can only perform digital signature functions; it cannot be used for encryption.

For one party to prove to another that it is the real owner of a public key, the proving party can present a certificate for verification by the other party. A **public-key certificate** is a digitally signed statement from one entity, saying that the public key (and some other information) of another entity has some specific value. A *chain* of certificates is possible, whereby each certificate contains a public key that is used to certify the public key in the succeeding certificate. The first certificate, often called the **root certificate**, does not have another public key to certify it. Thus it normally is a *self-signed certificate* in that its own public key is used to certify itself. Later chapters (especially Section 4.3) have more in-depth discussion about certificates.

1.6   Authentication

Another basic security issue is authentication. **Authentication** is the process of confirming the identity of the user (or machine operating on behalf of the user). It first became an issue when timesharing systems began to be deployed and the system needed to know the identity of a user logging in to the system. This knowledge is critical for enforcing access control policies, as most of the security models mentioned previously are based on granting access to certain users and not to others.

The importance of authentication increased when networked computer systems started to surface. The network often is shared or public, so it is crucial to authenticate or know the identity of the user at the other end of the wire. It is equally important for the users to know the identity of the system they are connecting to.

Numerous authentication protocols exist, but many of these have subtle security flaws, discovered even after many years of scrutiny by experts. As a result, authentication has become a major study subject.

The basic approach is first to ask the user at the other end of the wire to present a name and a password and then to check these against system records. Such a simple-minded solution, which amazingly is still widely used when more secure solutions are available, is vulnerable to eavesdropping and guessing attacks [47]. Anyone who is monitoring network traffic can learn the password and use it later. Variations of this approach exist, such as one-time passwords [40] and now an Internet Engineering Task Force (IETF) standard called OTP (evolved from S/Key) [31]. These are an improvement with limitations because one can carry only a limited number of one-time passwords.

This basic approach can be generalized to one based on challenge and response. It can also be extended to perform the function of key distribution such that different entities need to share keys only with certain designated key distribution centers. These centers can dynamically establish secret keys between any set of such entities that previously might not have communicated to each other. The earliest work in network-based authentication is the well-known Needham-Schroeder protocol [59]. As illustrated in Figure 1.5, with such a protocol, entities A and B can use the key distribution center as a trusted third party to

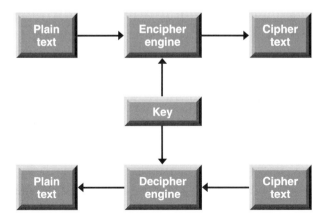

Figure 1.5   Network authentication.

establish a short-term secure session. This protocol is the basis of the Kerberos system implemented as part of the MIT Project Athena and later adopted as part of the DCE and as an IETF standard [56, 60].

Protocol design is full of peril. The Needham-Schroeder protocol, among many others, was later shown to be defective in a number of aspects [9, 26]. Attacks on security protocols include replay attacks and interleaving attacks, where an attacker listens and records legitimate network traffic and then reuses these messages (sometimes after some skillful modifications) to defeat security. But these can easily slip a protocol designer's mind and thereby lead to the possibility of attack later. As a result, formal and informal protocol analysis techniques have been suggested and applied [9, 15, 26, 50, 55], including the fairly recent application of model-checking tools.

One especially serious issue involves authentication protocols designed for use by human beings. These usually involve the use of passwords that people can remember. This approach has the disadvantage that such passwords are generally chosen from a fairly small space (such as all words in a dictionary) that can be mechanically searched and thus easily deduced. All of the authentication protocols examined by the security research community that were published prior to 1989 suffer from this problem of easily guessed passwords. As a result, an attacker who has monitored the network traffic and obtained a running record of an authentication protocol can then guess each candidate password and verify if the guess is correct, all off-line and thus undetectable. Technical solutions to this problem started to appear in late 1989 [21, 47] and include also EKE and A-EKE [4, 5]. Smartcards and other hardware-based security devices are often helpful in avoiding to use guessable passwords.

1.7 Mobile Code

Mobile code is not a fundamentally new concept—anything that causes a remote system to behave differently can in theory be viewed as mobile code. Thus the whole field of distributed computing works on the premise of mobile code. This includes data such as Domain Name Service (DNS) information, remote commands such as Remote Procedure Call (RPC), and executable scripts such as remote shell on UNIX. This section focuses on the last category: executable scripts, code that travels from one machine to another and gets executed as it travels. Such mobile code is widespread, partly because it helps to distribute the computation load among client as well as server machines and partly because it helps to reduce demand on network bandwidth.

PostScript files belong to this category because when a PostScript file is displayed and viewed, it is the file content that is being executed. The same is true for

Microsoft Word documents that contain macros—the macros are interpreted as the document is read. Another example is Lisp. Many people read their e-mail from within Emacs, a powerful text editor. Emacs interprets Lisp programs as it sees fit, so a Lisp program segment embedded in an e-mail message can become active when viewed inside Emacs. Other kinds of active components include ActiveX controls and Java applets.

Active contents do not pose a new category of threat. Instead, they help expose the inadequacies of commonly deployed security mechanisms. For example, when mobile code is a DNS update request, the interface is fairly narrow so that its security implication is more easily understood. However, when fully general mobile code such as an ActiveX control arrives, the interface becomes the entire Win32 APIs and any security holes in those APIs might be exploited.

The increasing use of mobile code has resulted in two responses. On the one hand, people try to enhance system security to better control and thus utilize the attractive aspects of mobile code. On the other hand, people get scared and want to block mobile code at their perimeters. The latter is at best a gap-stopper. This is because mobile code and active contents can travel through multiple channels such as e-mail and filtering every e-mail message and removing parts of messages is often unacceptable (to the e-mail users). One primary design goal of Java technology is to make Java a secure platform for mobile code.

1.8   Where Does Java Security Fit In

The previous sections painted, in rather broad strokes, the large security jigsaw puzzle that today's systems use, from firewalls to access control, from encryption to authentication. Java security is a very important piece of this puzzle. This is because Java is pervasive both as a platform-independent technology and as the best vehicle to program mobile code and executable content for the Internet and the Web. The rate of Java adoption is phenomenal. It is being deployed, for example, in financial institutions, in on-line e-commerce software, and as part of other critical applications. All these mean that the Java platform must fulfill its promise as a safe Internet programming platform.[3]

The Java platform can be viewed as a client-side application (such as when running Java inside a browser), a server-side application (such as when running server software programmed in Java), or an operating system (such as when running the JavaOS directly on MS-DOS or bare hardware). Because different usage

---

[3]   I should make it clear that JavaScript is not based on Java and is related to it only by name. JavaScript does not have the comprehensive security considerations and mechanisms that Java has.

scenarios might require different or even conflicting security features, JDK 1.2 is designed to build in common functionalities while leaving sufficient hooks so that it can be extensible to handle specific requirements.

When Java technology is available within an operating system such as Solaris 2.6 or Microsoft Windows 95 or 98 (collectively called, "MS-Windows"), its presence does not alter the basic security characteristics of the underlying system. For example, on Solaris 2.6 an instance of the Java virtual machine (JVM) will have access only to resources that would be available to the user running the JVM. However, if the entire application interface is limited to Java, then usually the overall system security is improved. This is very obvious if one compares the lack of security features on MS-Windows with the rich security features available in Java. If all applications on such a system are restricted to be 100 percent Java code, then many security problems on MS-Windows suddenly disappear (actually, they are hidden behind the Java interface and thus cannot be exploited directly).

Finally, I want to emphasize that security features on the Java platform are not limited to what is available in JDK 1.2. Further versions of JDK no doubt will continue to enrich the security features. In addition, a whole range of standard Java interfaces have been or are being designed to include such functionality as cryptography, secure sockets layer (SSL), user authentication, and others. Thus Java is becoming not just one but actually many pieces of the security puzzle. Just as SSL and the browser finally brought cryptography to the mass market, Java has played an important role in pushing computer security into the technology mainstream.

CHAPTER 2

Basic Security for the Java Language

Never forget class struggle.
—Mao Ze-Dong

Since the inception of Java technology [30, 46], strong and growing interest has centered on its security, in part because this has been publicized as one of its critical design goals and cited as a significant means of differentiating Java from other technologies.

A new technology rarely includes reasonably good security features in its initial release. Thus the positioning of Java as the best platform for secure Internet programming has attracted a lot of attention from both security professionals and the computer industry in general. Long-time security researchers, academics, and students have poured over design details and source code of the JDK, which was released by Sun Microsystems for just such purposes. Even the popular media have caught the frenzy; both *The Wall Street Journal* and *The New York Times* have covered it prominently.[1]

From a technology provider's point of view, Java security provides two features [23]:

♦ The Java platform (primarily through JDK) as a secure, ready-made platform on which to run Java-enabled applications in a secure fashion

♦ Security tools and services implemented in Java that enable a wider range of security-sensitive applications in such arenas as enterprises

---

[1] Refer to [49] for some quotes and citations.

The deployment of the Java technology also raised an array of interesting security issues, which are covered in later chapters. This chapter focuses primarily on the basic security features provided by the Java language and platform.

2.1   The Java Language and Platform

The Java language was designed originally for use in embedded consumer electronics applications such as handheld devices and set-top boxes. It is a general-purpose object-oriented programming language and is simple enough that many programmers can become fluent in it fairly quickly. It is specifically designed to be platform-independent so that application developers can write a program once using Java and then run that program securely everywhere on the Internet. It is related to C and C++, but it is rather different, with a number of aspects of C and C++ omitted and a few ideas from other languages included.

The Java language is strongly typed. It does not include any unsafe constructs, such as array accesses without index checking, because such unsafe constructs might result in unspecified and unpredictable program behavior.[2] It comes with automatic storage management, typically done by a garbage collector. Further, it avoids the safety problems, such as those posed by C's "free" or C++'s "delete," concerning the explicit deallocation of memory that is no longer needed.

Java is normally compiled to a bytecoded instruction set and binary format defined in the Java Virtual Machine Specification [30]. It also defines a number of packages for more complete programming support. A Java program is normally stored as binary files representing compiled classes and interfaces. The binary class files are loaded into a JVM, and then linked, initialized, and executed. Here is an example of a simple program.

```java
class Test {
    public static void main(String[] args) {
        for (int i = 0; i < args.length; i++)
            System.out.print(i == 0 ? args[i] : " " + args[i]);
        System.out.println();
    }
}
```

---

[2]   A recent study concluded that about 50 percent of all CERT-issued alerts are due in part to buffer-overflow errors.

On a Sun workstation running the Solaris operating system, the class `Test`, stored in the file `Test.java`, can be compiled and executed by giving these commands:

```
javac Test.java
java Test Hello
```

The program will print out `Hello`.

The Java platform is network-centric and is born of the idea that the same software should run on many different kinds of computers, consumer gadgets, and other devices such as smart cards. With Java technology, you can use the same application on a Sun SparcStation running the Solaris operating system, a personal computer (PC) running MS-Windows, a Macintosh computer, a network computer, or even a cellular phone or an Internet screen phone.

The original HotJava browser demonstrated Java's power by making it possible to embed Java programs inside HTML pages. These programs, called *applets*, are transparently downloaded, to be run inside the browser. The Java platform has been incorporated into all major Web browsers and soon will be built into next-generation telephones and TV set-top boxes. Java programs can also run directly on a computer without depending on a browser and are being written to run on servers and large mainframe computers.

The Java platform consists of the Java language, the JVM, and the application programming interfaces (API libraries). The JVM is an abstract computing machine and does not assume any particular implementation technology or host platform. It also knows nothing of the Java programming language; it knows only of a particular file format, the *class file format*. A class file contains JVM instructions (or bytecodes) and a symbol table, as well as ancillary information. Bytecodes can be either interpreted or compiled for a native platform. The JVM may also be implemented either in microcode or directly in silicon. The current release of Sun's implementation of the JVM, inside JDK 1.2, emulates the JVM on Win32 and Solaris platforms.

2.2   Basic Security Architecture

In the original Java release, the basic security architecture centered on allowing a user to dynamically import and run Java applets without undue risk to the user's system. An **applet** is loosely defined to be any code that does not reside on the local system and must be downloaded to be run. Code that does reside on the local system is commonly called a **Java application**. Because applets are downloaded dynamically and often without your awareness, and because you may not know who the applets, authors are, you cannot blindly trust an applet not to attempt to cause harm. Thus a downloaded applet's actions are restricted to its **sandbox**, an area of the Web browser allocated specifically to the applet. The applet may play around within its sandbox but cannot reach beyond it. For example, it cannot read or alter any file stored on the user's system. In this way, if a user accidentally imports a hostile applet, that applet cannot damage the user's system. Thus this sandbox model provides a very restricted environment in which to run untrusted code (that is, applets) obtained from the open network.

In the sandbox model, all applications (as opposed to applets) are completely trusted to have full access to vital system resources (such as the file system). Security comes from maintaining physical control over the systems, for example by preventing end-users from installing suspicious software. Note that the distinction between an applet and an application, or "outside" versus "inside," is not always absolute. With a networked file system, a class file appearing to reside on the local file system actually might be located thousands of miles away, whereas an applet can be downloaded from within the local area network (LAN), possibly from the same host on which the user is running it.

The sandbox model is deployed through JDK 1.0.*x* and is generally adopted by applications built with JDK, including Java-enabled Web browsers.

The original basic security architecture is enforced through a number of mechanisms. First, the Java language is designed to be type safe and easy to use. Thus the programmer is less likely to make subtle mistakes, compared with those possible when using other programming languages such as C or C++. Language features such as automatic memory management, garbage collection, and range checking on strings and arrays are examples of how the language helps the programmer to write safer code.

Second, a bytecode verifier ensures that only legitimate Java code is executed. A compiler translates Java programs into a machine-independent bytecode representation. Before a newly downloaded applet is run, a bytecode verifier is invoked to check that the applet conforms to the Java language specification and that there are no violations of the Java language rules or name space restrictions. This is because, for the sake of security, the JVM imposes strong format and structural constraints on the code in a class file. The verifier also checks for violations of memory management, stack underflows or overflows, and illegal data type casts. These might allow a hostile applet to corrupt part of the security mechanism or to replace part of the system with its own code. The bytecode verifier, together with the JVM, is designed to guarantee language type safety at runtime. For example, Java uses a runtime type check when storing references in arrays to ensure complete type safety.

Moreover, note that runtime activities include the loading and linking of the classes needed to execute a program, any optional machine code generation and dynamic optimization of the program, and the actual program execution. During this process, a class loader defines a local name space, which is used to ensure that an untrusted applet cannot interfere with the running of other Java programs.

Finally, access to crucial system resources is mediated by the JVM and is checked in advance by a security manager class that restricts to a minimum the actions of untrusted code. Class loader and security manager classes are discussed in greater detail later in Section 3.8.

2.3   Bytecode Verification and Type Safety

This section takes a closer look at the general issue of type safety and in particular bytecode verification because this subject has been the focus of some well-publicized discoveries of potential security holes. A review of specific bugs and their fixes is in Section 2.4.

Although a trustworthy compiler can ensure that Java source code does not violate safety rules, someone could use a rigged compiler to produce code that does violate them. A web browser with Java enabled that can import code fragments from anywhere does not know whether a code fragment comes from a trustworthy compiler. Thus, before executing any code fragment, the runtime system subjects it to a series of tests.

The tests range from verifying that the format of the fragment is correct to passing it through a simple theorem prover to establish that the code plays by the rules. Approximately, the code is checked to ensure the following.

♦ It does not forge pointers.

♦ It does not violate access restrictions. For example, a private field should not be accessible from outside of the object.

♦ It accesses objects as what they are. (For example, the tests ensure that `Input-Stream` objects are always used as `InputStreams` and never as anything else.)

♦ It calls methods with appropriate arguments of the appropriate type and there are no stack overflows.

♦ No illegal data conversions are done, such as converting integers to pointers.

Note that a static bytecode verifier is not strictly necessary to ensure type safety because the JVM can, in theory, perform complete type checking during runtime. However, runtime checks often can slow down the execution of a program significantly because such checks have to be done repeatedly for each method invocation. Thus moving some checks up front to class loading time, where those checks are done only once, seems an appealing strategy. Knowing that any downloaded code satisfies these properties makes the runtime system operate much faster because it does not have to check for them. Note that the verifier is independent of the Java language or compiler, so it can also examine bytecode that is generated from non-Java source languages.

The five checked points above obviously do not tell the whole story and are not meant to be formal or precise. Space limitations do not permit a description of the considerable work that covers the finer details of the Java language design, the inner workings of the JVM, the background of flow analysis, and the art of theorem proving, all of which are necessary background for a complete understanding of how type safety is enforced.

For the present discussion, it is sufficient to understand the following points. The most fundamental goal of the Java security architecture is to ensure that the Java Language Specification and the Java Virtual Machine Specification are observed and implemented correctly. One way to think about this is to imagine that you are writing a calendar application. You typically will have interfaces that expect to take an integer between 1 and 12 to represent a month within the year. You might also have an initialization interface that prompts the user to type in the current date. Because your other interfaces assume that the month integer will be between 1 and 12, it is prudent that you check and ensure, from inside the initialization procedure, that the user's input is indeed a valid number. If you do not check for this and as a result do not reject invalid numbers, your calendar application might not work with an out-of-range month number and might behave in strange ways.

This same principle applies to the Java platform. The JVM expects the bytecode that it runs to have certain properties, and it is the job of the bytecode verifier to ensure that those properties are met. The JVM also decides to check additional properties itself, perhaps because these are difficult or impossible to analyze statically by the bytecode verifier. There is no mystery in ensuring type safety, just mountains of detail and tons of work.

You might ask what type safety has to do with computer security. This question can be addressed in a couple of ways. First, type safety contributes toward program correctness. If a program that is implementing some security functionality does not accomplish what it is intended to do, because the program cannot be correctly executed, then security may not be provided correctly. For example, a security decision may be embodied in an equality test, of the following form.

```
if (the name is James Gosling) {
   open the door to Hacker's Lounge
} else {
   throw the person out
}
```

Here, security reasoning is written and performed in the Java language. Thus it is critical that a yes answer is not possible when a string such as `James Gosling` is compared with a different string, say `Scott McNealy`. Otherwise, a trivial incorrectness in string comparison leads to a security hole.

On the other hand, it is important to note that not all type safety problems inevitably result in a security breach. For example, if a virtual machine implementation has a single bug that equates string `acegikmoqsuwy` with string `bdfhjlnprtvxz`, what security compromise this will cause is not immediately clear. Nevertheless, the type safety issue needs close attention and should not be left to chance.

Yellin, in an early paper, included some details of the verifier and other type checking mechanisms [82]. However, you need a fairly good understanding of the bytecode instructions in order to fully digest them. More recently, Liang and Bracha wrote about a new mechanism, implemented in JDK 1.2, that solves a problem with type safety regarding dynamic class loading [45]. This subject of bytecode verification is still evolving, with ongoing work occurring within the JDK development team, as well as at research labs and universities. A more formal and precise exposition of the entire language type safety subject is anticipated for the future.

2.4 Signed Applets

JDK 1.1 introduced the concept of *signed applets*. Recall that in the original sandbox model, all remote code—that is, all applets—are automatically untrusted and are restricted to running inside the sandbox. Such restrictions, although contributing to a safe computing environment, are too limiting for some applets. For example, a company might deploy, within a LAN, an applet that is used to maintain employee pension data. An employee who downloads and runs the applet to change the plan allocation would want the applet to automatically update his own accounting record stored in his own file directory.

To facilitate such features, JDK 1.1 added support for digital signatures so that an applet's class files, after their development, could be signed and stored together with their signatures in the JAR (Java Archive) format. For each JDK installation, you can specify which signers (or their public keys) are trusted. When a correctly digitally signed applet is downloaded, and if its signers can be verified and recognized as trusted, the applet is treated as if it is trusted local code and is given full system access (Figure 2.1).

Both the original sandbox model and the trusted applet model have been extended into a new security architecture in JDK 1.2 that implements fine-grained access control based on security policies and permissions. This new architecture is covered extensively in Chapter 3.

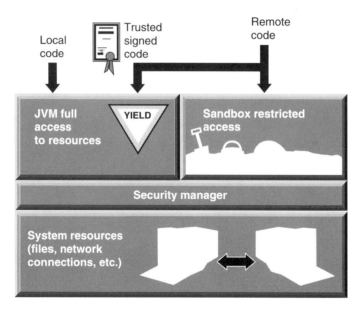

Figure 2.1   JDK 1.1 security model.

2.5   A Brief History of Security Bugs and Fixes

It is often said that those who forget history are bound to repeat it. As part of understanding the new security architecture in JDK 1.2, you need to understand the series of Java security-related bugs, what caused them, and what has been done to fix them. This review, set out in the following list, is based on the archive that JavaSoft keeps on its public Web site. All known bugs are fixed, normally shortly after their discovery, and the fixes are issued in the next release of JDK. Bugs and fixes that are technically obscure are not explained in detail here. McGraw and Felten [49] provide additional background such as media coverage and stock market movement that might have been related to some of the bug reports.

It is worth emphasizing that for all of the bugs discussed here, the problem is a bug in the implementation of the security model, not with the model itself. As a result, no major "surgery" is necessary and fixes are quickly developed and deployed. Sun's policy of "security through openness," according to which all source code is made available for public review, has attracted very capable people to invest their time and energy in Java security research. This policy, which has resulted in security bugs being found and fixed more quickly, has been a great success.

♦ **February 1996**. Drew Dean, Ed Felten, and Dan Wallach of Princeton University (hereafter called "the Princeton team") described an attack that exploits the way in which the applet security manager in JDK 1.0 uses the DNS (Domain Name Service) for hostname-to-IP address resolution. This attack is called the *DNS spoofing attack*. Steve Gibbons also independently suggested this attack scenario.

The attack uses the fact that DNS allows one hostname to match to multiple IP addresses. Thus a malicious party can take control of a DNS server and falsely advertise its attack host with its actual IP address and a fake address, which belongs to the target machine. The attack also exploits a weakness in the applet security manager that allows an applet to connect to any of the IP addresses associated with the name of the computer from which it came. Thus an applet from the attack host could open a connection to the fake address and connect to the target machine, even though it was not supposed to.

The fix for the applet security manager is to make it more strict about deciding to which computers an applet is allowed to connect. In particular, it notes the actual IP address from which the applet truly came and thereafter allows the applet to connect only to that exact same numerical address.

♦ **March 1996**. David Hopwood at Oxford University found a bug in the JDK 1.0 class loader that could be exploited to load illegal bytecode, which could then be used to load a class referenced by an absolute pathname. This meant that if in cases such as an FTP upload, the attacker could install a malicious class file on the target system with a known pathname, then the attack applet would be able to load the malicious class file.

♦ **March 1996**. The Princeton team found an implementation bug in the Java bytecode verifier in JDK 1.0.1. Through a sophisticated attack, a malicious applet could exploit this bug to delete a file or do other damage.

♦ **April 1996**. A security problem in JDK 1.0.1 was reported to JavaSoft by a software engineer from Sprint. For a specific firewall-protected network configuration, an outside applet downloaded by a client inside the firewall could connect to a single specific host behind the firewall. This was due to a bug in the Uniform Resource Locator (URL) name resolution code. For the attack to succeed, the target network and the attacker's network must have an identical domain name, with the attacker's domain being the official (InterNIC), registered network. In other words, the target network must use an internal name that has not been registered with InterNIC and the attacker must have control over the InterNIC-registered name.

- **May 1996**. The Princeton team found another way to get past system restrictions on creating a class loader in JDK 1.0.1. (Section 3.8 discusses that a class loader is a sensitive and powerful object, so you must carefully control who can create instances of a class loader.) This attack builds on earlier work done by Tom Cargill.

- **June 1996**. David Hopwood uncovered a bug in JDK 1.0.2, based on illegal type casting, to manipulate how objects are assigned and how they collaborate.

- **March 1997**. The JavaSoft engineering team came across a bug in the implementation of the JDK 1.1 bytecode verifier. To exploit this bug, someone would have to handcraft specially formatted bytecode. The theoretical attack is complex and appears extremely difficult to accomplish.

- **March 1997**. It was reported that an applet can call a method named `getLocalHost()` to determine the IP address of the computer in which it is running. This turned out to be a false alarm, even though the media showed great interest. Since the May 1996 JDK 1.0.2 release, an applet that calls `getLocalHost()` will get the loopback host (`"localhost/127.0.0.1"`) as an answer. This is a generic handle to the local computer, which does not reveal any private information.

- **April 1997**. The Princeton team (now with a new member Dirk Balfanz) found a flaw in the JDK 1.1.1 digital signature handling code used to manage identities of signers that signed class files. The attack used digitally signed code for impersonation, and made the code appear to be signed by anyone from the list of signers that were recorded in the Java runtime system.

- **May 1997**. Brian Bershad, Sean McDirmid, and Emin Gun Sirer of the University of Washington (hereafter called "the Washington team") discovered a bug in the JDK 1.1.1 verifier. The verifier was not checking that the number of arguments passed into a method invocation is less than the amount of space allocated to local variables for that method. Thus an excessive number of arguments could cause a stack overflow, most likely leading to the JVM's crashing. There was no known security attack based on this bug, but since the bug relates to class loading, it was important enough to fix immediately.

- **June 1997**. The Washington team reported another implementation bug in the JDK 1.1.2 bytecode verifier. This bug allowed a type-unsafe applet to execute and to search and locate strings that are stored in the browser's address space.

♦ **March 1999**. Karsten Sohr, a graduate student at the University of Marburg in Germany discovered a bug in the implementation of the bytecode verifier. This bug could allow an untrusted applet to run with excess privileges, and affects JDK 1.1.*x* and JDK 1.2.

In retrospect, these bugs have a high probability to be caught earlier by more complete and careful design specification and quality assurance measures.

In summary, note the following points. First, there was a fair amount of confusion over the details of the sandbox security model. For example, applets were not allowed to do certain actions. But the list of forbidden actions was not exhaustive and was not given in precise language. Consequently, there was occasional debate on whether something was a security bug.

Second, not all Java bugs are security bugs, even though they potentially all are. On the one hand, we treat all bugs seriously; on the other hand, we all should keep things in the right perspective.

Third, not all bugs are strictly Java security bugs because they interplay with other aspects of the computing environment, such as the operating system, the Web browser, Web spoofing, and some installed software. In fact, a lot of media coverage has centered on bugs that have nothing to do with Java technology, but because they are related to the Internet, some observers commonly issue warnings about potential Java security problems before the real cause of the problems is discovered. In addition, some people confuse ActiveX with Java, while others (wrongly) think that JavaScript is the same as Java.

Finally, the current Java security technology does not attempt to monitor and control resource consumption by applets and applications. For example, it is hard to automatically tell the difference between an MPEG decompressor that takes a long time to execute and a hostile applet that is intentionally wasting resources. Note that resource consumption attacks can be mounted with or without Java and sometimes do not require complicated programming. For example, a malicious Web server can serve an infinitely long Web page, thus filling up the client browser's cache space. And a junk mailer can spam gigantic e-mail messages and saturate a user's mail box. Nevertheless, Sun recognizes that in some situations, it is desirable to control the impact of denial-of-service attacks, and it is actively researching this subject area.

CHAPTER 3

JDK 1.2
Security Architecture

The state is nothing but an instrument of
oppression of one class by another.
—Friedrich Engels

This chapter focuses on the inner workings of the JDK 1.2 security architecture that supports policy-driven, permission-based, flexible and extensible access control. I will go over the designs of the `Policy` and `Permission` classes, the internal mechanisms for secure class loading, and the access control algorithm. But first I will outline the motivations of the new architecture and its development timeline.

3.1   From the Beginning

Planning for the JDK 1.2 security architecture started in late August 1996; actual code development got under way in the following February. The first permission-controlled Appletviewer `appletviewer` prototype ran in March, and the first-cut feature completion was achieved by May 1997. This time line roughly coincides with the publication of the new architectural directions for Java security. I presented a paper at IEEE COMPCON in February 1997 [29], which later was revised and expanded for the *IEEE Micro* May/June issue [23]. During my Java-One talk in April 1997, I was able to confidently give some technical details based on the prototype already in hand. For the subsequent twelve months, the security architecture remained stable. The APIs, however, have been undergoing constant refinement. An overview paper was presented at a USENIX conference in December 1997 [25], while aspects of implementation details were presented at an Internet Society symposium in early 1998 [28].

The JDK 1.2 security project was named "Gibraltar."[1] This was because we, that is, the Java security development team at Sun Microsystems, viewed it as an important foundation stone for Java technology. But also, we anticipated major, though not quite Herculean, efforts to complete it. We also intended to use the other Herculean pillar (called "Abyla" in ancient times and today known as Mount Hacho) to name the next major security project of this scale.

3.2   Why a New Security Architecture

As discussed in Chapter 2, it was critical that the original release of JDK 1.0 consider security seriously and provide the sandbox security model. Not many technologies have security as a design goal, so Java technology, together with the Internet and the promise of e-commerce, helped to finally move security technology into the mainstream of the computer industry. This was a significant achievement. The next step was to improve the original design to make the security solutions on the Java platform easier to use, as well as more robust. The new architecture corrects several limitations of earlier versions.

3.2.1   Sandbox Restrictions on Applets Too Limiting

By default, the sandbox model severely restricts the kind of activities that an applet may perform. Although this model was the catalyst that created the atmosphere for safe Internet computing, it treats all applets as potentially suspicious. Thus some applets, such as those created by a corporation's finance group to handle internal transactions, are also limited in what they can do, even though they are likely to be more trustworthy than an arbitrary applet downloaded from an unfamiliar Web site.

Such a blanket restriction on all applets can be limiting. For example, suppose a customer of Charles Schwab, a brokerage firm headquartered in San Francisco, runs an applet loaded from Charles Schwab's Web page to make stock trades. This customer might want to let the applet update local files that contain her portfolio at Charles Schwab; however, access to the client-side file system is prohibited by the sandbox model. Thus this customer needs *flexible access control*, whereby certain applets can have access that is outside of the sandbox or in other words, the sandbox can be customized (for example, by the client system) to have flexible shapes and boundaries.

---

[1]   Gibraltar: The "calpe" of the ancients and one of the two pillars of Hercules, from *Brewer's Dictionary of Phrase & Fable*.

However, the Charles Schwab customer might also have Quicken software installed on the local desktop that handles income tax issues. She might not feel comfortable letting the Charles Schwab applet have free reign on her entire desktop system. In this case, it would be best to confine the applet to limited file system access, perhaps to only the Charles Schwab file folder. In other words, she needs *fine-grained access control.*

Prior to JDK 1.2, one could, in theory, implement a more flexible and finer-grained access control on the Java platform. To accomplish this, however, someone (such as an application writer) had to do substantial programming work, for example by subclassing and customizing the `SecurityManager`, `ClassLoader`, and other classes. The HotJava browser is an example of such efforts; it has a limited range of user-definable security properties. However, such programming is extremely security-sensitive and requires in-depth knowledge of computer security and robust programming skills.

The JDK 1.2 architecture aims to eliminate the need to write custom security code for all but a small number of environments, such as the military, which requires special security properties (such as multilevel security [44]). And even then, writing custom security code would be simpler and safer.

3.2.2 Insufficient Separation Between Policy and Enforcement

The sandbox model, as codified by the `SecurityManager` class, implements a specific security policy that is expressed in the software that does the policy enforcement. This means that to enforce a different security policy, a special version of the software must be used—clearly this is not desirable. Instead, what is needed is an infrastructure that supports a range of easily configurable security policies.

The JDK 1.2 security architecture cleanly separates the enforcement mechanism from the security policy statement. In this way, application builders and users can configure their own flavors of security policies without having to write special programs.

3.2.3 Security Checks Not Easily Extensible

The original design hard coded the types of security checks that the JDK performs. For example, to check if a file can be opened for reading, you would call the `checkRead()` method on the `SecurityManager` class. Such a design is not easily extensible because it does not accommodate the handling of new types of checks that are introduced as after-market add-on to JDK. It also is not very scalable. For example, to create a new access check, such as one that checks to see if money can be withdrawn from a bank account, you would have to add a new `checkAccountWithdraw()` method to the `SecurityManager` class or one of its subclasses. Thousands of various kind of checks are possible. If methods were created for this large number, they would overcrowd the `SecurityManager` class. In fact, because many checks are application-specific, not of all them can be defined within JDK. What is needed is an easily extensible access control structure.

The JDK 1.2 architecture introduces typed access-control permissions and an automatic permission handling mechanism to achieve extensibility and scalability. In theory, no new method ever needs to be added in the `SecurityManager` class. So far, throughout the development of JDK 1.2, when numerous new types of security checks were introduced, we have not encountered a situation requiring a new method. Instead, a single method, called `checkPermission()`, is now sufficient to handle all security checks.

3.2.4   Locally Installed Applets Too Easily Trusted

The original security model has the built-in assumption that all locally installed Java applications are fully trusted and therefore should run with full privileges. As a result, the sandbox model applies only to downloaded applets. However, software installed locally should not be given full access to all parts of the system. For example, often a user installs a demo program on the local system and then tries it out. It is a good idea to limit the potential damage such a demo program could cause by giving it less than full system access. In another example, caching applets on the local file system will improve performance, but caching should not change the security model by treating cached applets as trusted code, even though it now resides on the local system. Furthermore, the distinction between what is local code and what is remote code is fast becoming blurred. In the modern world of software components, one application could utilize multiple components, such as JavaBeans, that reside in all corners of the Internet. So security checks must be extended to all Java programs, to include applets as well as applications.

In the new architecture, local code is subjected to the same security controls as applets, although users can choose to give full system access to certain (or all) local or remote code, thus running them effectively as completely trusted. Such a choice can be made by simply configuring a suitable security policy.

3.2.5   Internal Security Mechanisms Fragile

In the original release JDK 1.0 and the subsequent JDK 1.1, a number of internal security mechanisms are designed and implemented using techniques that are rather fragile. Although they work reasonably well in those versions, maintaining and extending them is difficult. Thus we made a few important internal structural adjustments in order to reduce the risks of creating subtle security holes in programs. This involved revising the design and implementation of the `Security-Manager` and `ClassLoader` classes, as well as the underlying access control checking mechanism. Later Sections 3.8 and 3.9 touch on some historical details.

3.2.6 Summary

To summarize, the need to support flexible and fine-grained access-control security policies, with extensibility and scalability, called for a new and improved security architecture. The result is JDK 1.2. This new architecture uses a security policy to decide which individual access permissions are granted to running code. These permissions are based on the code's characteristics, for example where the code is coming from, whether it is digitally signed, and if so by whom. Later, attempts to access protected resources will invoke security checks that will compare the granted permissions with the permissions needed for the attempted access. If the former includes the latter, access will be permitted; otherwise, access will be denied. If a security policy is not explicitly given, then the default policy is the classic sandbox policy implemented in JDK 1.0 and JDK 1.1. There are various caveats, refinements, and exceptions to this model that are discussed in later chapters.

The JDK 1.2 security architecture has not invented a new computer security theory, even though we have had to design new ways to deal with many subtle security issues that are unique to object oriented systems. Instead, it offers a real-world example in which well-known security principles [17, 61, 63, 70] are put into engineering practice to construct a practical and widely deployed secure system.

The remainder of this chapter describes the details of the implementation classes. The major components of the new security model include security policy, access permission, protection domain, access control checking, privileged operation, and Java class loading and resolution. Security policy and access permissions define what actions are allowed, whereas protection domain and access control checking provide the actual enforcement. Privileged operation and class loading and resolution are valuable assistants in the overall protection mechanisms.

3.3 `java.security.GeneralSecurityException`

First, we specified a new exception class called `GeneralSecurityException`. Why introduce this class when there was already `java.lang.Security-Exception`? `SecurityException` and its subclasses are runtime exceptions that are thrown only to signify that a security check has failed, for example when someone attempts to illegally access a protected file. Such runtime exceptions are not declared or checked and will cause the execution of a program to stop unless application developers write code to explicitly catch them.

However, other error conditions, such as syntax errors, are related to the security mechanisms but do not correspond to failed security checks. In these cases, throwing a `SecurityException` is inappropriate. Instead, a `GeneralSecurity-Exception` should be thrown. For example, passing in an invalid `Policy` object is security related but nonvital, and the exception here should probably not be a security violation and should be caught and dealt with by a developer.

`GeneralSecurityException` is a subclass of `java.lang.Exception` and must be declared or caught. This exception should be thrown in all cases from within the security packages, except when some sort of security violation is detected, in which case a `SecurityException` should be thrown.[2]

3.4   Security Policy

The security behavior of a Java runtime system is specified by its security policy. In abstract terms, the security policy is a typical access-control matrix that says what system resources can be accessed, in what fashion, and under what circumstances. For example, one entry in the matrix shown in Figure 3.1 says something

Code	Permissions
CharlesSchwab applets, signed	read and write/tmp and/home/gong/stock
CharlesSchwab applets, signed and unsigned	connect and accept bankofamerica.com
local applications	read and write to /tmp
. . .	. . .

Figure 3.1   Policy matrix.

---

[2] The `java.security` package contains two places in which exceptions thrown are subclassed directly from `java.lang.RuntimeException`. These were introduced in JDK 1.1 and, to maintain backward compatibility, we do not change them to subclass from `GeneralSecurityException`.

like "when running an applet downloaded from http://java.sun.com, allow it to read the following file *x*." More specifically, a security policy is a mapping from a set of properties that characterizes running code to a set of access permissions granted to the code.

When JDK 1.2 is run, a system security policy is in place that is really composed of a set of policies that can be configured by the user or by a system administrator. There can be multiple forms of representation of such a policy outside of the Java runtime environment. For example, the default implementation of JDK 1.2 uses an ASCII format and the policy is stored in an ASCII file. The policy file can then be retrieved via HTTP or other protocols. The specification of the format of the policy file is in Chapter 4.

So that the security mechanism inside the Java runtime environment can consult the policy, the policy contents are necessarily represented internally in the form of a Policy object, which is instantiated from a subclass of the class java.security.Policy. Because there is no limitation on who can instantiate such an object, multiple instances of the Policy object could exist at the same time. Nevertheless, only one Policy object is in effect at any time, in the sense that it is the one of which the security mechanism asks questions.

The Policy class is an abstract class, so a Policy object is instantiated not from Policy but from one of its subclasses. The security policy is represented by a Policy subclass that provides an implementation of the abstract methods in this Policy class. Following are Policy's four most important methods:

```
public static Policy getPolicy();
public static void setPolicy(Policy policy);
public abstract Permissions getPermissions(CodeSource
                                           codesource);
public abstract void refresh();
```

The currently installed Policy object can be obtained by calling the getPolicy method. This object maintains a runtime representation of the policy and is typically instantiated either at the JVM start-up time or when the security policy is used for the first time. It may be changed later via a secure mechanism, such as by calling the setPolicy method.

The source location for the policy information utilized by the Policy object is up to Policy's implementation. It may be stored, for example, as a flat ASCII file, as a serialized binary file of Policy, or as a database.

The refresh method causes the Policy object to refresh or reload its current configuration. How this is done is implementation-dependent. For example, if the Policy object stores its policy content in configuration files, a call to refresh will typically cause it to reread the configuration policy files. However, the default implementation in JDK 1.2 does not affect classes that have already been loaded in the sense that they retain the permissions they have already been granted, even if these permissions may conflict with the new security policy. Also, new classes that are loaded after the policy update may not be granted permissions under the new policy, depending how the class loaders are implemented. For example, if they cache the old policy content, then this content and not the new policy content gets used. Section 3.6 further elaborates policy update issues.

The default `Policy` implementation can be changed by setting the value of the `policy.provider` security property (in the Java security properties file) to the fully qualified name of the desired `Policy` implementation class. The Java security properties file is located in the file named

```
JAVA-HOME/lib/security/java.security
```

where JAVA-HOME refers to the directory in which the JRE (Java Runtime Environment) is installed. For example, if you have JDK 1.2 installed on Solaris, the security properties file is located in the file named

```
jdk1.2/jre/lib/security/java.security
```

If instead you installed JRE 1.2 on Solaris, the file is named

```
jre1.2/lib/security/java.security
```

We designed the policy component as a provider structure because we wanted to instill enough flexibility so that the policy content can be obtained in arbitrary ways. It would have been impossible to anticipate the various possible ways for doing this and then design sufficient APIs for them.

Policy content can be sensitive, and the method `getPolicy()` is public static so that anyone can call it. Thus a suitable security check is installed so that only code that has the permission to obtain the policy can successfully call the method.

Similarly, a security check is invoked when the `setPolicy()` method is called. If the calling code does not have the required permission, a `Security-Exception` is thrown, thereby indicating that a security-sensitive operation was attempted and then denied due to insufficient access permission.

The security checks are based on the new security architecture introduced in JDK 1.2 (so we practice what we preach) and are illustrated in the following code segments. These code segments use the new permission model, details of which are explained later in Sections 3.5, 3.7, 3.8, and 3.9.

```
public static Policy getPolicy() {
    SecurityManager sm = System.getSecurityManager();
    if (sm != null) sm.checkPermission(new
        SecurityPermission ("getPolicy"));
    return policy;
}
```

```
public static void setPolicy(Policy policy) {
    SecurityManager sm = System.getSecurityManager();
    if (sm != null) sm.checkPermission(new
        SecurityPermission("setPolicy"));
    Policy.policy = policy;
}
```

Note that because the `getPermissions` and `refresh` methods are abstract, they must be implemented by a subclass of the `Policy` class and in which the appropriate security checks should be done to protect the contents of the `Policy` object.

An example of how `Policy` is used is the following code fragment of `java.lang.ClassLoader`, whose `defineClass` method indirectly executes as follows when defining a class that is granted with the default permissions.

```
...
Class c = defineClass0(name, b, off, len);
c.setProtectionDomain0(getDefaultDomain());
...
```

where `getDefaultDomain()` is implemented as follows.

```
...
CodeSource cs = new CodeSource(null, null);
PermissionCollection p = Policy.getPolicy().getPermissions(cs);
return new ProtectionDomain(cs, p);
```

3.5   CodeSource

Recall that the security policy is essentially an access control matrix that describes code according to its characteristics and the permissions it is granted. This section examines how to describe code.

Currently, a piece of code is fully characterized by two things. One is its origin (its location as specified by a URL). The second is the set of digital certificates containing the public keys that correspond to the set of private keys that have been used to sign the code using one or more digital signature algorithms. Such characteristics are captured in the class `java.security.CodeSource`, which can be viewed as a natural extension of the concept of a codebase within HTML. It is important not to confuse the `CodeSource` class with the `CodeBase` tag in HTML.

For example, the `CodeSource` of an applet packaged in a JAR file called `foo.jar` that resides at the Web address `http://java.sun.com/classes/` contains the URL

```
http://java.sun.com/classes/foo.jar
```

If the JAR file is signed, it will contain digital signatures for individual entries in the JAR file or for the entire JAR file itself. In this case, the corresponding Code-Source will also contain the certificates that correspond to the signature keys. Note that if signatures cannot be verified, the JAR file will be viewed as unsigned and the certificates will effectively be null. Verification could fail either because the content of the JAR file was modified so that an entry no longer matches its signature or because the signature keys are unrecognizable.

Following are the most important method calls for the CodeSource class:

```
CodeSource(URL url, java.security.cert.Certificate certs[]);
public boolean equals(Object obj);
public boolean implies(CodeSource codesource);
```

We intentionally made CodeSource immutable by including both the URL and the certificates in the constructor and by making copies of the certificates (instead of merely keeping references to those certificate objects). Note that the URL itself is already immutable, so there is no need to make a clone of it. Making a CodeSource object immutable ensures that it can be passed around without its integrity being compromised. Its integrity is important because, as I discuss in Section 3.6, access control decisions are made partly based on the CodeSource of running code. For example, a code fragment from a designated CodeSource can be allowed to write to the local file system, while code from other places is prohibited local file system access. If a latter kind of CodeSource object can be mutated, illegally, to become identical to the former CodeSource object, then code from the latter would gain illegal access to the local file system, thereby causing a security breach.

You might have noticed that because you need only private keys to create signatures and only public keys to verify them, certificates are sometimes unnecessary. So why does the interface in CodeSource deal with only certificates and not public keys? The answer is, for simplicity. In theory, both interfaces can exist, where one interface deals with public keys and the other with certificates. But having both is redundant and adds complexity to the underlying algorithm and code. Until JDK 1.2 beta3, we decided to use public keys exclusively. From beta4 onward, we generalized to using certificates exclusively.

Using certificates exclusively should not cause any problem because given any public and private key pair, you can easily produce a self-signed certificate that encloses the public key. In fact, the tool used to generate keys in JDK 1.2, called keytool, always generates a self-signed certificate when generating a key. A self-signed certificate normally would not convey any significance to the key enclosed inside, except to serve as a medium to transport the key.

Moreover, using certificates instead of public keys makes it easier to carry around important information that might be contained inside a certificate but cannot be expressed by the public key itself. For example, because CodeSource objects contain not only certificates but also their supporting certificate chains, one can validate an entire certificate chain all the way up to the root CA. Such validation information is valuable for auditing purposes.

3.5.1 Testing for Equality and Using Implication

Testing for equality between two CodeSource objects is important because such a comparison is central to security policy decision. Two CodeSource objects are considered equal if their URL locations are identical and if the two sets of certificates contained in the two objects are identical. In other words, the two sets of certificates might not be stored in the same order (in the array), but the two sets must be identical.

Sometimes, it is convenient to specify a first CodeSource object that is more general than a second CodeSource object so that any code coming from the second can be considered also coming from the first. In this case, the first CodeSource "implies" the second CodeSource. For example, CodeSource of http://java.sun.com/classes/ is more general than a more specific CodeSource of http://java.sun.com/classes/foo.jar.

With such a relationship based on "implication," security policy can be simplified by granting permissions to a general CodeSource object, which will implicitly grant the same permissions to any more specific CodeSource object. For example, you can give to http://java.sun.com/classes/ permission to access the local file system, meaning that you give the same permission to all code residing on that Web page.

Obviously, strict and precise rules must be followed in order to determine if one CodeSource object implies another. When the this.implies(CodeSource codesource) method is called, it returns true if "this" CodeSource object implies the specified codesource passed in as the parameter. More specifically, this method makes the following checks, in the following order. If any check fails, it returns false. If they all succeed, it returns true.

1. codesource must not be null.

2. If this object's certificates are not null, then all of them must be present in codesource's certificates.

3. If this object's location (getLocation()) is not null, then the following checks are made against its location and codesource's location.

   a. codesource's location must not be null.

   b. If this object's location equals codesource's location, then immediately return true. Otherwise, continue.

c. This object's protocol (`getLocation().getProtocol()`) must be equal to `codesource`'s protocol.

d. If this object's host (`getLocation().getHost()`) is not null, then the `SocketPermission` constructed with this object's host must imply the `SocketPermission` constructed with `codesource`'s host.

e. If this object's port (`getLocation().getPort()`) is not equal to −1 (that is, if a port is specified), it must equal `codesource`'s port.

f. If this object's file (`getLocation().getFile()`) does not equal `code-source`'s file, then the following checks are made.

- If this object's file ends with a "/", then `codesource`'s file must contain this object's file as a prefix.

- If this object's file ends with "/*", then `codesource`'s file must reference a class or JAR file in the directory pointed by this object's file without the trailing "*".

- If this object's file ends with "/-", then `codesource`'s file must reference a class or JAR file in the directory pointed by this object's file without the trailing "*" or recursively any of its subdirectories.

- In all other cases, `codesource`'s file must, as a prefix, contain this object's file with a "/" appended.

g. If this object's reference (`getLocation().getRef()`) is not null, it must equal `codesource`'s reference.

For example, consider `CodeSource` objects with the following locations and null certificates:

```
http:
http://*.sun.com/
http://java.sun.com/classes/
http://java.sun.com/classes/foo.jar
```

All of these imply the `CodeSource` object with the location `http://java.sun.com/classes/foo.jar` and null certificates. This is because `http:`, `http://*.sun.com/`, and `http://java.sun.com/classes/` all include `http://java.sun.com/classes/foo.jar` as a special case.

Two different `CodeSource` objects refer to the same code source if they imply each other.

Because `CodeSource` implements the interface `java.io.Serializable`, we provided customized methods `writeObject()` and `readObject()` for serialization.

Following is a sample usage of the `CodeSource` class. When defining a class that is loaded from either the local host or a remote host, you need to calculate its code source in order to consult the security policy to figure out the permissions to grant to the code. Thus the method `findClass()` in class `java.net.URLClass-Loader` executes the following code segment.

```
...
URLClassPath ucp = new URLClassPath(urls);
...
Resource res = ucp.getResource(path, false);
...
byte[] b = res.getBytes();
java.security.cert.Certificate[] certs = res.getCertificates();
CodeSource cs = new CodeSource(url, certs);
...
return defineClass(name, b, 0, b.length, cs);
```

3.6   Permission Hierarchy

The previous sections introduced the security policy, as well as the code source that comprises half of the policy content. The remaining part of the policy describes the permissions granted to each different code source. This section covers first the design of the `Permission` class hierarchy and then the various specific permission classes.

The permission classes represent access to system resources. Currently, all permission classes are positive in that they represent approvals, rather than denials, of access. This design choice greatly simplifies the implementation and improves efficiency. The root class of the `Permission` class hierarchy, `java.security.Permission`, is an abstract class and is subclassed, as appropriate, to represent specific accesses. For example, the following Java code can be used to produce a permission to read the file named abc in the `/tmp` directory:

```
perm = new java.io.FilePermission("/tmp/abc", "read");
```

New permissions are subclassed either from the `Permission` class or one of its subclasses, such as `java.security.BasicPermission` (Figure 3.2). Subclassed permissions (other than `BasicPermission`) generally belong to their own packages. Thus `FilePermission`, which describes access permission for the file system, is found in the `java.io` package, which holds the APIs for file system access.

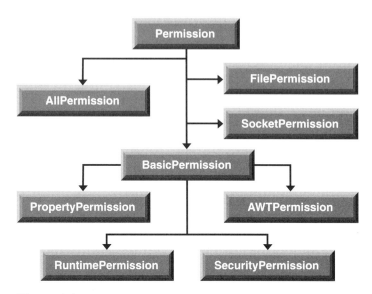

Figure 3.2   Permission subclasses.

3.6.1   `java.security.Permission`

Following are the constructor and the method calls of the `Permission` class at the root of the `Permission` class hierarchy:

```
public Permission(String name);
public abstract boolean implies(Permission permission);
public abstract boolean equals(Object obj);
public String toString();
public PermissionCollection newPermissionCollection();
```

Each `Permission` instance is typically generated by passing one or more string parameters to the constructor. In a common case with two parameters, the first parameter is usually the name of the target (such as the name of a file for which the permission is aimed) and the second parameter is the action (such as reading a file). Generally, a set of actions can be specified as a comma-separated composite string.

All permissions have a target name, whose interpretations depend on the subclass. It is conceivable that for certain types of permissions, the target name is of no importance and is thus not interpreted. `Permission` objects are similar to `String` objects in that they are immutable once they have been created. Subclasses should not provide methods that can change the state of a permission once it has been created.

Whether two `Permission` objects are considered equal is left entirely up to each subclass of the `Permission` class. The same is true for those abstract methods for defining the semantics of the particular `Permission` subclass.

An important method that must be implemented by each subclass is the `implies` method to compare permissions. Basically, "permission p1 implies permission p2" means that if you are granted permission p1, you are naturally granted permission p2. Thus this is not really an equality test, but rather more of a subset test.

It is important to remember that object equality differs from permission equivalence. Object equality is useful, for example, when you store objects in hash tables and later need to determine if an entry already exists. This can be done by calling the `equals` method. Permission equivalence, on the other hand, means that two objects semantically represent the same permission. To determine permission equivalence, you must use the `implies` method and check to see if one `Permission` object implies another, and vice versa.

Most `Permission` objects also include a list that gives the actions that are permitted on the permission target. For example, for a `java.io.FilePermission` object, the permission name (and target) is the pathname of a file (or directory) and the list of actions specifies which actions (such as `read` and `write`) are granted for the specified file (or for files in the specified directory).

The actions list is optional for those `Permission` objects that do not need such a list. One example is `java.lang.RuntimePermission`, where the named permission (such as `"exitVM"`) is either granted or not. There is no further subdivision of different actions. Admittedly, for these special cases, quite often the name embodies both the target of the permission (for example, VM is the target from which to exit) and the action (`exit`). For simplicity, they are merged as one string. The design of such permission classes typically subclasses from `java.security.BasicPermission`.

Sometimes it is desirable to present a permission's content in a human-readable fashion. The `toString()` method returns a string describing the permission. The convention is to specify the class name, the permission name, and the actions in the following format:

```
("ClassName" "name" "actions")
```

The `Permission` class implements two interfaces: `Guard` and `java.io.Serializable`. For the latter, the intention is that `Permission` objects may be transported to remote machines, such as via RMI, and thus a `Serializable` representation is useful. `Guard`, which is related to the class `GuardedObject`, is discussed in Chapter 6. Applications (and applets) are free to introduce new categories of `Permission` classes beyond those that the system always supports. How to add such application-specific permissions is discussed in Chapter 5.

The method newPermissionCollection() returns an empty Permission-Collection object for a given Permission object, or null if a corresponding PermissionCollection() class is not defined. The next section deals with permission sets.

3.6.2   Permission Sets

Often it is more convenient to deal with sets of permissions rather than one permission at a time. The abstract class java.security.PermissionCollection represents a collection (that is, a set that allows duplicates) of Permission objects for a single category (such as file permissions), for ease of grouping. Each PermissionCollection object holds a homogeneous collection of permissions. In other words, each instance of the class holds only permissions of the same type. Following are its more important method calls:

```
public abstract void add(Permission permission);
public abstract boolean implies(Permission permission);
public abstract Enumeration elements();
public void setReadOnly();
public boolean isReadOnly();
```

The add method adds a Permission object to the current collection of Permission objects. How this is done is left to each subclass. For example, file permissions can be added to a PermissionCollection object in any order.

Similar to its purpose in the Permission class, the implies method here checks whether the specified permission is implied by one or more of the permissions in the current PermissionCollection object. If so, we say that the permission is implied by the PermissionCollection object. Note that in this case, the specified permission, say to read and write file *x*, might not be implied by any single permission but rather by a collection of permissions in the Permission-Collection object, such as one permission to read file *x* and another to write file *x*. Thus it is crucial that any concrete subclass of PermissionCollection ensures that the correct semantics are followed when the implies method is called.

The setReadOnly method marks this PermissionCollection object as read-only. After this, no new Permission objects may be added to it using addPermission.

To group a number of Permission objects of the same type, you should first call the newPermissionCollection method on that particular type of Permission object. The default behavior (from the Permission class) is simply to return null. Sometimes, subclasses of Permission need to store their permissions in a particular PermissionCollection object in order to provide the correct semantics when the `PermissionCollection.implies` method is called. In this case, they override the method. If a non-null value is returned, that `PermissionCollection` must be used. If null is returned, then the caller of `newPermissionCollection` is free to store permissions of the given type in any `PermissionCollection` it chooses (one that uses a `Hashtable`, one that uses a `Vector`, and so on).

The `java.security.Permissions` class represents a collection of collections of `Permission` objects, that is, a super collection of heterogeneous permissions. A subclass of `PermissionCollection` and final, it basically is a collection of `PermissionCollection` objects. That is, it contains different types of `Permission` objects organized into `PermissionCollections`. For example, any `java.io.FilePermission` objects added to an instance of this class are all stored in a single `PermissionCollection`. This is the `PermissionCollection` returned by a call to the `newPermissionCollection` method in the `FilePermission` class. Similarly, any `java.lang.RuntimePermission` objects are stored in the `PermissionCollection` returned by a call to the `newPermissionCollection` method in the `RuntimePermission` class. Thus this class represents a collection of `PermissionCollections`.

Following are two of the methods worth examining:

```
public void add(Permission permission);
public boolean implies(Permission permission);
```

When the add method is called to add a `Permission`, the `Permission` is stored in the appropriate `PermissionCollection`. If no such collection yet exists, the `Permission` object's class is determined and the `newPermissionCollection` method is called on that class to create the `PermissionCollection` and add it to the `Permission` object. If `newPermissionCollection` returns null, then a default `PermissionCollection` that uses a hash table will be created and used. Each hash table entry has a `Permission` object's name as the key and the `Permission` object as the value.

Similar to its action with `PermissionCollection`, the `implies` method checks to see if this object's `PermissionCollection` for permissions of the specified permission's type implies the permission expressed in the passed-in `Permission` object. It returns `true` if the combination of permissions in the appropriate `PermissionCollection` (for example, a `FilePermissionCollection` for a `FilePermission`) together imply the specified permission.

Note, neither of the two permission set classes is a subclass of `java.security.Permission`.

3.6.3   java.security.UnresolvedPermission

Recall that the policy for a Java runtime environment (specifying which permissions are available for code from various code sources) is represented by a Policy object. In particular, the internal state of a security policy is normally expressed by the Permission objects that are associated with each code source CodeSource. Thus, whenever a Policy object is initialized or refreshed, Permission objects of appropriate classes may need to be created for all permissions allowed by the policy.

Many Permission class types referenced by the policy configuration exist locally (that is, those that can be found on CLASSPATH). Objects for such permissions can be instantiated during Policy initialization. For example, it is always possible to instantiate a java.io.FilePermission, since the FilePermission class is found on CLASSPATH.

However, the dynamic nature of Java technology makes it possible that when the Policy object is constructed, the actual code that implements a particular Permission class has not yet been loaded (or is not even available for loading). For example, a referenced Permission class might be in a JAR file that will later be loaded. In this case, the Permission class cannot be defined in the Java runtime environment at this point. For each such class, an UnresolvedPermission object is instantiated instead, as a placeholder that contains information about the permission. Thus the UnresolvedPermission class is used to hold such "unresolved" permissions. Similarly, the class UnresolvedPermissionCollection stores a collection of UnresolvedPermission permissions.

Unresolved permissions of a particular type are resolved when access control decisions are made regarding a permission of the same type that was previously unresolved, but whose class has since become available (it either is already loaded or is now loadable). That is, for each such UnresolvedPermission, a new object of the appropriate class type is instantiated, based on the information in the UnresolvedPermission. This new object then replaces the stored Unresolved-Permission. If the permission is still unresolvable at this time, it is considered invalid in the sense that the permission is not granted and the request to access is denied. Of course, an UnresolvedPermission may get resolved eventually (after a few tries) when the relevant permission class finally becomes available.

Note that it is not necessary to instantiate all loadable permission classes at Policy initiation. This is because typically only a small portion of the Policy's contents is needed to run the virtual machine. Thus it is quite legitimate, and even sometimes desirable for performance and efficiency, to make extensive use of UnresolvedPermission even when the Permission class is loadable, thus delaying the actual instantiation of the Permission objects until right before they are used. Nevertheless, you must pay close attention to the complexity that UnresolvedPermission adds, especially when an UnresolvedPermission can be resolved into different implementations at different times.

A few methods in the UnresolvedPermission class need explaining:

```
public UnresolvedPermission(String type,
        String name, String actions,
        java.security.cert.Certificate certs[]);
public boolean implies(Permission p);
public boolean equals(Object obj);
```

Note that the constructor takes an array of certificates, which can be used to verify the signatures on the Permission class binary files. This feature does not exist for other Permission classes. This is because for permissions that are not resident on CLASSPATH or other system paths, the permissions are more than likely defined by a third party and are delivered as part of an extension or application. In this case, the authenticity of the Permission classes, such as whether they respect the intentions of the root class java.security.Permission and whether their implementation is not malicious, can be questionable and are difficult to verify from within an application. The certificates, if present, can provide additional assurance. This assurance depends on the trust conveyed by the signature keys that signed the Permission classes and on how an application chooses to interpret the certificates.

The certificates also are useful when a Permission class does not reside locally and is downloaded each time it is used. On the one hand, ensuring that the same class file is downloaded each time is often desirable. However, this could be difficult to verify unless local storage is used to keep a copy or at least a fingerprint (a hash value) of a prior class file. On the other hand, software tends to get upgraded often, so it is not uncommon to expect the same named Permission class file to change over time, albeit in a consistent way. But again this consistency is difficult to check by examining the class files. The certificates, which can be used to verify a class file's digital signature, normally change less often and can be managed more efficiently than the actual class files.

The by now familiar implies() method always returns false for unresolved permissions. This is because an UnresolvedPermission is never considered to imply another permission.

Finally, when comparing two UnresolvedPermission objects for equality, you need to check that the second Permission object is also an Unresolved-Permission and has the same type (class) name, permission name, actions, and certificates as the first object, the one doing the comparison.

3.6.4   `java.io.FilePermission`

The `java.io.FilePermission` class represents access to a file or directory. A `FilePermission` consists of a path name and a set of actions valid for that path name. The path name is that of the file or directory on which the specified actions are granted. It can be specified in the following ways, where directory names and file names are strings that cannot contain whitespaces.

`file`	The named file
`directory`	Same as directory /
`directory/file`	The named file
`directory/*`	All files in this directory
`*`	All files in the current directory
`directory/-`	All files in the file system under this directory
`-`	All files in the file system under the current directory
`"<<ALL FILES>>"`	All files in the file system

In other words, a pathname that ends in "/*" indicates a directory and all of the files contained in that directory. Here, "/" is the file separator character, implemented as `File.separatorChar`. A pathname that ends with "/-" indicates a directory and (recursively) all files and subdirectories contained in that directory. A pathname consisting of the special token `"<<ALL FILES>>"` matches any file. Note that a pathname consisting of a single "*" indicates all of the files in the current directory. A pathname consisting of a single "-" indicates all of the files in the current directory and (recursively) all files and subdirectories contained in the current directory.

The actions to be granted are passed to the constructor in a string containing a list of zero or more comma-separated keywords. Following are the possible keywords. The actions string is converted to lowercase before processing.

- `read` refers to read permission.

- `write` refers to write permission.

- `execute` refers to execute permission, which allows `Runtime.exec` to be called. It corresponds to the security check done within the `Security-Manager.checkExec()` method.

- `delete` refers to delete permission, which allows `File.delete` to be called. It corresponds to the security check done within the `SecurityManager.check-Delete` method.

Here are the important method calls in the `java.io.FilePermission` class:

```
public FilePermission(String path, String actions);
public boolean implies(Permission p)
public boolean equals(Object obj)
public PermissionCollection newPermissionCollection()
```

The `implies()` method checks to see if this `FilePermission` object implies the specified permission. More specifically, this method returns `true` if p is an instance of `FilePermission`, p's actions are a proper subset of this object's actions, and p's pathname is implied by this object's pathname. For example, `/tmp/*` implies `/tmp/foo`, since `/tmp/` encompasses the `/tmp` directory and all files in that directory, including the one named `foo`.

When checking two `FilePermission` objects for equality using the `equals` method, you must check that `obj` is a `FilePermission` and has the same pathname and actions as the object on which `equals` is invoked. Slightly more complicated is the method that returns a new `PermissionCollection` object for storing `FilePermission` objects. `FilePermission` objects must be stored in a manner that allows them to be inserted into the collection in any order and that also enables the `PermissionCollection`'s `implies()` method to be implemented in an efficient (and consistent) manner.

For example, suppose that you have two `FilePermissions`:

```
"/tmp/-", "read"
"/tmp/scratch/foo", "write"
```

and you are calling the `implies()` method with this `FilePermission`:

```
"/tmp/scratch/foo", "read,write"
```

In this case, the `implies` method must take into account both the `/tmp/-`, `read` and the `/tmp/scratch/foo,write` permissions, so the effective permission includes `/tmp/scratch/foo,read,write`, and `implies` returns `true`. The semantics of the `implies` method for `FilePermissions` are handled properly by the `PermissionCollection` object returned by this `newPermission-Collection` method.

Note that `"<<ALL FILES>>"` is a special string denoting all files in the system. On a UNIX system, this includes all files under the root directory. On an MS-DOS system, this includes all files on all drives.

Thus the following are valid code samples for creating file permissions.

```
import java.io.FilePermission;
FilePermission p = new FilePermission("myfile", "read,write");
FilePermission p = new FilePermission("/home/gong/", "read");
```

```
FilePermission p = new FilePermission("/tmp/mytmp",
                                      "read,delete");
FilePermission p = new FilePermission("bin/*", "execute");
FilePermission p = new FilePermission("*", "read");
FilePermission p = new FilePermission("/-", "read,execute"");
FilePermission p = new FilePermission("-", "read,execute");
FilePermission p = new FilePermission("<<ALL FILES>>", "read");
```

The `implies` method in this class correctly interprets the file system. For example, `FilePermission("/-", "read,execute")` implies `FilePermission("/home/ gong/public-html/index.html", "read")`, while `FilePermission("bin/*", "execute")` implies `FilePermission("bin/emacs19.31", "execute")`.

Note that most of these strings are given in a platform-dependent format. This, unfortunately, will be necessary until a universal file description language is in common use. For example, to represent read access to the file named `foo` in the `temp` directory on the C drive of an MS-Windows system, you would use

```
FilePermission p = new FilePermission("c:\\temp\\foo", "read");
```

The double backslashes, "\\", are necessary to represent a single backslash because the strings are processed by a tokenizer (`java.io.StreamTokenizer`). The tokenizer allows "'"" to be used as an escape string (for example, ""n" to indicate a new line) and thus requires two backslashes to indicate a single backslash. After the tokenizer has processed the `FilePermission` target string, converting double backslashes to single backslashes, the end result is the actual path `"c:"temp" foo"`.

Note also that the use of meta symbols such as "*" and "–" precludes the use of some specific file names with those symbols. We consider this a small limitation that can be tolerated for the moment.

Also note that "/–" and "<<ALL FILES>>" are the same target on UNIX systems in that they both refer to the entire file system. They can refer to multiple physical file systems that are organized as one virtual file system. Conversely, on a Unix system that divides the file system into volumes or slices, "/–" may refer to only the current slice while "<<ALL FILES>>" refers to all slices. The two targets are potentially different on other operating systems, such as MS-Windows and MacOS.

Finally, note that a target name that specifies just a directory with a `read` action, as in

```
FilePermission p = new FilePermission("/home/gong/", "read");
```

means that you are giving permission only to list the files in that directory, not to read any of them. To allow read access to the files, you must specify either an explicit filename or an "*" or "-", as in

```
FilePermission p = new FilePermission("/home/gong/myfile",
                            "read");
FilePermission p = new FilePermission("/home/gong/*",
                            "read");
FilePermission p = new FilePermission("/home/gong/-",
                            "read");
```

To illustrate how file permissions are used in the real world, here is a code segment from the constructor of the class `java.io.FileInputStream`.

```
public FileInputStream(String name)
     throws FileNotFoundException {
   SecurityManager security = System.getSecurityManager();
   if (security != null) {
      security.checkRead(name);
   }
(now open the file)
}
```

The corresponding `checkRead()` method in class `SecurityManager` does the following.

```
public void checkRead(String file) {
   checkPermission(new FilePermission(file, "read"));
}
```

This example shows how to create a corresponding file permission and use it to invoke the security check. You could obtain the same result by bypassing `checkRead()` and having the `FileInputStream` constructor call `checkPermission()` directly. We chose to keep `checkRead()` in order to provide backward compatibility. More is said on compatibility issues where the `SecurityManager` class is discussed in Section 3.10.

3.6.5   `java.net.SocketPermission`

The `java.net.SocketPermission` class represents access to a network via sockets. A `SocketPermission` consists of a host specification and a set of actions specifying ways to connect to that host.

Informally, the host can be given as `hostname:port-range`, where hostname can be given in the following ways:

`hostname`	A single host
`IP address`	A single host
`localhost`	The local machine
`" "`	Equivalent to `localhost`
`hostname.domain`	A single host within the domain
`hostname.subdomain.domain`	A single host within the domain
`*.domain`	All hosts in the domain
`*.subdomain.domain`	All hosts in the domain
`*`	All hosts

More precisely, the host is specified in BNF format as

```
host = (hostname | IPaddress)[:portrange]
portrange = portnumber |-portnumber | portnumber-[portnumber]
```

The host is expressed as a DNS name, as a numerical IP address, or as `local-host` (for the local machine). The wildcard "`*`" may be included once in a DNS host specification. If it is included, it must be in the leftmost position, as in `*.sun.com`.

`portrange` is optional and can be given as follows:

`N`	A single port
`N-`	All ports numbered N and above
`-N`	All ports numbered N and below
`N1-N2`	All ports between N1 and N2, inclusive

Here N, N1, and N2 are non-negative integers ranging from 0 to 65535.

The possible action by which to connect with a host are

- ◆ `accept`
- ◆ `connect`
- ◆ `listen`
- ◆ `resolve`

`listen` actions are meaningful only when used with `localhost`. Note that implicitly, the action `resolve` is implied by `accept`, `connect`, and `listen` when any of the other actions are present. In other words, anyone that can listen or accept incoming connections from or initiate outgoing connections to a host should be able to look up the name of the remote host.

You might question why there is both a `listen` action and an `accept` action. Why not have just `accept`, which would imply `listen`? Both actions are necessary because `listen` is an action that applies only to ports on the local host, whereas `accept` is an action that applies to ports on both the local and remote hosts.

Following are the more interesting methods for the java.net.Socket-Permission class:

```
public SocketPermission(String host, String action);
public boolean equals(Object obj);
public boolean implies(Permission p);
```

Here are the various ways to construct socket permissions.

```
import java.net.SocketPermission;
SocketPermission p =
    new SocketPermision("java.sun.com","accept");
p = new SocketPermission("204.160.241.99","accept");
p = new SocketPermission("*.com","connect");
p = new SocketPermission("*.sun.com:80","accept");
p = new SocketPermission("*.sun.com:-1023","accept");
p = new SocketPermission("*.sun.com:1024","connect");
p = new SocketPermission("java.sun.com:8000-9000",
    "connect,accept");
p = new SocketPermission("localhost:1024-",
    "accept,connect,listen");
```

Suppose you try the following:

```
SocketPermission("java.sun.com:80,8080","accept");
SocketPermission("java.sun.com,javasun.sun.com","accept");
```

You will encounter a runtime exception, IllegalArgumentException. This is because comma-separated lists are not accepted in hostnames or port ranges.

Checking two SocketPermission objects for equality is easy. You simply check to see if both are of the type SocketPermission and have the same hostname and actions. Checking if this SocketPermission object implies another specified permission is more complicated.

First, the implies method ensures that both of the following are true (and returns false if one is not).

1. p is an instance of SocketPermission.

2. p's actions are a proper subset of this object's actions, and its port range is included in this portrange.

Then it checks the following, in order. When a stated condition is true, it skips the remaining checks and returns true. If none are true, it returns false.

1. If this object was initialized with a numeric IP address and one of p's IP addresses is equal to this object's IP address

2. If this object is a wildcard domain (such as *.sun.com) and p's canonical name (the name without any preceding *) ends with this object's canonical hostname; for example, *.sun.com implies *.eng.sun.com

3. If this object was initialized with a host name (instead of a numeric address), and one of the IP addresses corresponding to the host name equals one of p's IP addresses

4. If this canonical name equals p's canonical name

Here it becomes clear that the meaning of having the same host name can be subtle. When comparing host names, you sometimes must compare the corresponding IP addresses instead. However, when initializing a SocketPermission object, there is no need to do a DNS lookup right then. It is sufficient if you delay the lookup until the implies method is called, since that is when the authenticity of the hostname and other information matters. Of course, if DNS records change during the delay, the delayed check might yield unexpected results. If you choose to use your own mechanism to compare two SocketPermission objects, you should be wary of taking the host names at their face value.

To illustrate how socket permissions are used in the real world, here is a code segment from a constructor of the class java.io.Socket.

```
SecurityManager security = System.getSecurityManager();
if (security != null) {
    security.checkConnect(address, port);
}
```

The corresponding checkConnect() method in the SecurityManager class does the following.

```
public void checkConnect(String host, int port) {
    if (port == -1) {
        checkPermission(new SocketPermission(host,"resolve"));
    } else {
        checkPermission(new SocketPermission(host+":"+port,
    "connect"));
    }
}
```

3.6.6 `java.security.BasicPermission`

The `java.security.BasicPermission` class extends the `Permission` class and offers a very simple naming convention that is often encountered when creating permission classes. It can be used as the base class for other permission classes that want to follow the same naming convention.

The name of a `BasicPermission` is the name of the given permission (for example, `exitVM`, `setFactory`, and `queuePrintJob`). The naming convention follows the hierarchical property naming convention. An asterisk may appear at the end of the name, following a "." or by itself, to signify a wildcard match. For example, `java.*` and `*` are valid but `*java` and `a*b` are invalid.

Thus `BasicPermission` is commonly used as the base class for **named** permissions. A named permission is a permission that contains a name but no actions list; you either have the named permission or you do not. `BasicPermission` is an abstract class, so you cannot really construct it and must construct one of its subclasses instead. Subclasses may implement actions on top of `BasicPermission`, if desired. Following are the subclasses of `BasicPermission`:

```
java.util.PropertyPermission
java.lang.RuntimePermission
java.awt.AWTPermission
java.net.NetPermission
java.lang.reflect.ReflectPermission
java.io.SerializablePermission
java.security.SecurityPermission.
```

Note that even though the action string (inherited from `Permission`) is unused, you must provide a constructor for `BasicPermission`. Thus the following two constructors are equivalent:

```
public BasicPermission(String name);
public BasicPermission(String name, String actions);
```

The `implies()` method checks to see if the specified permission to be compared with is an instance of `BasicPermission`, and if so, whether its name is implied by the name of the comparing permission. Here, name string comparison takes into account of wildcards, so that, for example, `"a.b.*"` implies `"a.b.c"`.

When checking two `BasicPermission` objects for equality, you check to see if their name strings are equal.

3.6.7 `java.util.PropertyPermission`

The `java.util.PropertyPermission` class represents the permission to access Java properties set in various property files. For example, the property called `user.home` is typically set to be the home directory of a user.

A subclass of `BasicPermission`, `PropertyPermission`, similar to a `FilePermission`, contains a target and an action. The targets for this class are basically the names of Java properties, such as java.home and os.name. The naming convention follows the hierarchical property naming convention. Also, an asterisk may appear at the end of the name, following a "." or by itself, to signify a wildcard match. For example, java.* and * are valid, while *java and a*b are invalid. Thus targets can be specified as * (any property), "a.*" (any property whose name has a prefix "a."), "a.b.*", and so on.

This class is one of the BasicPermission subclasses that implements actions on top of BasicPermission. The actions are read and write. Their meanings are defined as follows.

♦ Read permission allows the getProperty() method in java.lang.System to be called to get the property value.

♦ Write permission allows the setProperty() method to be called to set the property value.

There is nothing surprising about the methods in this class, listed as follows:

```
public PropertyPermission(String name, String actions)
public boolean implies(Permission p)
public boolean equals(Object obj)
```

The actions to be granted are passed to the constructor in a string containing a list of zero or more comma-separated keywords. The actions string is converted to lowercase before processing.

The following code segment shows how this permission is used. The java.System class implements two static methods, getProperties() and set-Properties(), as follows.

```
public static String getProperty(String key) {
    if (security != null) {
        security.checkPermission(new
                      PropertyPermission(key, "read"));
    }
    return props.getProperty(key);
}


public static String setProperty(String key, String value) {
    if (security != null)
        security.checkPermission(new
                      PropertyPermission(key, "write"));
    return (String) props.put(key, value);
}
```

3.6.8   `java.lang.RuntimePermission`

The `java.lang.RuntimePermission` class is a straightforward subclass of `BasicPermission`. The target for a `RuntimePermission` can be represented by any string, and there is no action associated with the targets. For example, `RuntimePermission("exitVM")` denotes the permission to exit the JVM.

The naming convention follows the hierarchical property naming convention. Also, an asterisk may appear at the end of the name, following a "." or by itself, to signify a wildcard match. For example, `package.*` and `*` are valid, while `*package` and `a*b` are invalid.

Currently, the following target names are used:

```
createClassLoader
getClassLoader
setContextClassLoader
createSecurityManager
setSecurityManager
exitVM
setFactory
setIO
modifyThread
modifyThreadGroup
getProtectionDomain
readFileDescriptor
writeFileDescriptor
loadLibrary.{library name}
accessClassInPackage.{package name}
defineClassInPackage.{package name}
accessDeclaredMembers.{class name}
queuePrintJob
stopThread
```

To see how this `Permission` class is used, consider the situation in which some code tries to link in a native library. A native library is not under JVM's supervision, so once linked in, it can perform security sensitive tasks. Thus linking a native library must be a controlled operation. In the `java.lang.Runtime` class is the following code segment.

```
public void loadLibrary(String libname) {
    ...
    SecurityManager security = System.getSecurityManager();
```

```
   if (security != null)
      security.checkLink(libname);
   ...
}
```

The `checkLink()` method in `SecurityManager` class is implemented as follows.

```
public void checkLink(String lib) {
   checkPermission(new RuntimePermission("loadLibrary."+lib));
}
```

3.6.9   `java.awt.AWTPermission`

The `java.awt.AWTPermission` class is very similar to `RuntimePermission`. An `AWTPermission` contains a name but no actions list. Following are some of the targets for this class:

```
showWindowWithoutWarningBanner
accessClipboard
accessEventQueue
listenToAllAWTEvents
readDisplayPixels
```

The naming convention follows the hierarchical property naming convention. Also, an asterisk may be used to represent all AWT permissions.

In the `java.awt.Window` class, creating a top-level window requires the following code segment to be exercised.

```
...
SecurityManager sm = System.getSecurityManager();
if (sm != null) {
   if (!sm.checkTopLevelWindow(this)) {
      ...
   }
   ...
}
```

This check method translates into the following in the `SecurityManager` class.

```
public boolean checkTopLevelWindow(Object window) {
   try {
      checkPermission(topLevelWindowPermission);
      return true;
```

```
    } catch (SecurityException se) {
        // Fall through to return false.
    }
    return false;
}
```

Note that this check method returns a boolean rather than either returning silently or throwing a security exception, as other check methods do. For backward compatibility reasons, we did not change this interface.

3.6.10 java.net.NetPermission

The java.net.NetPermission class is yet another subclass of BasicPermission that contains targets but no actions. The targets represent various network permissions. The naming convention follows the hierarchical property naming convention. Also, an asterisk may appear at the end of the name, following a "." or by itself, to signify a wildcard match. For example, foo.* and * are valid, while *foo and a*b are invalid. Following are some of its targets:

```
setDefaultAuthenticator
specifyStreamHandler
requestPasswordAuthentication
```

In the java.net.Authenticator class, the requestPasswordAuthentication() method asks the authenticator that has been registered with the system for a password. Obviously, passwords must be safely guarded. Thus the following check is performed.

```
SecurityManager sm = System.getSecurityManager();
if (sm != null) sm.checkPermission(new
    NetPermission("requestPasswordAuthentication"));
```

3.6.11 java.lang.reflect.ReflectPermission

The java.lang.reflect.ReflectPermission class is one more subclass of BasicPermission and is used for reflective operations. A ReflectPermission is a named permission (like RuntimePermission) and has no actions. The only name currently defined is suppressAccessChecks, which allows you to suppress the standard Java language access checks performed by reflected objects at their point of use. Normally, access checks are done when someone tries to access a class's public, default (package) access, protected, and private members.

In the `java.lang.reflect.AccessibleObject` class is a convenience method, `setAccessible()`, that sets the accessible flag for an array of objects with a single security check (for efficiency). This method implements the following check.

```
SecurityManager sm = System.getSecurityManager();
if (sm != null) sm.checkPermission(new
        ReflectPermission("suppressAccessChecks"));
```

3.6.12 `java.io.SerializablePermission`

The `java.io.SerializablePermission` class is very similar to `ReflectPermission` and contains the following targets and no actions:

```
enableSubclassImplementation
enableSubstitution
```

For example, in the `java.io.ObjectOutputStream` class, the following code segment checks to see if a subclass can completely reimplement `ObjectOutputStream`.

```
SecurityManager sm = System.getSecurityManager();
if (sm != null) sm.checkPermission(new
    SerializablePermission("enableSubclassImplementation"));
enableSubclassImplementation = true;
```

3.6.13 `java.security.SecurityPermission`

The `SecurityPermission` class controls access to security-related objects, such as `Security`, `Policy`, `Provider`, `Signer`, and `Identity`. It contains the following targets and no actions:

```
getPolicy
setPolicy
getProperty.{key}
setProperty.{key}
insertProvider.{provider name}
removeProvider.{provider name}
setSystemScope
setIdentityPublicKey
setIdentityInfo
```

```
addIdentityCertificate
removeIdentityCertificate
printIdentity
clearProviderProperties.{provider name}
putProviderProperty.{provider name}
removeProviderProperty.{provider name}
getSignerPrivateKey
setSignerKeyPair
```

The `java.security.Policy` class contains a static method to set the default system `Policy` object. Because the `Policy` object now defines what sort of security is enforced, this object cannot be changed without the appropriate permission.

```
public static Policy setPolicy() {
    SecurityManager sm = System.getSecurityManager();
    f (sm != null)
        sm.checkPermission(new SecurityPermission("setPolicy"));
    ...
}
```

Note that the classes `java.security.Identity` and `java.security.IdentityScope` have been deprecated in JDK 1.2 and should not be used.

3.6.14 `java.security.AllPermission`

The new `java.security.AllPermission` class represents all permissions. We introduced it to simplify the work of system administrators who might need to perform multiple tasks that require all (or numerous) permissions and it would be inconvenient to require the security policy to iterate through all permissions.

Since `AllPermission` does not care about the actual targets and actions, its constructors ignore all passed-in parameters. By definition, `AllPermission` permission implies all permissions. Moreover, two `AllPermission` objects are always considered equal. Thus the `AllPermission` class implements the following two methods specially.

```
public boolean implies(Permission p) {
    return true;
}

public boolean equals(Object obj) {
    return (obj instanceof AllPermission);
}
```

Note that `AllPermission` also implies new permissions that are defined in the future. Clearly, granting this permission must be done with caution.

3.6.15 Implications of Permission Implications

Recall that permissions are often compared with each other. To facilitate such comparisons, each permission class must define an `implies()` method that represents how the particular permission class relates to other permission classes. For example, `java.io.FilePermission("/tmp/*", "read")` implies `java.io.FilePermission("/tmp/a.txt", "read")`, but it does not imply any `java.net.NetPermission`. However, there is another deeper implication that might not be immediately obvious to some readers.

Suppose that an applet is granted permission to write to the entire file system. Presumably, this allows the applet to replace the system binary, including the JVM runtime environment. This effectively means that the applet has been granted all permissions. Or suppose an applet is granted runtime permission to create class loaders. It effectively is granted many more permissions, since a class loader can perform sensitive operations.

Other permissions that are potentially dangerous to give out include these:

♦ `AllPermission` (of course)

♦ Those that allow the setting of system properties

♦ Runtime permissions for defining packages and for loading native code libraries (because the Java security architecture is not designed to and does not prevent malicious behavior at the level of native code)

3.7 Assigning Permissions

Previous sections covered the basics of security policy, code source, and the `Permission` class hierarchy. This section discusses how permissions are actually granted to running code.

When loading a new class that originated from a particular `CodeSource`, the security mechanism consults the `Policy` object to determine what permissions to grant. It does this by calling the `getPermissions()` method of the `Policy` object:

```
public abstract Permissions getPermissions(CodeSource
    codesource);
```

In other words, the permissions are *generally* granted before the class is defined in the Java runtime. There are a couple of exceptions. First, it is perfectly legitimate to delay the instantiation of the granted permission classes and objects until a security check occurs. This optimization allows a Java program that does not call for security checks to execute faster and with a smaller footprint. Even for a Java program that does trigger a security check, this optimization allows it to start up faster. Note that if the content of the policy is changed between the time the policy class is instantiated and the time the first security check is invoked, the presence of this optimization technique will result in a `Policy` object's having more up-to-date content. Keeping the policy content up to date is of course a good thing. Section 3.3 discusses policy update using the `refresh` method.

Second, it is possible that the permissions already granted to a class will be changed or even withdrawn after the class is defined, such as during a revocation procedure after a security incident. Although the JDK 1.2 default implementation does not alter permissions once they are granted, such alterations are considered legal, as long as they are also controlled with the appropriate permissions.

It is worth emphasizing that permissions are granted to classes, which are static Java code, and not to objects, which are instances of classes. The primary reasons for this are to reduce complexity and increase manageability. Objects are runtime entities, so they do not exist in a static state. But the security policy must exist in a static state and independent of any particular Java runtime environment, so it cannot possibly refer to objects. Also, for the sort of security policies considered here, the same policy should be enforced no matter how objects are instantiated. In addition, the number of different classes tends to be a lot smaller than the number of different objects. Even if you want to support a security policy that is dependent on the runtime environment, the right way is not to grant permissions to objects but rather to perform security checks that take into account the actual runtime environment.[3] I return to this subject in Section 3.10.

Finally, recall that the security policy, in essence, can be represented with a list of entries, each being of the form (codeSource, `Permission`), thereby indicating that code from the named code source is given the named permission. Clearly, for a given piece of code, its code source can match multiple entries in the policy. In this case, the code is granted the union of all permissions granted in each matched entry in the policy. In other words, permission assignment is *additive*. For example, if code signed with key A gets permission X and code signed by key B gets permission Y, then code signed by both A and B gets permissions X and Y. Similarly, if the URL `http://java.sun.com` is given permission X and

---

[3] The security policy can grant permissions to interfaces, too, but this is immaterial, as interfaces alone do not get instantiated into objects that cause security checks to occur.

the URL http://java.sun.com/people is given permission Y, then an applet from http://java.sun.com/people/gong gets both X and Y (assuming that the signers match).

For details of the matching algorithm, refer to the implies() method in the CodeSource section (Section 3.5). Note that URL matching here is purely syntactic and does not deal with proxies or redirects. For example, a policy can give an entry that specifies a URL ftp://ftp.sun.com. Such an entry is useful only when you can obtain Java code directly from FTP for execution. If the Web server redirects this URL to a different one, this policy entry might have no effect. To specify URLs for the local file system, you can use a file URL. For example, to specify files in the /home/gong/temp directory on a Solaris system, you can use file:/home/gong/temp/*. To specify files in the temp directory on the C drive on an MS-Windows system, you can use file:/c:/temp/*. One more note: Code base URLs always use slashes (no backlashes), regardless of the platform to which they apply. Of course, you can also use an absolute pathname such as /home/gong/bin/MyWonderfulJava.

3.7.1   Positive versus Negative Permissions

It is important to observe that the Permission class hierarchy currently denotes positive permissions only. This means that if a permission is present in the security policy, the said permission is granted. The denial of a permission is implicitly expressed by the absence of the said permission, rather than by the presence of a "negative" permission. The lack of negative permissions today does not mean that they cannot be introduced in the future.

However, restricting oneself to only positive permissions has significant benefits for simplicity and good performance. This is because no conflict can exist between two positive permissions in the sense that there is no danger that access granted by one permission is denied by the other. Consequently, when you examine a security policy to decide what permissions to grant to some code, you do not need to check for conflict. Section 3.10 discusses how to perform access control checking and the need to examine if a set of permissions implies a particular permission. Without negative permissions, you can determine that the set implies the said permission as soon as you find one permission within the set that implies the said permission. These benefits to JDK implementation are also benefits to security policy administration.

The lack of negative permissions, on the other hand, does not allow you to specify a policy conveniently, such as "grant all file system access except for this particular file." However, this loss of convenience is not really a loss of functionality because a negative can be expressed by the complement of a positive. It seems that with additional "syntactic sugar" in more powerful policy processing tools, one can preprocess a policy with negative permissions and translate the policy into one with only positive permissions. How this issue plays out in practice remains to be seen.

3.8 ProtectionDomain

When implementing the permission assignment algorithm, you can follow the straightforward approach of encapsulating all of the permissions granted to a class, which are represented by various Permission objects, in a Permissions object and then associating the permission set with the class via an interface in the base class java.lang.Class. However, linking a permission set with a class so directly leads to a rigid API that cannot be easily extended. For example, suppose that you want to perform access control checks based on not only permissions granted to the class but also on the name of the principal (for example, a user) running the code. To do this, you would have to extend the Class class with additional interfaces, thus cluttering the base class.

To facilitate extensibility, JDK 1.2 allows permissions to be granted to protection domains; classes and objects belong to protection domains and indirectly "inherit" the granted permissions. According to the classical definition of a protection domain [70], a domain is scoped by the set of objects that is currently directly accessible by a principal, where a principal is an entity in the computer system to which authorizations (and as a result, accountability) are granted. Thus the Java sandbox in JDK 1.0 is, in a sense, a protection domain with a fixed boundary. In JDK 1.2, each class belongs to one and only one domain. The Java runtime maintains the mapping from code (classes and objects) to their protection domains and then to their permissions. The mapping from a class to its domain is set only once, before the class is usable, and cannot be changed during the lifetime of the Class object.

The definition of the class java.security.ProtectionDomain is fairly simple, as follows.

```
public ProtectionDomain(CodeSource codesource,
    PermissionCollection permissions);
public boolean implies(Permission permission);
```

The implies() method checks to see if the ProtectionDomain implies the permissions expressed in the Permission object.

The following code segment from java.lang.Class is one example of how protection domains are used.

```
public java.security.ProtectionDomain getProtectionDomain() {
    SecurityManager sm = System.getSecurityManager();
    if (sm != null) {
        getPDperm = new RuntimePermission("getProtectionDomain");
        sm.checkPermission(getPDperm);
    }
    return protectiondomain;
}
```

Note that because a `ProtectionDomain` object may contain sensitive information, access to it is security checked with a runtime permission.

A number of finer points are worth discussing. First, in JDK1.2 protection domains are created on demand as new classes are loaded into the runtime. In the JDK 1.2 default implementation, classes belonging to the same domain are loaded by the same class loader. This implementation detail is natural but not necessary. Classes belonging to the same domain are granted the same permissions, but the reverse is obviously not true, since there may be classes that have the same permissions but that are from different code sources and thus belong to different domains.

Second, out of the many protection domains created during the lifetime of the Java runtime, one protection domain is special: the **system domain**. The system domain is a domain consisting of all code that is considered part of the system core (or kernel, in operating system terminology). For historical reasons, system code is always loaded by a primordial class loader that is written entirely in C. This has the effect that system classes appear to be loaded with a special null class loader. JDK 1.2 largely maintains this backward compatibility. Details of class loading are covered in Section 3.9. For the time being, you need remember only that code in the system domain is automatically granted all permissions. It is important that all protected external resources, such as the file system, the networking facility, and the screen and keyboard, are directly accessible only via system code, which mediates access requests made by less trustworthy code. Note that although system classes have a special null class loader (this is discussed in Section 3.9), their protection domain is a non-null object that has been granted `AllPermission`.

Moreover, the indirection between a class and its permissions via a protection domain has an interesting benefit for Java virtual machine vendors to perform implementation optimizations. For example, recall that it is desirable in some cases to change the permissions granted to some code during the lifetime of a Java runtime. This can be achieved by changing the contents but not the reference of the `ProtectionDomain` object that is associated with a class. By maintaining stability in the reference of the `ProtectionDomain` object, you can determine if two classes belong to the same domain and then apply various optimization techniques.

Finally, note that the protection domains also serve as a convenient point for grouping and isolating units of protection within the Java runtime. For example, different domains may be prevented from interacting with each other. This can be done by using distinct class loaders to load classes belonging to different domains in such a way that any permitted interaction must be either through system code or explicitly allowed by the domains concerned. This is because in the JVM, a class is distinguished by itself plus the ClassLoader instance that loaded the class. Thus a class loader defines a distinct name space. It can be used to isolate and protect code within one protection domain by refusing to load code from different domains (and with different permissions).

This point brings up the issue of accessibility, that is, what is visible to an object and what methods can an object invoke and on what other objects. In defining the new security architecture, we examined existing coding practices that utilize accessibility features that makes one object visible to another. We found that accessibility needed to remain flexible, especially in server programs, without regard to the particular security policy being enforced. So we decided to maintain existing accessibility customs and rules, thus making accessibility orthogonal to security. In other words, it is up to the application programmer to decide if and how objects and methods should be hidden from one another. In this sense, the Java security mechanism is much more than a classical capability system.

Note that, technically, we could have enforced stricter isolation between domains. However, this would have created a need for a new set of interfaces for interdomain communication (similar to IPC, or interprocess communication). Also, existing applications would have had to be rewritten to utilize the new interfaces. To enforce complete isolation, we might have had to redesign some shared system classes and their static fields [33]. Thus the decision to leave accessibility separate from security is the best available solution.

3.9 Securely Loading Classes

Dynamic class loading is an important feature of the JVM because it provides the Java platform with the ability to install software components at runtime [45]. This feature has a number of unique characteristics. One is **lazy loading**, which means that classes are loaded on demand and at the last moment possible. Another is **dynamic class loading**, which means that the type safety of the JVM is maintained by adding link-time checks, which are performed only once, while avoiding additional runtime checks.

In addition, because class loaders are first-class objects, programmers can define class loaders, for example, that specify the remote location from which certain classes are loaded. They also can assign appropriate security attributes to class loaders.

Finally, class loaders can be used to provide separate name spaces for various software components. For example, a browser can load applets from different Web pages by using separate class loaders, thus maintaining a degree of isolation between those applet classes. In fact, those applets may contain classes of the same name; they are treated as distinct types by the JVM.

Section 2.3 briefly touched on language type safety, which is enforced by a variety of techniques, including bytecode verification, class loading, and runtime checks. This section focuses on the algorithms and APIs for locating the class files, determining the appropriate class loaders to use, and assigning suitable security attributes to loaded classes.

3.9.1   Class Loader Hierarchy

When a class loader loads Java software components, the smallest component unit is a class. A class is defined in a machine-independent, binary representation called **class file format**. The representation of an individual class is called a **class file**, even though it need not be stored in an actual file.

A class file may contain bytecode, as well as symbolic references to fields, methods, and names of other classes. An example is a class C declared as follows:

```
class C {
    void f() {
        D d = new D();
        ...
    }
}
```

The class file representing C contains a symbolic reference to class D. Such symbolic references are resolved at link time (of class C) to actual class types. To do this, the JVM must load the class file of D and create the class type.

A class loader instance L that loads class C is called the class's **defining class loader**. The actual type of the class is fully qualified by both itself and its defining class loader, <C, L>. In other words, two types in the Java runtime are equal if both the class types are equal and their defining class loaders are identical. Further, multiple instances of class loader objects may exist in one JVM, so an important question when loading a class is how to determine which class loader to use as the defining loader.

As a further complication, JDK 1.2 introduces multiple class loader classes that have distinct properties. Thus another important question to ask when loading a class is what type of class loader you should use. The next subsection introduces the class loader hierarchy and explains the similarities and differences between classes within the hierarchy.

Comparisons among the Class Loader Hierarchy

Recall that each class is loaded by its defining a class loader. Because each class loader is itself a class and must be loaded by another class loader, a chicken-and-egg question arises, that is, from where does the first class loader come. The answer is, a *primordial class loader* that bootstraps the class loading process. This class loader is generally written in a native language, such as C, and does not manifest itself within the Java context in that it is not directly visible or accessible from within the Java language. This primordial class loader often loads classes from the local file system in a platform-dependent manner.

Some classes, such as those defined in the java.* package, are essential for the correct functioning of the JVM and Java runtime system, and are often referred to as **system classes**. For historical reasons, all system classes have a defining class loader that is a null object. This null class loader, sometimes called the **system class loader**, is perhaps the only sign of the existence of a primordial class loader. In fact, it is easier to simply view the null class loader as the primordial class loader. Fairly late during JDK 1.2 development, there was a terminology shift. All classes that reside on the CLASSPATH are now called system classes. These classes are loaded by either the primordial (or null) class loader or a non-null instance of a subclass of java.lang.ClassLoader. A new term, bootstrap class loader, refers to the class loader that loads the classes necessary to bootstrap the Java virtual machine. In the default implementation of JDK 1.2, the bootstrap class loader is the primordial class loader.

With all classes in one Java runtime environment, a class loading tree can easily be formed to reflect the class loading relationship (Figure 3.3). Each class that

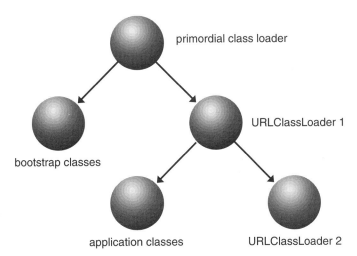

Figure 3.3   Class loader tree.

is not a class loader is a leaf node. Each class's parent node is its defining class loader, with the null class loader being the root class. Such a structure is a tree because there cannot be cycles; that is, a class loader cannot load its own ancestor class loader.

Recall that class loaders are ordinary objects that can be defined in Java code. The root of the class loader class hierarchy is an abstract class called `java.lang.ClassLoader`, originally defined in JDK 1.0 and has since been expanded (see Section 3.9.2). Class `java.security.SecureClassLoader`, introduced in JDK 1.2, is a subclass and a concrete implementation of this abstract `ClassLoader` class. The class `java.net.URLClassLoader`, also introduced in JDK 1.2, is a critical component of the extensions mechanism [1] and a subclass of `SecureClassLoader`.

A utility program called `appletviewer` that is built with the JDK uses a private class, `sun.applet.AppletClassLoader`, to load applets. In JDK 1.0, `AppletClassLoader` is a subclass and concrete implementation of `ClassLoader`. In JDK 1.2, it is a subclass of `URLClassLoader`. Note that interposing new classes between an existing class and its subclass is binary backward compatible [30].

When creating a custom class loader class, you can subclass from any of the class loader classes mentioned in this section, depending on the particular needs of the custom class loader (Figure 3.4). Note that because the `AppletClass-Loader` class is a private class defined in the `sun.*` package, it is not supported and is subject to change, so you should not subclass from it.

3.9.2   `java.lang.ClassLoader` and Delegation

To understand how the abstract class `java.lang.ClassLoader` functions, you need to understand a particular relationship existing among `ClassLoader` objects: delegation.

When one class loader is asked to load a class, it either loads the class itself or asks another class loader to do so. In other words, the first class loader can delegate to the second class loader. The delegation relationship is virtual in the sense that it has nothing to do with which class loader loads which other class loader. Instead, the delegation relationship is formed when `ClassLoader` objects are created; it takes the form of a parent-child relationship. Nevertheless, the primordial (or bootstrap) class loader is the delegation root ancestor of all class loaders.

The first group of `ClassLoader` APIs concerns the constructors:

```
protected ClassLoader(ClassLoader parent)
protected ClassLoader()
```

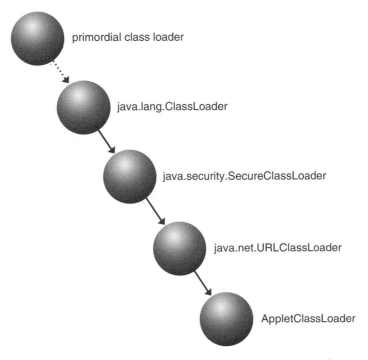

primordial class loader

java.lang.ClassLoader

java.security.SecureClassLoader

java.net.URLClassLoader

AppletClassLoader

Figure 3.4 Subclassing `ClassLoader`.

The first constructor creates a class loader, with a particular class loader as the delegation parent. The second constructor uses a default delegation parent. Because class loaders can perform sensitive operations such as defining classes, you should strictly control who may create class loaders by invoking a security check in the constructors, when a security manager is present. Because all class loaders are subclasses of `ClassLoader` and constructors in the subclasses always call the `super()` method, security checks placed here are always invoked.

The default delegation parent is determined by the method call `getSystem-ClassLoader()`, which is typically the class loader used to start the application. You can obtain the parent of a class loader using the method call `getParent()`.

```
public static ClassLoader getSystemClassLoader()
public ClassLoader getParent()
```

You also should tightly control who can successfully invoke these methods. This is primarily because from within any object, you can call `this.get-Class.getClassLoader()` to obtain its own defining class loader. With a reference to this class loader, you might attempt to "reach over" to its delegation parents and then invoke methods on them. Uncontrolled reach-over is clearly undesirable. Thus if a security manager is present, the two methods will succeed only if the caller's class loader is the same as or is a delegation ancestor of the current class loader, or if the caller has `RuntimePermission("getClassLoader")` permission. Otherwise, a security exception will be thrown. Note that allowing a delegation ancestor to have access is reasonable because a delegation child, upon its creation, must designate its delegation parent. Obviously, one has to be very careful about which parent to adopt.

For similar reasons, the same security check is placed in the method call `Class.getClassLoader()` because you do not want anything with a reference to a `Class` object to reach over to its `ClassLoader` object. This security check is new to JDK 1.2.

The next group of methods deals with actual class loading:

```
public Class loadClass(String name)
protected synchronized Class loadClass(String name,
                                       boolean resolve)
protected native final Class findLoadedClass(String name)
protected final Class findSystemClass(String name)
protected Class findClass(String name)
protected final void resolveClass(Class c)
```

The first two methods take a class name as argument and return a `Class` object that is the runtime representation of a class type. The default implementation will search for classes in the following order (Figure 3.5). If at any step a class is located, the methods return the class.

1. Call `findLoadedClass()` to check if the class has already been loaded.

2. If the current class loader has a specified delegation parent, call the `loadClass()` method of the parent to load the class. Otherwise, call the `findSystemClass()` method to see whether the class can be found among system classes.

3. Call the `findClass` method to find the class.

Here, `findLoadedClass()` looks into the class loader's local cache (or its equivalent) to see if a loaded class matches the target class. However, it is critical for type safety that the same class is not loaded more than once by the same class loader. If the class is not among those already loaded, the current class loader will attempt to delegate the task to the parent class loader; this can occur recursively. This ensures that the appropriate class loader is used. For example, when locating a system class the delegation process continues until the system class loader is

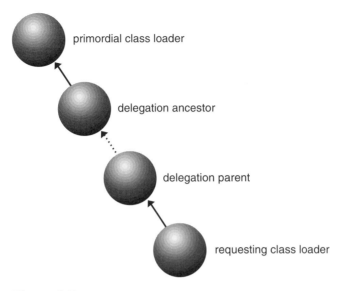

Figure 3.5   `ClassLoader` searching for classes.

reached. If the target class is indeed a system class `findSystemClass()` uses the null system class loader to load the class.

The `findClass()` method provides a way to customize the mechanism for looking for classes, thus a custom class loader can override this method to specify how a class should be looked up. For example, an applet class loader can override this method to go back to the applet host to try to locate the class file and load it over the network.

If the class was found using the previous steps and the `resolve` flag is `true`, the `loadClass()` method will then call the `resolveClass()` method on the resulting `Class` object.

Yet another issue to be clarified concerning class loading is which class loader do you start with when trying to load the class, when given the name of any class? Following are the rules implemented in JDK 1.2.

◆ When the first class of an application is being loaded, a new instance of the `URLClassLoader` is used.

◆ When the first class of an applet is being loaded, a new instance of the `Applet-ClassLoader` is used.

◆ If the request to load a class is triggered by a reference to it from an existing class, the class loader for the existing class is asked to load the class.

The rules about the use of `URLClassLoader` and `AppletClassLoader` instances have exceptions and can vary depending on the particular system environment. For example, a Web browser may choose to reuse an existing `AppletClassLoader` to load applet classes from the same Web page.

The next group of methods convert an array of bytes into an instance of class `Class`:

```
protected final Class defineClass(String name, byte[] b,
      int off,    int len, ProtectionDomain protectionDomain)
protected final Class defineClass(String name, byte[] b,
      int off,    int len)
protected final void setSigners(Class c, Object[] signers)
```

Recall from Section 3.8 that access control permissions are granted to protection domains and that each class belongs to one and only one protection domain. The class loader, when defining a class, consults the security policy to obtain a reference to the `ProtectionDomain` object that the class belongs to and then calls the `defineClass()` method with the `ProtectionDomain` object as a parameter. Note that the second `defineClass()` method does not explicitly mention a `ProtectionDomain` because this method existed before JDK 1.2. In this case, a default `ProtectionDomain` is used. This domain typically contains the set of permissions granted when a call to `Policy.getPolicy().getPermissions()` is made with a `CodeSource` of (`null`, `null`).

The result of class definition is that a class is marked as belonging to a specific protection domain. You can later query a class on its protection domain by calling the `Class.getProtectionDomain()` method. Obviously, `Protection-Domain` objects are sensitive, so you must be cautious regarding who can obtain references to them. Thus, if a security manager is present the `getProtection-Domain()` method invokes a security check to ensure that the caller has the `RuntimePermission("getProtectionDomain")` permission. If it does not, a security exception is thrown.

When a class file is correctly signed with one or more digital signatures, the runtime class created from the class file is marked by its signers. This is done by calling the method `setSigners()`. You can query a class for its signers by calling the `Class.getSigners()` method. There is no security check placed in this method because it is usually not a security risk to reveal who signed the class.

The rest of the methods in the `ClassLoader` class are mostly related to finding resources and packaging. They are given next but not explained further.

```
protected String findLibrary(String libname)
public URL getResource(String name)
public final Enumeration getResources(String name)
```

```
public Enumeration findResources(String name)
public URL findResource(String name)
public static URL getSystemResource(String name)
public static Enumeration getSystemResources(String name)
public InputStream getResourceAsStream(String name)
public static InputStream
    getSystemResourceAsStream(String name)
protected Package definePackage(...)
protected Package getPackage(String name)
protected Package[] getPackages()
```

3.9.3   `java.security.SecureClassLoader`

The `java.security.SecureClassLoader` class extends `ClassLoader` with additional support for defining classes with an associated code source. During JDK 1.2 development, this class initially had a richer design with a comprehensive set of method calls. Gradually, those functionalities have been moved either to the base class `ClassLoader` or to the newly created class `URLClassLoader`. The class currently has two interesting methods:

```
protected PermissionCollection getPermissions(CodeSource
                                        codesource)
protected final Class defineClass(String name, byte[] b,
                 int off,    int len, CodeSource cs)
```

The first method returns the permissions for the given `CodeSource` object. The default implementation of this method invokes the `Policy.getPermissions()` method to get the permissions granted by the policy to the specified codesource. This method is invoked by the `defineClass` method that takes a `CodeSource` object as an argument when it is constructing the `ProtectionDomain` for the class being defined. A class loader can override this method. For example, this method in the `AppletClassLoader` automatically grants a permission that allows the applet to connect back to the host from which the applet is downloaded, even though the security policy does not specify this permission. The next section describes how the `URLClassLoader` customizes this method.

The second method defines a class from a particular code source. In some sense, this method duplicates certain functionality of the `defineClass()` method in `ClassLoader` that takes a `ProtectionDomain` as an argument. However, sometimes it is convenient not to have to worry about protection domains. For example, the caller of this method might not be able to determine which protection domain to use but might still want to define the class. In this case, `codesource` is the only piece of information available about the origin of the class that can be used to determine the permissions to be granted.

3.9.4   `java.net.URLClassLoader`

The `java.net.URLClassLoader` class extends `SecureClassLoader` and is used to load classes and resources from a search path of URLs referring to both JAR files and directories. Here are the two constructors:

```
public URLClassLoader(URL[] urls, ClassLoader parent)
public URLClassLoader(URL[] urls)
```

The first method constructs a new `URLClassLoader` for the given URLs. The URLs will be searched in the order specified for classes and resources but only after it first delegates to its parent by searching in the specified parent class loader.

The second method constructs a new `URLClassLoader` for the specified URLs using the default delegation parent class loader.

```
public Class loadMainClass()
```

This method loads the main class for an application. The URL class path is searched for the first JAR file containing a `Main-Class` manifest attribute specifying the name of the class to load for the application's main method. It returns the resulting class, or null if no Main-Class manifest attribute is found.

The `java.net.URLClassLoader` class also overrides the method `findClass(String name)` and a few resource-related loading methods to find and load the class or resource with the specified name from the URL search path. Any URLs that refer to JAR files are loaded and opened as needed until the class is found.

More interesting from a security perspective, this class overrides the method

```
protected PermissionCollection getPermissions(CodeSource cs)
```

This method, in returning the permissions for the given `CodeSource` object, first calls `super.getPermissions()` to get the permissions granted by the security policy. It also adds additional permissions based on the URL of the code source, according to the following rules.

♦ If the protocol specified by the URL is "file" and the path specifies a file, then read permission to that file is granted.

♦ If the protocol specified by the URL is "file" and the path is a directory, read permission is granted to all files and (recursively) all files and subdirectories contained in that directory.

♦ If the protocol specified by the URL is not "file," then a permission to connect to and accept connections from the URL's network host is granted.

In other words, by default, classes loaded by a URLClassLoader are granted permission to access the URLs specified when the URLClassLoader was created.

Another distinguishing feature of URLClassLoader is the pair of static methods to create new URLClassLoader instances:

```
public static URLClassLoader newInstance(URL[] urls,
ClassLoader parent)
public static URLClassLoader newInstance(URL[] urls)
```

As stated earlier in the chapter, security concerns compel severe restrictions on who can create ClassLoader instances. However, it is convenient to provide a mechanism for applications or applets to specify URL locations, and to load classes or resources from them. These static methods allow any program to create instances of the URLClassLoader class, although not other types of class loaders. This is considered acceptable, given the available public methods and the delegation mechanism. Note that an application or applet still cannot call the protected methods in URLClassLoader or its super classes.

Typically in a Web browser and specifically in appletviewer, an applet class loader is used to load classes and resources needed for applets. In JDK 1.2, this class is defined in the private sun.* package and is a straightforward subclass of URLClassLoader.

3.9.5 Classpaths

The class loader classes described previously provide programmable ways to locate and load classes and resources. To simplify the task of installing software components on a Java-enabled system, common and user-specific places are available in which to put such components in order to allow them to be automatically discovered by the Java runtime system.

In JDK 1.0 and 1.1 is a well-known, built-in, system-wide search path called CLASSPATH that is set in a platform-specific way. For example, on UNIX systems CLASSPATH can be set via the Shell environment variable CLASSPATH. Essentially, all classes or JAR files containing classes on the local file system must reside on this path to be discovered. It also is where all system classes reside. As a result, all classes from the local file system are treated as system classes and are given full privileges to access all resources. In other words, those local classes that really belong to the system code are not distinguished from other local classes that are merely part of some locally installed applications.

This is clearly not perfect. One can imagine many scenarios in which a locally installed application should not be given full system privilege, for example, a demo program newly received in the mail. As another example, when displaying an important document you might want to run the display application in read-only mode to ensure that the content of the document is not altered or lost due to software bugs in the application.

The security architecture in JDK 1.2 includes provisions to treat locally resident classes in the same way as remotely downloaded applet classes, that is, by granting them specific and fine-grained permissions. For this to work, true system classes must be distinguishable from all other classes. The JDK 1.2 approach is to have separate class paths, one for system classes and one for the rest.

The earliest design for this path separation, which was released in a beta version of JDK 1.2, called for a search path—the application class path—in addition to the existing CLASSPATH. As with JDK 1.1, all classes on CLASSPATH were treated as system classes. All classes on the application class path are nonsystem classes, however, and are loaded with instances of the SecureClassLoader, which grants them permissions according to the security policy. The application class path can be specified by either setting a Java property called java.app.class.path or using a command-line option when invoking the application. Command-line options and other deployment issues are discussed in Chapter 4.

This design has the advantage that it is fully backward compatible. An existing application can be migrated from sitting on CLASSPATH to the new application class path at its own pace and without affecting other installed software components. Before migration, the application runs exactly as in JDK 1.0 and JDK 1.1. Once migrated, the application become subject to fine-grained access control. However, it can be argued that such migration effort should not be placed on the shoulders of users. Also, the backward compatibility might simply lead users to do nothing at all; thus they would miss out on a much better security architecture and a very powerful extensions mechanism.

Because of such concerns, in the eventual design of JDK 1.2 CLASSPATH is interpreted as the application class path. Thus deployed applications do not have to be moved. When JDK 1.2 is installed, classes on this path are loaded by instances of the URLClassLoader. The security policy can be configured to grant different permissions to different classes on the application path.

As the system class path, a new path Xbootclasspath has been created. Users or developers should rarely or never have to install classes on this path except those classes included in JDK. Note, this design might not provide full backward compatibility for some existing applications, even though the number of such applications is expected to be very small. This is because up to and including JDK 1.1, all classes on CLASSPATH were treated as system classes and were loaded with the null class loader. In JDK 1.2, they are loaded with instances of URL-ClassLoader. An application that checks for null class loaders might need to be upgraded to reflect the presence of URLClassLoader.

You might question why there remains a separate system class path. If system classes need all permissions, why not simply use the policy to grant them `AllPermission` and thus treat them as just a special kind of application. The real situation is somewhat more complicated than this. As noted, system classes are accustomed to being loaded by the null class loader. Determining whether a class is a system class by whether it has a null class loader is not good practice, yet there remains legacy code that is best not broken in the new security architecture. Moreover, there are bootstrapping and other issues that can be technically solved, but the solutions are judged to be too destabilizing to attempt for JDK 1.2. We hope that, in the future, different parts of the system classes can be granted only those fine-grained permissions that they really need. This subdivision of system classes will constrain the power of each system component and further reduce the consequence of a programming error in system classes.

3.10 `java.lang.SecurityManager`

The `java.lang.SecurityManager` class, designed into the original release of JDK 1.0, is the focal point of access control. Recall that the bytecode verifier, the class loader, and other runtime checks ensure type safety. The security manager is called whenever you decide whether to grant or deny a request for accessing sensitive resources. For example, this class implements the sandbox security model in JDK 1.0. Recall from Chapter 1 that according to this model, applications (classes residing on the local file system) are given full system access, while applets (remote classes loaded over the network) are denied all but the most essential privileges.

This class went through perhaps the biggest conceptual change during the development of JDK 1.2. This section explains the APIs that existed in JDK 1.1 and remain unchanged in JDK 1.2 and covers a few methods that have been deprecated in JDK 1.2. Then it covers newly introduced APIs and how they relate to existing ones.

3.10.1 Example Use of the Security Manager

A program idiom for performing a security check is first to see if a `Security-Manager` is installed, and if so, to call the appropriate `check()` method on it. For example, the following code segment checks to see if you have permission to read a file before opening it.

```
public FileInputStream(String name) throws
        FileNotFoundException {
```

```
    SecurityManager security = System.getSecurityManager();
    if (security != null) {
        security.checkRead(name);
    }
    (proceed to open the file for read)
}
```

The SecurityManager is thereby given an opportunity to prevent completion of the operation by throwing an exception. A SecurityManager routine, such as checkRead(), simply returns if the operation is permitted, but it throws a SecurityException if the operation is not permitted. Note that because a SecurityException is a runtime exception, it is not declared, although it can be caught.

3.10.2 Unchanged APIs in JDK 1.2

Following are the APIs existing in JDK 1.1 that remain unchanged in JDK 1.2, except that the constructor has been changed from protected to public:

```
public SecurityManager()
protected native Class[] getClassContext()
public Object getSecurityContext()
```

Prior to JDK 1.2, the SecurityManager class was abstract, so a vendor must subclass it and create a concrete implementation. This is inconvenient. In JDK 1.2, the class is concrete, with a public constructor. A security check is placed in the constructor because SecurityManager has sensitive methods so that not just any-one can invoke them. The required permission to pass the security check is RuntimePermission("createSecurityManager").

The getClassContext() method returns the current execution stack as an array of classes. The length of the array is the number of methods on the execution stack. The element at index 0 is the class of the currently executing method, the element at index 1 is the class of that method's caller, and so on. Such a context is useful for determining the current method calling sequence, which is essential knowledge for making an access control decision. This method is necessarily native because introspection should not disturb the Java execution context.

The getSecurityContext() method creates an object that encapsulates the current execution environment. Its purpose is to create a snapshot of the context so that later you can query whether a security check would have passed if invoked within that context. The default implementation of this method is to return an AccessControlContext object. The special context class AccessControl-Context is explained later in Sections 3.10.3.1 and 3.11.6.

Recall that there may be a system-wide security manager. The `java.lang.System` class manages this security manager, with the following relevant method calls:

```
public static synchronized void
    setSecurityManager(SecurityManager s)
public static SecurityManager getSecurityManager()
```

In the `set` method, if a security manager has not been established for the currently running Java application, the argument passed in is established as the current security manager. This process is sometimes called *installing the security manager*. If the argument passed in is null and no security manager has been established, then no action is taken and the method simply returns. If a security manager has already been installed, a security check is invoked to see if the caller has the permission `RuntimePermission("setSecurityManager")`. If it does, the passed-in argument is installed as the new security manager. Otherwise, a `SecurityException` is thrown. Note that prior to JDK 1.2, the system-wide security manager could be set only once—this can be limiting in some cases.

The `get` method returns the established or installed security manager, or null if no security manager has been installed. Allowing a security manager to be null is not a perfect design; its shortcomings are discussed later in the chapter. But this design feature has become a sort of de facto API, so we decided not to change it.

3.10.3 Deprecated Methods in JDK 1.2

The following APIs have been deprecated in JDK 1.2.

```
public boolean getInCheck()
protected boolean inClass(String name)
protected Class currentLoadedClass()
protected native ClassLoader currentClassLoader()
protected native int classDepth(String name)
```

These methods were used for determining which class made a particular method call. This generally was done on an inconsistent and often ad-hoc basis. Typically, it involved determining whether a class somewhere on the stack existed that was defined by a non-null class loader and/or determining how deep—that is, how many method calls—a class was from the current method. This led to very fragile code.

It also led to several security holes in the past. For example, in object-oriented programming, an extra layer of indirection or interface is often added between two existing method calls. But inserting another method call into the call chain changes the class depth. Thus it is very difficult to use the class depth as a reliable indicator, especially when the software code is frequently revised. As one potential consequence, a miscalculated class depth can make it appear that the code trying to access a protected resource is trusted system code when in fact it is really an untrusted applet.

The new security architecture in JDK 1.2 completely eliminates the need for these deprecated methods. While we have not removed but only deprecated them—for backward compatibility reasons—we strongly recommend that you do not use them.

SecurityManager contains 29 methods that have names that begin with the word "check." These check methods are called by various methods in the Java libraries before they perform certain potentially sensitive operations. The only exception to this convention is checkTopLevelWindow, which returns a boolean value. Following are the check methods.

```
public void checkCreateClassLoader()
public void checkAccess(Thread t)
public void checkAccess(ThreadGroup g)
public void checkExit(int status)
public void checkExec(String cmd)
public void checkLink(String lib)
public void checkRead(FileDescriptor fd)
public void checkRead(String file)
public void checkRead(String file, Object context)
public void checkWrite(FileDescriptor fd)
public void checkWrite(String file)
public void checkDelete(String file)
public void checkConnect(String host, int port)
public void checkConnect(String host, int port, Object context)
public void checkListen(int port)
public void checkAccept(String host, int port)
public void checkMulticast(InetAddress maddr)
public void checkMulticast(InetAddress maddr, byte ttl)
public void checkPropertiesAccess()
public void checkPropertyAccess(String key)
public boolean checkTopLevelWindow(Object window)
public void checkPrintJobAccess()
public void checkSystemClipboardAccess()
public void checkAwtEventQueueAccess()
public void checkPackageAccess(String pkg)
public void checkPackageDefinition(String pkg
public void checkSetFactory()
public void checkMemberAccess(Class clazz, int which)
public void checkSecurityAccess(String action)
```

Most of these methods are self-explanatory by their names. Such a design style with one distinctly named method for each different security check tends to accumulate a large number of methods. A bigger problem is that, because each existing method is designed for a particular type of resource, whenever a new type of protected resource is added to the system, an appropriate security check is needed but is normally not anticipated by the existing check methods. Thus a new check method must be added to the SecurityManager class. This is a serious design flaw because it is often not possible to extend an existing Security-Manager; an example is a Web browser with a fixed SecurityManager class. Thus an application cannot extend the runtime system with a new protected resource without having to invent something similar to SecurityManager. Even when extending SecurityManager is feasible, the new security check method often involves complicated JVM internal mechanisms and is difficult to implement, or implement correctly.

Such difficult situations can lead to the overloading of an existing check method. For example, in JDK 1.1 the System.setIn(InputStream) method call invokes the checkExec() call, which is normally used to see if someone is allowed to execute a file. Another overloaded method is the checkConnect() method. Calling this method with a port of –1 means that the caller is attempting to resolve an IP address to a host, or vice versa. Overloading check methods is extremely undesirable and indeed can be very dangerous.

In JDK 1.2, all check methods are reimplemented cleanly using the following new methods:

```
public void checkPermission(Permission perm)
public void checkPermission(Permission perm, Object context)
```

checkPermission() with a single permission argument always performs security checks within the context of the currently executing thread. When a security check is being invoked within a given context (for example from within a worker thread A), often the check should actually be done against a different context (such as thread B). In this case, checkPermission() should be used with an appropriate context argument (such as the AccessControlContext of thread B).

In a sense, all existing check methods are superseded by checkPermission. For backward compatibility, we did not deprecate the check methods. However, we reimplemented them with checkPermission methods and removed all occurrences of check method overloading. The next subsections examine the new checkPermission methods and then see how they relate to the existing check methods.

New checkPermission Methods

The first method, public void checkPermission(Permission perm), checks to see if the requested access, specified by the given permission, is permitted based on the current security policy. If it is permitted, the method returns silently; otherwise, it throws a security exception. The default implementation forwards all calls to the checkPermission() method to java.security.Access-Controller, which is explained in Section 3.11.

The second method, public void checkPermission(Permission perm, Object context), checks to see if the requested access, specified by the given permission, is permitted based on the current security policy, if the request is issued in the execution context passed in. Recall that the method getSecurity-Context() creates an object that encapsulates the current execution environment and can return an AccessControlContext. If the context passed in is an instance of AccessControlContext, the checkPermission method on that Context object is called. If the request is permitted, the method returns silently. Otherwise, it throws a security exception.

AccessControlContext has the following APIs:

```
public AccessControlContext(ProtectionDomain context[])
public void checkPermission(Permission perm)
```

The public constructor creates an AccessControlContext object with the given set of ProtectionDomain objects, thus mimicking the execution context in which objects, which instantiate classes from different protection domains, call each other in the sequence given in the array. The first element in the array corresponds to the most recent class's protection domain. Duplicate domains will be removed from the context, and the context array must not be null.

A single checkPermission() method can replace the many check methods because the semantics of the required check are no longer hard coded in the names (and implementation code) of those methods. Instead, they are encoded in the permission argument passed to the checkPermission() method. This simple idea has a tremendous advantage. The implementation of the checkPermission() call typically involves examining Java runtime internal state and performing complicated algorithms. That implementation can now be reused for all permission types, including those yet to be invented. Thus, to (dynamically) add a new protected resource, you can simply introduce a new Permission class and then place a checkPermission() call in the appropriate place. The new Permission class can be written entirely in the Java language, thereby resulting in the existing SecurityManager class no longer needing to be modified.

To utilize the new checkPermission method, we must match each method call with a suitable permission. Table 3.1 lists the check methods replaced by

Table 3.1 Check Methods Replaced by `checkPermission`

Name of Check Method	Content of `RuntimePermission`
checkCreateClassLoader	createClassLoader
checkExit	exitVM
checkSetFactory	setFactory
checkAccess(Thread)	modifyThread
checkAccess(ThreadGroup)	modifyThreadGroup
checkRead(FileDescriptor)	readFileDescriptor
checkWrite(FileDescriptor)	writeFileDescriptor
checkLink	loadLibrary.{library name}
checkPackageAccess	accessClassInPackage.{package name}
checkPackageDefinition	defineClassInPackage.{package name}
checkMemberAccess	accessDeclaredMembers
checkPrintJobAccess	queuePrintJob
java.lang.System.{setIn,setOut,SetErr}	setIO

`checkPermission` with a suitable `RuntimePermission`. For each check method, it lists the category (or type) of the permission, followed by the actions and targets of the permission, if any. Permission names are given within double quotation marks, such as `"fproperty nameg"`, to represent an actual property name.

As an example of a permission translation, here is how `checkLink()` is reimplemented.

```
public void checkLink(String lib) {
    checkPermission(new
        RuntimePermission(''loadLibrary.''+lib));
}
```

Table 3.2 lists the remaining check method calls that are matched.

Table 3.2 Matching the Check Method Calls

Method Name	Permission Class	Content of the Permission
checkPropertiesAccess	PropertyPermission	
checkPropertyAccess	PropertyPermission	{property name}
checkTopLevelWindow	AWTPermission	showWindowWithoutWarningBanner
checkSystemClipboardAccess	AWTPermission	accessClipboard
checkAwtEventQueueAccess	AWTPermission	accessEventQueue
checkSecurityAccess	SecurityPermission	{action}
checkExec	FilePermission	{file or directory pathname}

Table 3.2   Matching the Check Method Calls *(Continued)*

Method Name	Permission Class	Content of the Permission
checkRead(String)	FilePermission	{file or directory pathname}
checkWrite(String)	FilePermission	{file or directory pathname}
checkDelete	FilePermission	{file or directory pathname}
checkConnect	SocketPermission	{host:port}
checkListen	SocketPermission	{host:port}
checkAccept	SocketPermission	{host:port}

Because JDK 1.2 has permission classes, such as NetPermission, that are created for security checks new in JDK 1.2, these permission classes do not correspond to any check methods in JDK 1.1.

One question that we expect many developers will ask is, when writing new code to perform a security check, should they call the old check methods or the new checkPermission method. This mostly concerns backward compatibility. If you intend to defer security decisions to a pre-JDK 1.2-style customized security manager, calling the old check methods is best because the security manager might have overridden and customized certain check calls. In fact, for backward compatibility, we did not revise JDK code that calls the check methods. This is because an existing application that installs a customized SecurityManager might have been expecting the appropriate JDK code to call its own check methods. If we had revised the JDK code to call the checkPermission method, the customized SecurityManager would have been bypassed.

However, if you want to ensure that the new JDK 1.2-style security manager is consulted, you should call the new checkPermission method. We recommend the new method for new application code because it is safer and cleaner. But we expect that, for the foreseeable future, all check() methods in SecurityManager will be supported.

3.11 java.security.AccessController

Although the SecurityManager class defines the checkPermission class and the check methods as interfaces to invoke an appropriate security check, these interfaces do not specify how the security checks are done. In particular, they do not specify under what circumstances a request should be granted or denied. This is necessary because it is almost impossible to anticipate all reasonable ways to enforce a security check. For example, one application might want to implement a multilevel security policy [3], while another wants to implement support for separation-of-duty policies [44]. One way to achieve the goal of supporting multiple policies is to provide a Policy object with a sufficiently rich expressive power to include all possible policy specifications. This might not be possible, or at best, it might be very difficult. Another way is to override the check methods defined in `SecurityManager` to implement particular flavors of the security policy and to install the appropriate security managers depending on the application environment.

Not fully specifying how security checks are done has its drawbacks. One is that developers might write security managers that have inconsistent behavior. For example, two custom `SecurityManager` classes might implement totally opposite semantics of a check method, thus resulting in inconsistent, ad-hoc, and possibly dangerous behavior. Another problem is that `SecurityManager` is difficult to get right, especially for application developers who are not deeply versed in security. Some programmers tend to hard code a security policy in the check methods without leaving enough room for smooth evolution, while others might commit subtle security bugs.

Thus there is an urgent need to provide a default implementation that specifies a complete access control algorithm and that is general enough to be used in a majority of applications. Developers can readily utilize such as implementation, while users can expect consistent behavior across different applications and platforms. The default implementation, introduced in JDK 1.2, is the `Access-Controller` class. In other words, by default, `SecurityManager` invokes methods defined in `AccessController` and essentially delegates security decision making.

The next section examines the interface design of `AccessController`. Later sections cover in detail the general access control algorithm that is embodied in this new class.

3.11.1 Interface Design of `AccessController`

The `AccessController` class is declared final, so it cannot be further subclassed. It has no public constructor; thus no one can instantiate it. It has only static methods, listed next:

```
public static void checkPermission(Permission perm)
public static native Object
    doPrivileged(PrivilegedAction action)
public static native Object
    doPrivileged(PrivilegedAction action,
 AccessControlContext context)
public static native Object
    doPrivileged(PrivilegedExceptionAction action)
        throws PrivilegedActionException
public static native Object
    doPrivileged(PrivilegedExceptionAction action,
        AccessControlContext context)
        throws PrivilegedActionException
public static AccessControlContext getContext()
```

The now-familiar `checkPermission()` method checks to see if a requested access, as specified by the permission argument, is allowed in the current execution context. If it is, the method returns silently. Otherwise, it throws an `Access-ControlException`, which is a subclass of `SecurityException` and provides details of the reason for failure.

3.11.2   The Basic Access Control Algorithm

The decision of granting access to controlled resources can be made only within the right context, which must provide answers to such questions as who is requesting what and on whose behalf. Often, a thread is the right context for access control. Less often, access control decisions must be carried out among multiple threads that must cooperate in obtaining the right context information. A thread of execution may occur completely within a single protection domain (that is, all classes and objects involved in the thread belong to the identical protection domain) or might involve multiple domains, such as an application domain and also the system domain. For example, an application that prints a message will have to interact with the system domain that is the only access point to an output stream.

The current execution context is entirely represented by its current sequence of method invocations, where each method is defined in a class that belongs to a protection domain. Thus you can form a sequence of protection domains for the execution context. The basic access-control algorithm can be summarized in one sentence. That is, *a request for access is granted if, and only if, every protection domain in the current execution context is granted the said permission.*

The term *caller* is used to denote a protection domain within the context of the current execution, since a protection domain can be associated with multiple contexts. The basic algorithm can be expressed in the following constructive manner.

```
for each caller in the current execution context {
    if the caller does not have the requested permission
        throw an AccessControlException
}
return normally
```

To examine this basic algorithm, suppose a game applet has a method named `openHighScoreFile()` that calls the constructor of `FileInputStream` to open the high score file, the file that keeps the scores of the top ten players of the game. The constructor calls `checkRead()`, which in turn calls the `checkPermission()` method inside the security manager. The security manager in turn calls the `checkPermission()` method in `AccessController`. At this point, the execution context looks like the snapshot in Figure 3.6.

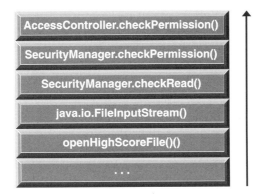

Figure 3.6 Stack frame snapshot.

In this example, two distinct protection domains exist within the execution context: the system domain and the domain assigned to the applet. The algorithm says that the file can be opened if, and only if, both domains have the file permission. Because the system domain by default has all permissions, the algorithm is reduced to checking whether the applet has been granted the file permission. If the applet has not been granted the permission, the file will not be opened, even though the applet tries to enlist the help of system code to do so.

This last point is critical because an application domain should not gain additional permissions simply as a result of calling the system domain. Serious security implications could result otherwise.

In a reverse situation, a system domain invokes a method from an application domain. For example, the AWT system code calls an applet's `paint()` method to display the applet. Suppose the applet then tries to open the high-score file from within `paint()`. Figure 3.7 shows the execution context.

Again, even though it appears that the AWT code triggers the call to `FileInputStream`, the file will not be opened if the applet has not been granted the necessary file permission. Otherwise, the applet will gain immense power simply because system code calls back to its own code. The access control algorithm built into the access controller in JDK 1.2 prevents such mishaps.

Thus a less powerful domain cannot gain additional permissions as a result of calling a more powerful domain, whereas a more powerful domain must lose its power when calling a less powerful domain. This *principle of least privilege* is applied to a thread that transverses multiple protection domains.

Prior to JDK 1.2, any code that performed an access control decision relied on explicitly knowing its caller's status (that is, whether the caller was system code or applet code). This arrangement was fragile because, often, knowing only the caller's status is insufficiently secure. You frequently need also to know the status

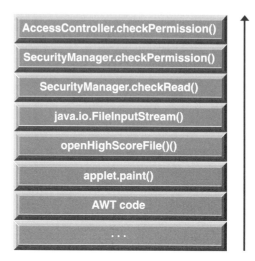

Figure 3.7   Stack frame execution context.

of the caller's caller, and so on. At this point, placing this discovery process explicitly on the typical programmer becomes a serious burden and can be error-prone. It also means that the AWT code writer must worry about scenarios under which an applet might behave. The algorithm implemented in AccessController relieves this burden by automating the access checking process.

3.11.3   Method Inheritance

The subtle issue of method inheritance needs clarification. The basic algorithm, and its extended versions discussed later in the chapter, are defined in terms of a sequence of callers, each represented by a method invocation. The method invocation identifies the class in which the method is defined; the class is linked to the protection domain to which it belongs. The protection domain has been granted permissions, against which an access control decision is made. Suppose class B is a subclass of class A. Class A defines a method x(), which B inherits but does not override. Further assume that classes A and B belong to two different protection domains. When someone invokes a call on B.x(), who is the caller that corresponds to this method invocation? Is it class A, which defined and implemented this method? Or is it class B, which simply inherited the method unchanged?

Either choice might seem more reasonable than the other under certain conditions, but on balance, associating the caller according to where the method is implemented is more natural. This is because a more powerful class can write its methods in a secure way that allows less powerful classes to inherit them and accomplish tasks for which the less powerful classes themselves would not have

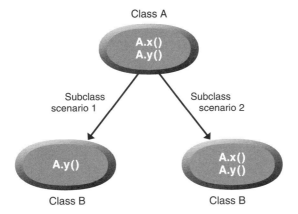

Figure 3.8   Method inheritance.

had the permissions. Thus, in the scenario just given, class A is regarded as the real caller and its protection domain is examined for the necessary access permissions. Note that if, in class B, method x() was overridden but otherwise does nothing other than call its parent's x(), then the caller for B.x() would be B instead of A, even though the override will not have changed the implementation of the method. This is because once a subclass overrides a method call, the superclass cannot be held responsible for the eventual implementation of the method call. In other words, B could have changed the implementation of x() in arbitrary ways, so its protection domain should be examined. Both of these scenarios are depicted in Figure 3.8.

3.11.4 Extending the Basic Algorithm with Privileged Operations

The basic algorithm is simple and secure because all code involved in the computation must be granted sufficient permission for the requested access. However, the algorithm can be too restrictive. For example, consider a password-changing application. When a piece of user code calls this application, the user is prompted to type a new password twice (to ensure that the correct password is entered) and then to enter the old password. If the old password matches the one stored in the password file, the new password is stored in the updated password file. Note that the application needs to open the password file for read and write access, and assume that the application has been granted sufficient access. Under the basic algorithm, the application cannot open the password file because it is called by the user code, which does not (and should not) have permission to directly access the password file. In this case, the application should be given a way to opt out of the basic algorithm in order to open the file, knowing full well what it is doing.

In another, similar, example, an applet might not have direct access to certain system properties, but the system code servicing the applet might need to obtain some properties in order to complete its tasks.

To deal with such exceptional cases, the AccessController class includes a static method, doPrivileged(). A piece of code that calls doPrivileged() is telling the Java runtime system to ignore the status of its callers and that it itself is taking responsibility in exercising its own permissions. Following is an extended access control algorithm that takes into account privilege status.

```
for each caller in the current execution context {
    if the caller does not have the requested permission
        throw an AccessControlException;
    if the caller is privileged, return normally;
}
return normally
```

In this extended algorithm, callers must be checked in the same order that they call each other, starting with the most recent caller.

Armed with the call to "invoke one's own privilege," the password-changing application can use the following code segment to open the file, even if the user code does not have access permission.

```
public void changePassword() {
    // Use own privilege to open the password file.
    AccessController.doPrivileged(new PrivilegedAction() {
        public Object run() {
            // Open file for reading and writing.
            ...
            return null;
        }
    });
    // Verify user's old and new passwords.
    ...
}
```

Here is a detailed look at doPrivileged. When executing this method, the JVM marks the calling thread's stack frame as privileged. In the previous example, the stack frame corresponding to the changePassword() method is marked privileged. Just before completing the execution of this method, the JVM unmarks the calling thread's stack frame, thereby indicating it is no longer privileged.

By calling doPrivileged, the caller is merely enabling privileges it already has. This is important to understand. A block of code never gains more permissions than the set of permissions it has been granted. Being privileged simply tells AccessController to ignore its callers. For example, AccessController can stop checking after it has already verified that the privileged code holds the requested permission.

Moreover, a privileged block is specific to the thread that enabled its privileges. That is, the effect of some code's being privileged in one thread does not have any impact on other concurrently running threads, even though those other threads might be executing code that belong to the same protection domain.

Another subtlety to consider is that the doPrivileged method can be invoked reflectively by using java.lang.reflect.Method.invoke(). In this case, the privileges granted in privileged mode are not those of Method.invoke() but those of the nonreflective code that invoked it. Otherwise, system privileges could erroneously (or maliciously) be conferred on user code.

Let us dig a little deeper into the proper and careful use of doPrivileged. In the password-changing application example, suppose that the code to open the password file is actually in another method named openPasswordFile(), which opens the password file and returns the object reference to the file input stream. The example code would become the following.

```
public void changePassword() {
    // Use own privilege to open the password file.
    AccessController.doPrivileged(new PrivilegedAction() {
        public Object run() {
            // Open file for reading and writing.
            f = openPasswordFile();
            return null;
        }
    });
    // Verify user's old and new passwords.
    ...
}
```

This code should operate exactly as before. Calling doPrivilege from inside openPasswordFile() would be a mistake. Why? Because the user code can then call it directly. Further, because of the privilege inside that method, the user code gets a reference to the password file. The lesson here is that a method, such as openPasswordFile(), should not invoke its own privilege if it does not know or have full control over who can call it, since the method returns some resource that is protected. On the other hand, changePassword() may safely invoke its own privilege, even if anyone can call it. This is because it takes care not to reveal the password file to the outside world and will process it internally only after password checking succeeds.

You might have noticed that the design of the privilege feature is asymmetrical. That is, you can choose to exercise your own privilege and tell the access controller to ignore those callers before your method, but you cannot tell the access controller to ignore those callers that you subsequently call (after you enable your privilege). Thus if you later call a method whose corresponding protection domain does not have a permission, that method call cannot gain the permission even if you have it. This asymmetry is designed to protect you. If the access controller also ignores those callers that you subsequently call, then you effectively have granted your permissions to those callers. You might have control over which caller you call directly but not over who that caller will call later. Your privileges and granted permissions could be misused or abused if any of those callers are malicious or incompetent. It is a very bad idea to trust a series of unknown parties. The algorithm is designed to prevent you from accidentally falling into such traps.

3.11.5 Three Types of Privileged Actions

The code example in the previous section demonstrates the simplest usage of doPrivileged by passing in a PrivilegedAction interface as the argument. That usage pattern, repeated next, is useful only when the code within the privileged block does not need to return a value.

```
somemethod() {
    ...normal code here...
    AccessController.doPrivileged(new PrivilegedAction() {
        public Object run() {
            // Privileged code goes here, for example:
            System.loadLibrary("awt");
            return null; // Nothing to return.
        }
    });
    ...normal code here...
}
```

Here, PrivilegedAction is an interface with a single method, named run, that returns an Object. The example shows a concrete implementation of the run method is supplied. When the call to doPrivileged is made, an instance of the PrivilegedAction implementation is passed to it. The doPrivileged method calls the run method from the PrivilegedAction implementation after enabling privileges and then returns the method's return value as the doPrivileged return value (which is ignored in this example).

If the code from within the privileged block needs to return a value, the following is one way to write the code.

```
somemethod() {
    ...normal code here...
    String user = (String) AccessController.doPrivileged(new
        PrivilegedAction() {
        public Object run() {
            return System.getProperty("user.name");
        }
    });
    ...normal code here...
}
```

This usage requires a dynamic cast on the value returned by doPrivileged.

An alternative is to use a final local variable as follows.

```
somemethod() {
    ...normal code here...
    final String user[] = {null};
    AccessController.doPrivileged(new PrivilegedAction() {
        public Object run() {
            user[0] = System.getProperty("user.name");
            return null; // Still need this.
        }
    });
    ...normal code here...
}
```

A third solution is to write a nonanonymous class that handles typing information safely, such as the following.

```
somemethod() {
    ...normal code here...
    GetPropertyAction gpa = new GetPropertyAction("user.name");
    AccessController.doPrivileged(gpa);
    String user = gpa.getValue();
    ...normal code here...
}
```

```
class GetPropertyAction implements PrivilegedAction {
    private String property;
    private String value;

    public GetPropertyAction(String prop) {
        property = prop;
    }

    public Object run() {
        value = System.getProperty(property);
        return value;
    }

    public String getValue() {
        return value;
    }
}
```

In this example, there is no type cast. Since the run method still returns a value, you can abbreviate somemethod to the following.

```
somemethod() {
    ...normal code here...
    String user = (String) AccessController.doPrivileged(new
                        GetPropertyAction("user.name"));
    ...normal code here...
}
```

Finally, the interface PrivilegedAction is for privileged code that does not throw checked exceptions (such as FileNotFoundException). If the code can throw such an exception, which must be declared in the throws clause of a method, then you must use PrivilegedExceptionAction instead.

```
somemethod() throws FileNotFoundException {
    ...normal code here...
    try {
        FileInputStream fis = (FileInputStream)
            AccessController.doPrivileged(new
            PrivilegedExceptionAction() {
            public Object run() throws FileNotFoundException {
                return new FileInputStream("someFile");
            }
        });
```

```
    } catch (PrivilegedActionException e) {
        // e.getException() should be an instance of
        // FileNotFoundException, as only "checked" exceptions
        // will be "wrapped" in a PrivilegedActionException.
        throw (FileNotFoundException) e.getException();
    }
    ...normal code here...
}
```

The use of doPrivileged is cumbersome. But there is a reason for this. The rationale behind this design choice is discussed in Section 3.11.9. Meanwhile, remember that privileged operations should be used with great care because they utilize your own granted permissions even though you might be acting on behalf of untrusted code. The privileged code block should be as small as possible, and all code that can be executed outside of the block should not be inside the block.

3.11.6 The Context of Access Control

As mentioned earlier in the chapter, getContext() takes a snapshot of the current execution context, places it in an AccessControlContext object, and returns that object. In the Java runtime system, a piece of code can start any number of child threads, which can then start their own child threads, and so on. When a new thread is created, the JVM creates a fresh execution stack, but ensures that the current execution context is inherited by the new child thread. In other words, as far as the security context of the child thread is concerned, it goes back all the way to include all ancestors' contexts. More specifically, the snapshot of the current execution context includes the current thread's inherited AccessControlContext.

Note that, strictly speaking, the JVM does not have to force a thread to recursively inherit its parent context, since not inheriting it does not necessarily pose a security problem. However, our experience shows that a typical programmer expects the security context to be inherited—and surprising the programmer is undesirable. Automatic inheritance is in fact quite convenient in some cases. For example, in a server application a master thread might create slave threads to handle individual incoming requests when it would have been a burden to manually write the code for the slave threads to take into account the master's security context.

Another point that needs emphasizing is that the inherited context is the exact context in the parent thread at the moment when the child thread is created. The inherited context is essentially frozen for further references, and the parent thread is free to continue and change its context afterwards without impacting the content of the inherited context.

The doPrivileged method that takes an AccessControlContext as argument marks the calling thread's stack frame as privileged and associates the given AccessControlContext with the privileged frame. The context will be included in all future access control checks and will be checked after the privileged frame's ProtectionDomain is checked. Understanding the use of this method might be easier after you read the full access-control algorithm, discussed in the next subsection. Its use is illustrated next, where acc is the AccessControlContext object.

```
somemethod() {
    AccessController.doPrivileged(new PrivilegedAction() {
        public Object run() {
            // Code goes here. Any permission checks from this
            // point forward require both the current context
            // and the snapshot's context to have the desired
            // permission.
        }
    }, acc);
    ...normal code here...
}
```

3.11.7 The Full Access Control Algorithm

Suppose the current thread traverses m callers in the order caller 1 to caller 2 to caller m. Then caller m invokes the checkPermission method, which determines whether access is granted or denied based on the following algorithm.

```
i = m;
while (i <> 0) {
    if (caller i's domain does not have the permission)
        throw AccessControlException;
    if (caller i is marked as privileged) {
        if (a context was specified in the call to doPrivileged)
            context.checkPermission(permission);
        return;
    }
    i = i - 1;
};
return;
```

The full algorithm is slightly more complicated than the extended algorithm given in Section 3.10.4. They differ only in one way. When a privileged frame is being checked and an access control context is specified in the call to doPrivileged(PrivilegedAction, AccessControlContext), the security check will pass only if the requested permission is allowable in that specified access control context.

Thus doPrivileged(PrivilegedAction, AccessControlContext) can be used to enable a privileged frame, but only for those permissions that would have been granted in the specified access control context. In other words, this feature can be used to further restrict the extent of the privilege coverage. Without a context's being specified, a privileged frame may exercise all of the permissions granted to the caller. With a context specified, the exercisable permissions are further limited to those that would have been permitted within the specified context.

From a theoretical and abstract level, the access control algorithm says that, at any point in a thread of computation, the effective permission is the intersection of the permissions of all protection domains transversed by the execution thread, with the privilege status (and its associated access control context, if any) as well as inherited access control context taken into account. Many strategies for implementing this algorithm are possible. The two most obvious are discussed here: eager evaluation and lazy evaluation.

In an *eager evaluation* implementation, whenever a thread enters a new protection domain or exits from an existing one, the set of effective permissions is updated dynamically. The benefit is that checking whether a permission is allowed is simplified and can be faster in many cases. The disadvantage is that because permission checking occurs much less often than cross-domain calls, a large percentage of permission updates might be useless effort.

In the *lazy evaluation* implementation, which is what JDK 1.2 uses, whenever permission checking is requested, the thread state (as reflected by the current thread stack or its equivalent) is examined and a decision is reached either to deny or to grant the particular access requested. One potential downside of this approach is the performance penalty at permission checking time. However, this penalty would be incurred as well in the "eager evaluation" implementation (albeit at earlier times and spread out among each cross-domain call). In the JDK 1.2 implementation, performance of this algorithm is quite acceptable, so we feel that lazy evaluation is the most economical approach overall.[4]

Note that because access control is based on the protection domains associated with the current execution context, the context must be preserved intact when optimizing a static, or just-in-time (JIT), compiler, or a particular implementation of the JVM. For example, method inlining must be done with care so that protection domain information is not lost and the AccessController class can be correctly implemented.

---

[4]   For details of the implementation of protection domains and a discussion on performance and optimization techniques, scc [28].

3.11.8 SecurityManager versus AccessController

Recall from earlier in this chapter the difference, when invoking a security check, between calling checkPermission() and calling the other check methods defined in the SecurityManager class. The choice then was contingent on whether you depended on any pre-JDK 1.2 security manager classes. Now you have another choice, that of calling the checkPermission() method defined in SecurityManager or in AccessController. These methods differ in two major ways.

First, sometimes no installed SecurityManager exists, so you cannot invoke check methods on it. By contrast, the static methods in AccessController are always available to be called. Recall the following idiom for calling Security-Manager.

```
SecurityManager sm = System.getSecurityManager();
if (sm != null)
    sm.checkPermission(permission);
```

But you can always call

```
AccessController.checkPermission(permission);
```

Thus, if you want to ensure that your security check is always invoked (regardless of whether a system-wide SecurityManager has been installed), you should call AccessController. Note, however, that some existing applications test whether there is an installed instance of SecurityManager. Then, based on the result of this test, which signifies one or the other security states, these applications take different actions. For the backward compatibility of these applications, calling SecurityManager is more appropriate.

The second difference is that calling SecurityManager does not guarantee a particular access control algorithm—someone might have extended it and installed a custom security manager. By contrast, calling AccessController guarantees that the full access control algorithm specified earlier is used. Thus, if you do not want to delegate your security check to a custom security manager, you should call AccessController directly. Otherwise, call SecurityManager.

Also be warned that because the SecurityManager class defines a general interface for security checks, it does not provide the privilege mechanism that AccessController has defined. In fact, if you use the privilege mechanism in your code but later call SecurityManager to perform a security check, the privilege status might not be taken into account if the security manager you installed is not the one provided by JDK 1.2 and does not consult AccessController or its equivalent.

You might wonder why we provide these choices. Isn't one way of doing things good enough? These choices are based on experience. A balanced tradeoff between generality and consistency is needed. In the long run, we expect that custom security managers will not often be needed, and even when they are defined, they will be built on existing functionality in `AccessController`. In particular, they will provide additional functionality rather than promote incompatible behavior. Nevertheless, in a special environment in which a vastly different sort of security policy must be enforced, a customized security manager conceivably might not be able to utilize the algorithms implemented by `AccessController`.

3.11.9 A Mini-History of Privileged Operations

To cap the discussion on the `AccessController` class, this section provides more background on how the design of the privilege methods developed. The main goals were to help programmers write secure code and to guarantee security when a programmer makes a mistake.

It is helpful to compare the desired result with UNIX's setuid facility. Compared with such operating systems as MS-DOS and MS-Windows, UNIX has traditionally given security somewhat more comprehensive consideration. It limits what a user-invoked program/application may do to a user's privileges. In some cases, though, these limits are too restricting. The setuid mechanism is designed to circumvent those limits. However, the entire setuid-ed program is "armed," in that any software bug in a part of the (often large) program can potentially lead to a security hole. We wanted to avoid this possibility in JDK 1.2, so we created APIs that enable a programmer to limit, to just a few method calls, either the scope of the dangerous operations or the duration of the "armed" period. In this way, bugs outside of those sensitive methods are less likely to cause unintended harm.

We considered several design proposals. One was to extend the language with a method modifier, perhaps called "privileged." Privilege would be granted when entering the method and revoked upon returning from it. This was by far the cleanest design, but it required a major addition to the Java language that in turn required compiler vendors to update their compilers. Such a change cannot be made lightly. Moreover, a method modifier cannot take a context argument. So we decided against it. We also rejected a number of other proposals, which would have either changed the existing semantics of nonsecurity code or required support in the JVM that would have been difficult to implement on all platforms.

Up to JDK 1.2 beta3, we went with a design by which we provided the following two method calls in the `AccessController` class:

```
public static native void beginPrivileged()
public static native void endPrivileged()
```

Declaring a block of code to be privileged was to occur as follows.

```
somemethod() {
   (normal code here)
   try {
      AccessController.beginPrivileged();
      // Privileged code goes here, for example:
      System.loadLibrary("awt");
   } finally {
      AccessController.endPrivileged();
   }
   (more normal code here)
}
```

This design had the advantage of being fairly simple to use within the well-known try-finally block construct. Its downside was that the call to endPrivileged() could have been made only in the same method frame as the begin-Privileged() call and optimally would have been called as soon as the privilege was no longer needed. This limited the privilege period to one method invocation and ensured that the privilege was reversed as soon as possible. In the event a programmer accidentally forgot to call endPrivileged(), we built in a number of measures and checks to prevent mismatch between invocations of these begin and end methods from within different frames. For example, we would have reversed a privilege status if it was clear that the programmer should have reversed it but forgot to do so. In the end, the requirement to match frames was considered difficult to specify and enforce precisely in a platform-independent manner, so we abandoned that design in favor of the doPrivileged interface.

The design we eventually adopted works reasonably well, except for slightly added complexity in programming. We expect to improve the design later, for example, when suitable language constructs are made available.

3.12 Summary and Lessons Learned

As a summary of the overall process of how the JDK 1.2 security architecture works, this section takes you through the handling of an applet or application. The following steps occur when viewing an applet, either through a Web browser or appletviewer, or running a Java application, possibly from the command line by invoking the program called java.

1. A class file is obtained and accepted if it passes preliminary bytecode verification.

2. The class's code source is determined. This step includes signature verification, if the code appears to be signed.

3. The security policy is consulted, and the set of permissions to be granted to this class is determined, based on the class's code source. In this step, the `Policy` object is constructed, if it has not been already.

4. A protection domain is created to mark the code source and to hold the permission set. Then the class is loaded and defined to be associated with the protection domain. If a suitable domain has already been created, then that `ProtectionDomain` object is reused and no new permission set is created.

5. The class may be instantiated into objects, and their methods executed. The run-time type safety check continues.

6. When a security check is invoked and one or more methods of this class are in the call chain, the access controller examines the protection domain, and in particular, its permission set, to see if sufficient permission has been granted for the requested access. If it has been granted, the execution continues. Otherwise, a security exception is thrown. (This check is done for all classes whose methods are involved in a thread. See Section 3.11.7 for the complete algorithm.)

7. When a security exception, which is a runtime exception, is thrown and not caught, the JVM aborts.

There are variations to this flow of actions. For example, in a lazy approach, the creation of the `Policy` object, protection domains, and permissions can be delayed until the first security check occurs. This delaying tactic helps to reduce start-up time and the footprint of the runtime because objects are not instantiated until they must be used.

The fundamental ideas adopted in the new security architecture have roots in the last 40 years of computer security research; for example, the overall idea of the access control list [newref 1, 42]. We followed some of the UNIX conventions in specifying access permissions to the file system and other system resources. But significantly, our design was inspired by the concept of protection domains and the work dealing with mutually suspicious programs in Multics [69, 75] and "rights amplification" in Hydra [36, 81].

One novel feature not present in operating systems such as UNIX or MS-DOS is the implementation of the least-privilege principle by automatically intersecting the sets of permissions granted to protection domains that are involved in a call sequence. In this way, a programming error in system or application software is less likely to be exploitable as a security hole.

Note that although the JVM typically runs over another host operating system such as Solaris, it also may run directly over hardware, as in the case of the network computer JavaStation running JavaOS [66]. To maintain platform independence, the JDK 1.2 architecture does not depend on security features provided by an underlying operating system.

Furthermore, this architecture does not override the protection mechanisms in the underlying operating system. For example, by configuring a fine-grained access control policy, a user may grant specific permissions to certain software. This is effective, however, only if the underlying operating system itself has granted the user those permissions.

Another significant characteristic is that JDK 1.2's protection mechanisms are language-based, within a single address space. A major distinction from more traditional operating systems, this feature is very much related to recent work on software-based protection and safe kernel extensions (for example, [7, 10, 76]), whereby various research teams have lately aimed for some of the same goals but by using different programming techniques. In a typical operating system, a cross-domain call tends to be quite expensive. In JDK 1.2, a cross-domain call is just another method invocation and is as cheap as it can get.

The new design has the following significant benefits that are worth highlighting.

1. The content of the security policy is totally separated from not only the implementation mechanism but also the interfaces. This leaves maximum room for evolution. It also allows the policy to be configured entirely separately from the runtime environment, thus reducing the complexity of system administration.

2. The access control algorithm is cleanly separated from the semantics of the permissions that it is checking. This allows the reuse of the access controller code with (perhaps application-specific) permission classes that are introduced after JDK 1.2's release.

3. The introduction of a hierarchy of permission classes brings the full power of object orientation (and especially encapsulation) to bear. This means that access control permissions can be expressed both statically and dynamically and that each `Permission` class may define its own semantics, for example how it relates to a permission of its own type or of a different type or how to interpret wildcard symbols and other peculiarities that are specific to it.

4. The secure class loading mechanism coupled with the extensions mechanism extends security coverage to Java applications, thus resulting in a uniform security architecture and policy for any and all Java code, whatever its origin or status.

In addition to those technical benefits, we paid great attention to good interface design. We worked extensively on API design issues, such as the proper division of labor among various classes. We also tried to maintain a minimal set of classes and APIs, kept as many classes private as possible, created suitable names for classes and methods, and kept the names as short and concise as possible. We did not start prototyping the code until we had a good grasp of the APIs. All of this effort paid off well. We were able to respond to comments and suggestions, and we made extensive revisions to APIs throughout the project, all without much difficulty and without jeopardizing code quality or project delivery. Further, we superseded some fragile features, such as those methods we deprecated in the `SecurityManager` class, with more robust architecture.

One major goal for good interface design is ease of use. In this area, the JDK 1.2 design is superior to a few others proposed. An example of one of the others is a commercial browser that implements features similar to JDK 1.2's privileged method calls. However, it requires that an application explicitly enable its granted privilege in order to use it. In this case, to open a file for reading to which the application has been granted read access, the application cannot just open a `FileInputStream`. Instead, the application first must call a specific method—basically announcing, "I will now exercise my right to read this file"—and then proceed to open the file. Without the prior declaration, the subsequent open operation will fail [79]. Such an interface design has a number of drawbacks.

1. If JDK 1.2 had adopted such a design, all existing applications and applets would have had to be rewritten to explicitly make the declarations. This would have seriously broken backward compatibility.

2. In a multitier application environment, a common scenario involves a request made by the top tier application to obtain a document. This request might be met by the bottom tier application in a number of ways, such as by obtaining the document from the file system, retrieving it from a database, or downloading it from a Web server. In this case, no easy way exists for the top tier application to know ahead of time whether it should enable the privilege for the bottom tier application to read a file, to access a database, or to make a network connection.

   However, if the application uses JDK 1.2 features, it does not need to decide which privilege to enable. The request will be served in any one of the three ways, as long as the application has been granted the appropriate permissions. In other words, requiring a declaration of intent to exercise privilege does not work well in a complex environment, even though it might work reasonably well in a one-tier application situation.

3. If a new or revised security check is placed on a protected resource, any existing application or applet code must be rewritten to enable this new privilege by

a new declaration before it can run as it did previously. This means that the application or applet must be recompiled and redeployed just to continue accessing the same resource. This is a nightmare maintenance scenario.

By contrast, in JDK 1.2, you need only to revise the security policy to grant one more permission to the application. The application or applet will run as before.

We did encounter two artifacts in JDK 1.0 which, although inconvenient, were not changed. First, system classes have been traditionally loaded with a primordial class loader, which is typically written in native code. As a result, all system classes (now called bootstrap classes in JDK 1.2) are loaded from within the Java runtime with a null system class loader. This particular implementation feature, however, became a sort of de facto API. Some programmers started to test for the existence of class loaders as a way to distinguish between system and nonsystem classes, especially as part of the security decision making process. For backward compatibility, JDK 1.2 provides that system classes (or at least those classes necessary for bootstrapping the Java virtual machine) are loaded by the null class loader.

This association between system classes and the null class loader coupled with the difference in treatment of classes based on their class loader types, however, makes it difficult to subdivide system classes into various packages or JAR files and then give them separate sets of permissions. Such a subdivision can effectively reduce the amount of code you need to trust completely, as well as reduce the amount of trust in that code. In JDK 1.2, application classes residing on the local file system must now be loaded with non-null class loaders as part of the extension mechanism. Further, under the new security architecture a class being loaded with a non-null class loader does not say anything about its status, since the class might have been granted `AllPermission`. Hindsight tells us that it would have been much easier to evolve the design if all system classes were originally loaded with a special, but non-null, class loader.

The second artifact in JDK 1.0 that is not changed is that the runtime system does not always have a security manager installed, and in this case, a call to `System.getSecurityManager()` results in a null security manager. Again, for backward compatibility, we did not change this in JDK 1.2. However, this oddity has caused a few unnecessary complexities. For example, everywhere you invoke a security check, you must test for a null security manage; this clutters the code. Moreover, programmers soon started testing for this null security manager as a way to determine the state of the universe, rather like trying to distinguish the world before and after the so-called "big bang." This has led to unwarranted assumptions of how a virtual machine should behave when the security manager is null, partly because no security checks can be invoked on a null security manager. These assumptions should not have been made at a general level, but nevertheless they are being made by some programmers. The presence of such assumptions creates backward compatibility pressure.

The `AccessController` class introduced in JDK 1.2 makes it possible to invoke security checks in the absence of a security manager, but such checks might need to be deployed gingerly for fear of breaking backward compatibility. It would have been easier for us if the security manager had always been installed (that is, immediately after the bootstrap process), even though its behavior might change over time.

The lesson we learned from these two artifacts is that you cannot easily evolve the interface design of something that is null—and you definitely cannot invoke method calls on something that is null.

CHAPTER 4

Deploying the Security Architecture

Policy must be clear, consistent, and confident.
—Dwight D. Eisenhower

To utilize the new security architecture provided in JDK 1.2, you must upgrade your Java environment to the latest version. Generally, new versions of operating systems or Internet browsers (for example, upgrades that you install or software that comes with a new computer system) already support the latest JDK 1.2. However, to upgrade the JVM yourself to the 1.2 version, you can download and install either the Java runtime environment for running Java applications or applets, the JDK itself for development use, or the Java Plug-In that upgrades the JVM inside Microsoft Internet Explorer (IE) and the Netscape Navigator (Navigator).

4.1   Installing JDK 1.2

JDK 1.2 versions for both the Win32 platform (MS-Windows or Windows NT) and the Sun Solaris platform are available from Sun Microsystem's Java Web site at `http://java.sun.com/products/jdk/1.2/`. For demonstration purposes, the instructions in this chapter assume that you are using a Sun Sparc workstation running Solaris.

1. From the Web site, choose the Solaris version of JDK 1.2 for download and save it in a file named `jdk12-solaris2-sparc.sh`.

2. Follow the installation instructions at the site and unpack the downloaded software as follows.

```
% chmod a+x jdk12-solaris2-sparc.sh
% ./jdk12-solaris2-sparc.sh
```

A dialog box displays, asking if you agree to the license terms. Click Accept to proceed. Now you have all of the necessary binary programs unpacked in the directory ./jdk1.2/bin.

3. Add the directory ./jdk1.2/bin to the search path by typing (in a shell window)

```
% set path=($path ./jdk1.2/bin)
```

4. If you want to ensure that programs that are part of the newly installed JDK are located first by the UNIX shell, move the directory to the beginning of the search path:

```
% set path=(./jdk1.2/bin $path)
```

and verify this by typing (again in a shell window)

```
% which java
./jdk1.2/bin/java
%
```

5. Next, you can test by running an applet with appletviewer:

```
% appletviewer http://java.sun.com/applets/other/TumblingDuke/
index.html
```

The command above should be typed on one line in a shell window (but it does not fit under the type-setting system here). You also can run the test application described at the beginning of Chapter 2 from the command line as follows:

```
% java Test Hello
```

If you are using appletviewer or a new version of a browser that deploys this new security architecture, you can continue to do things in largely the same way as before. This means that the same sandbox policy in JDK 1.1.x will apply. If you are a "power user," you can use JDK 1.2's built-in policytool utility (or an equivalent tool shipped with the browser) to customize the security policy, thus utilizing the full benefit of the new security architecture. Such customization might involve setting up a certificate store, which can be done using the keytool utility, used to create and administer keystores. This utility is introduced later in the chapter and is available for the Solaris and MS-Windows platforms.

Application developers in general need to do nothing special to work with JDK 1.2's security features because when their applications run on top of JDK 1.2, those features are invoked automatically. A developer might want to use the built-in tools to package the resulting application into JAR files and might choose to digitally sign them.

A software library developer whose code controls certain resources might need to extend the existing permission class hierarchy to create application-specific permissions. The developer might also need to learn to use features provided by the `AccessController` class, such as the `doPrivilege` interface.

4.2   Policy Configuration

So far in the demonstration example, no security policy has been specified for running applets or applications. Thus the JVM will default to the pre-JDK 1.2 sandbox security model, whereby remote applets are untrusted and local applications are fully trusted. To utilize the new security model, you first must configure a security policy and then specify which policy to use when running Java programs.

The design of the policy APIs in JDK 1.2 does not mandate how a security policy is expressed externally to the Java runtime system. It specifies only the APIs to the `Policy` object. Thus a JDK implementation can choose to store the policy information in a database, a directory service, a file system, or other location.

The default JDK implementation supports the specification of a security policy in a flat-file format. Configuring a security policy consists of specifying first the location and then the content of the policy file. Obviously, policy files should be well protected against, for example, unauthorized modifications.

4.2.1   Configuring System-Wide and User-Specific Policies

The source location for the policy information utilized by the `Policy` object is up to the `Policy` class implementation. JDK 1.2's implementation obtains its information from the static locations at which policy configuration files can be found. A policy file can be composed using a simple text editor or `policytool`, which is a graphical tool. The next section discusses the content of a policy file.

A single system-wide policy file and a single-user policy file have default locations. The default system policy file is located at

```
<java.home>/lib/security/java.policy
```

where `<java.home>` is a system property specifying the directory into which the JDK was installed. The default user policy file is located at

```
<user.home>/.java.policy
```

where `<user.home>` is a system property specifying the user's home directory.

The default `Policy` object is initialized the first time its `getPermissions` method is called or whenever its `refresh` method is called. Initialization involves parsing the policy configuration files and then populating the `Policy` object. When the `Policy` object is initialized, the system policy is loaded in first followed by the user policy. If neither policy is present, a built-in policy is used. This built-in policy is the same as the original sandbox policy.

Policy file locations are specified in the security properties file, which is located at

```
<java.home>/lib/security/java.security
```

These locations are specified as the values of properties whose names are of the form `policy.url.n`, where n is a number. For example, the default system and user policy files are defined in the security properties file as follows.

```
policy.url.1=${java.home}/lib/security/java.policy
policy.url.2=${user.home}/.java.policy
```

Here `${java.home}` is a special designation for property expansion, which is discussed later in this chapter.

You can change the security properties file. For example, you can comment out the second line to skip the default user policy file. You can also specify multiple policy files to form a composite security policy. You do this by specifying several URLs (including ones of the form `http://`) that refer to the file locations. Then the content of all of the designated policy files will be used to populate the `Policy` object.

Note that n in `url.n` must start with 1 and be consecutive integers. When the `Policy` object is initialized, the first policy file must be given by `policy.url.1`, the second by `policy.url.2`, and so on until there are no more policy files. If you specify, for example `policy.url.1` and `policy.url.3` but not `policy.url.2`, then `policy.url.3` is never read.

4.2.2   Configuring Application-Specific Policies

The policy files given in the security properties file (as described in the previous section) are system-wide in the sense that the same set of policy files will be used when running any applet or application. You may specify an additional or a different policy file when invoking the execution of an application. This can be done via the `-Djava.security.policy` command line argument, which sets the value of the `java.security.policy` property; for example:

```
java –Djava.security.manager –Djava.security.policy=someURL someApp
```

Here, `someURL` is a URL specifying the location of another policy file. In this case, this policy file will be used in addition to all of the policy files specified in the security properties file.

The `–Djava.security.manager` argument ensures that the default security manager is installed so that the application is run with a security policy in effect. This option is not required if the application `someApp` itself installs a security manager. Suppose you use the following (note the double equals signs):

```
java –Djava.security.manager –Djava.security.policy==someURL someApp
```

Then only the specified policy file located at `someURL` will be used; all others will be ignored.

When running applets using `appletviewer`, you can specify a policy using the `–Djava.security.policy` argument as follows:

```
appletviewer –Djava.security.policy=someURL someApplet
```

The policy file value given in the `–Djava.security.policy` option will be ignored for both command `java` and `appletviewer` if the property, `policy.allowSystemProperty` is set to `false`. This property, which can be set in the security properties file, is by default set to `true`.

4.2.3 Configuring an Alternative Policy Class Implementation

An alternative policy class can be given to replace the default policy class, as long as this alternative class is a subclass of the abstract `Policy` class and implements the `getPermissions` method (and other methods as necessary).

You can change the default `Policy` implementation without changing the JDK code. A property named `policy.provider` can be given in the security properties file `java.security` as follows:

```
policy.provider=PolicyClassName
```

The default value of this property is

```
policy.provider=sun.security.provider.PolicyFile
```

By changing the property value to specify another class, you substitute a new `Policy` class, as in

```
policy.provider=com.mycom.MyPolicy
```

When the `Policy` object is to be initialized, this class is used, rather than the default implementation class `PolicyFile`. When indicating an alternative `Policy` class, you must specify the fully qualified name of the desired `Policy` implementation class, such as `com.sun.security.MyPolicyClass`.

4.2.4   Default Policy File Format

The policy configuration files for a JDK installation specify the permissions (which types of system resource accesses) that are allowed by code from specified code sources. For an applet or an application to be allowed to perform secured actions (such as reading or writing a file), it must be granted permission for that particular action. In the default `Policy` implementation, that permission must be granted by a grant entry in a policy configuration file.[1]

The syntax of the default policy configuration file format includes a list of entries. It contains zero or more entries that start with the `grant` keyword and optionally a `keystore` entry. A **keystore** is a protected database of private keys and their associated digital certificates, such as X.509 certificate chains, authenticating the corresponding public keys. The default keystore implementation in JDK 1.2 implements the keystore as a file. X.509 certificates are discussed in Section 4.4. You can use `keytool` to create and administer keystores. The keystore specified in a policy configuration file is used to look up the public keys of the signers specified in the grant entries of the file. A keystore entry must appear in a policy configuration file if any grant entries specify signer aliases.

At this time, only one keystore entry is allowed in the policy file—others after the first one are ignored. The entry may appear anywhere outside of the file's grant entries and has the following syntax:

```
keystore "some-keystore-url", "keystore-type";
```

Here, `"some-keystore-url"` specifies the URL location of the keystore and `"keystore-type"` specifies the keystore type. The URL is typically relative to the policy file location. Thus, if the policy file is specified in the security properties file as

```
policy.url.1=http://foo.bar.com/fum/some.policy
```

and that policy file has an entry `keystore ".keystore"`, then the keystore will be loaded from

---

[1]   One exception is that code always automatically has permission to read files from its own `CodeSource` and the subdirectories of that `CodeSource`. It does not need explicit permission to do so.

```
http://foo.bar.com/fum/.keystore
```

The keystore URL can also be given as absolute, such as

```
keystore "http://foo.bar.com/fum/.keystore".
```

A keystore type defines the storage and data format of the keystore information, and the algorithms used to protect private keys in the keystore and the integrity of the keystore itself. The default type supported in JDK 1.2 is a proprietary keystore type named "JKS".

Code being executed is always considered to come from a particular code source (represented by an object of type `CodeSource`). The code source includes not only the location (URL) from which the applet originated, but also a reference to the certificates containing the public keys corresponding to the private keys used to sign the code. Certificates in a code source are referenced by (symbolic) alias names from the user's keystore.

Each grant entry in a policy file consists essentially of a `CodeSource` and its permissions. To represent the set of certificates that may be part of a `Code-Source`, a policy file simply include a list of signer names, which are aliases that map to the actual certificates via a keystore. The alias design is useful because certificates can be large and can contain binary data and unprintable characters, while a policy file should be easy to view and to edit.

The permission segment of each `grant` entry can include a number of permission entries. Following is the basic format of a `grant` entry.

```
grant signedBy "signer-names", codeBase "URL" {
    permission permission-class-name "target-name", "action",
        signedBy "signer-names";
    ...
    permission permission-class-name "target-name", "action",
        signedBy "signer-names";
};
```

A grant entry must begin with the word "grant." The `signedBy` and `codeBase` name/value pairs are optional. The order of these fields does not matter.

The `signedBy` field is optional in that if it is omitted, it signifies "any signer," that is, whether the code is signed and by whom does not matter. Its value, when specified, is a string alias that is mapped (using the keystore) to a set of public keys that are associated with the signers. These keys are used to verify that classes from the specified code source are really signed by these signers. This value can be a comma-separated string containing names of multiple signers, for example

"Adam,Eve,Charles", which means "signed by Adam and Eve and Charles." Note that the relationship is AND, not OR.

Similarly, the absence of a codeBase entry signifies "any code," that is, where the code originates from does not matter.

An informal BNF grammar for the policy file format is given next (terms that are not capitalized are terminals).

```
PolicyFile --> PolicyEntry | PolicyEntry; PolicyFile
PolicyEntry -->     grant {PermissionEntry}; |
            grant SignerEntry {PermissionEntry} |
            grant CodebaseEntry {PermissionEntry} |
            grant SignerEntry, CodebaseEntry {Permission-Entry} |
            grant CodebaseEntry, SignerEntry {PermissionEntry} |
            keystore "url"
SignerEntry -->    signedBy (a comma-separated list of strings)
CodebaseEntry --> codeBase (a string representation of a URL)
PermissionEntry --> OnePermission | OnePermission Permission-Entry
OnePermission --> permission permission-class-name
            [ "target-name" ] [, "action-list"]
            [, SignerEntry];
```

Note that a codeBase value is a URL and thus a forward slash "/" (never a backslash, "\") should always be used as the directory separator, even when the code source is on an MS-Windows system. For example, if the source location for code on an MS-Windows system is C:"somepath"app", then the policy code-Base entry should look like this.

```
grant codeBase "file:/C:/somepath/api/" {
...
}
```

A permission entry must begin with the word "permission." permission-class-name in the previous grammar would actually be a specific permission type, such as java.io.FilePermission or java.lang.RuntimePermission.

The action, for example read, write, access, or other, is required for many permission types, such as java.io.FilePermission (which specifies the type of file access permitted). It is not required for categories for which it is not necessary, such as java.lang.RuntimePermission—you either have the permission specified by the "target-name" following permission-class-name, or you do not.

The signedBy name/value pair for a permission entry is optional. If present, it indicates a signed permission. That is, the Permission class itself must be signed by the given alias(es) in order for the permission to be granted. For example, suppose you have the following grant entry.

```
grant {
    permission Foo "foobar", signedBy "FooSoft";
}
```

This permission of type Foo is granted if the Foo.class permission has been signed by the "FooSoft" alias, or if Foo.class is a system class, since system classes are not subject to policy restrictions.

This per-permission signer field is included to prevent spoofing when a permission class does not reside with the Java runtime installation. For example, a copy of the com.abc.TVPermission class can be downloaded as part of a remote JAR file, and the user policy might include an entry that refers to it. Because the archive is not long-lived, the second time that the com.abc.TVPermission class is downloaded, possibly from a different Web site, the second copy absolutely must be authentic. This is because the presence of the permission entry in the user policy might reflect the user's confidence or belief in the first copy of the class bytecode.

We chose to use digital signatures to ensure authenticity, rather than storing (a hash value of) the first copy of the bytecode and using it to compare with the second copy. We did this because the author of the Permission class can legitimately update the class file to reflect a new design or implementation.

Items in a permission entry must appear in the following order:

```
(permission, permission-class-name, "target-name",
"action", signedBy "signer-names").
```

An entry is terminated with a semicolon. Case is unimportant for the identifiers (permission, signedBy, codeBase, and so on) but is significant for permission-class-name or for any string that is passed in as a value.

In the specification of a java.io.FilePermission, "target-name" is a file path. On an MS-Windows system, whenever directly specifying a file path in a string (but not in a codeBase URL), you need to include two backslashes "\\" for each single backslash in the path, as in this example.

```
grant {
    permission java.io.FilePermission
  "C:\\users\\cathy\\foo.bat", "read";
};
```

This is because the strings are processed by a tokenizer (`java.io.Stream-Tokenizer`), which allows "\" to be used as an escape string. An example, is "\n" to indicate a new line. Thus two backslashes are required to indicate a single backslash. After the tokenizer has processed the above file path string, in the process converting double backslashes to single backslashes, the result is `"C:\users\cathy\foo.bat"`.

4.2.5   Policy File Examples

This section offers several examples of policy files. Following are examples of two entries in a policy configuration file. As with Java programs, lines preceded with `//` are comments and are not interpreted.

```
// If the code is signed by "Duke", grant it read/write access
// to all files in /tmp:
grant signedBy "Duke" {
    permission java.io.FilePermission "/tmp/*", "read,write";
};


// Grant everyone the following permission:
grant {
    permission java.util.PropertyPermission "java.vendor";
};
```

Here are the contents of another sample policy configuration file.

```
grant signedBy "sysadmin", codeBase "file:/home/sysadmin/" {
    permission java.security.SecurityPermission
        "Security.insertProvider.*";
    permission java.security.SecurityPermission
        "Security.removeProvider.*";
    permission java.security.SecurityPermission
        "Security.setProperty.*";
};
```

This example specifies that only applet code that was loaded from a signed JAR file (whose signature can be verified using the public key referenced by the alias name "sysadmin" in the keystore) from beneath the /home/sysadmin/ directory on the local file system can call methods in the Security class to add or remove providers or to set security properties.

Since the code source contains two components, codeBase and signedBy, and either (or both) components may be omitted, the following policy is still valid.

```
grant signedBy "sysadmin" {
    permission java.security.SecurityPermission
        "Security.insertProvider.*";
    permission java.security.SecurityPermission
        "Security.removeProvider.*";
};
```

This policy says that code that comes in a JAR file signed by "sysadmin" can add or remove providers regardless of from where the JAR file originated. Here is an example without a signer.

```
grant codeBase "file:/home/sysadmin/" {
    permission java.security.SecurityPermission
        "Security.insertProvider.*";
    permission java.security.SecurityPermission
        "Security.removeProvider.*";
};
```

In this case, code that comes from anywhere beneath the /home/sysadmin/ directory on the local file system can add or remove providers. The code does not need to be signed.

Following is an example that does not mention codeBase or signedBy.

```
grant {
    permission java.security.SecurityPermission
        "Security.insertProvider.*";
    permission java.security.SecurityPermission
        "Security.removeProvider.*";
};
```

Under this security policy, any code (regardless of where it originated, or whether it is signed, or who signed it) can add or remove providers. Obviously, this policy is too liberal for many situations.

4.2.6 Property Expansion in Policy Files

To make policy configuration and specification easier, JDK 1.2 allows property expansion both in policy files and in the security properties file. Property expansion is similar to expanding variables in a UNIX shell. That is, when a string of the form {some.property} appears in a policy file or in the security properties file, it will be expanded to the value of the system property. Suppose you have

```
permission java.io.FilePermission "${user.home}", "read";
```

This entry, when processed, will expand "${user.home}" to the value of the user.home system property. If that property's value is "/home/cathy", then the previous permission line is equivalent to

```
permission java.io.FilePermission "/home/cathy", "read";
```

To assist in the creation of platform-independent policy files, JDK 1.2 introduces the special notation "${/}" as a shortcut for "${file.separator}". Thus you can write lines such as

```
permission java.io.FilePermission "${user.home}${/}*", "read";
```

If you are using a Solaris system and the value of the user.home system property is "/home/cathy", the previous line gets expanded to

```
permission java.io.FilePermission "/home/cathy/*", "read";
```

If you are using an MS-Windows system and the user.home system value is "C:\users\cathy", the expansion result is

```
permission java.io.FilePermission "C:\users\cathy\*", "read";
```

As a special case, if a property in a codeBase string, such as grant codeBase "file:${java.home}/lib/ext/" is expanded, the system assumes that you are on a UNIX system (due to the use of slashes) and then any file separator characters in that grant entry will be automatically expanded (or converted) to "/". If this entry is used on an MS-Windows system, the expansion result is

```
grant codeBase "file:C:/jdk1.2/lib/ext/"
```

even if java.home is set to C:\jdk1.2. As a result, when specifying a codeBase string, you should use ${/}.

Because property expansion can take place anywhere that a double-quoted string is allowed in the policy file, the fields "signer-names", "URL", "target-name", and "action" can all be expanded. You can disable property expansion by setting to false the value of the policy.expandProperties property in the security properties file. The default value of this property is true.

Nested properties do not expand properly. For example, "${user.${foo}}" does not result in ${user.home}, even if the foo property is set to "home". This is because the property parser does not recognize nested properties. Rather, it simply looks for the first "${" and then keeps looking until it finds the first "}". It tries to interpret the result (in this case, "${user.$foo}") as a property but fails when there is no such property.

If a property expansion is given in a grant entry and property expansion fails, the entry is ignored. For example, suppose the system property `foo` is not defined and you have the following.

```
grant codeBase "${foo}" {
    permission ...;
    permission ...;
};
```

then all of the permissions in this grant entry are ignored.

On the other hand, if you have the following:

```
grant {
    permission Foo "${foo}";
    permission Bar;
};
```

then only the `permission Foo` entry is ignored and `Permission Bar` is granted.

If you have keystore `"${foo}"` and the system property `foo` is not defined, then the entire keystore entry is ignored.

Expansion of a property in a string takes place after the tokenizer has processed the string, thus for string `"${user.home}\\foo.bat"`, the tokenizer first processes the string, converting the double backslashes to a single backslash, and the result is `"${user.home}\foo.bat"`. Then `${user.home}` is expanded and the end result is `"C:\users\cathy\foo.bat"`, assuming that the `user.home` value is `"C:\users\cathy"`. In this example, to achieve platform independence, the string should be initially specified without any explicit slashes, that is, by using the `"${/}"` property instead, as in `"${user.home}${/}foo.bat"`.

4.3   Digital Certificates

Within a security policy, a `signedBy` keyword is used to specify that a piece of code must be digitally signed by an entity. The entity may be a person, organization, program, computer, business, bank, or other. `signedBy` merely gives an alias of the entity, whereas a database called keystore maintains a mapping between an alias and its public key. In practice, the public key is often stored inside a public-key certificate.

A **public-key certificate** is a digitally signed statement from one entity that says the public key (and some other information) of another entity has some specific value. According to this description, a public key and its associated information is certified by another public key. So there can be a chain of certificates,

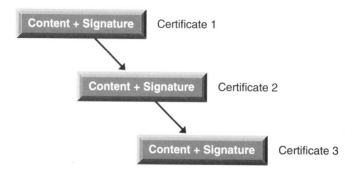

Figure 4.1   Certificate chain.

depicted in Figure 4.1, in which each certificate contains a public key that is used to certify the public key in the succeeding certificate. The first, top-level, certificate, often called the **root certificate**, does not have another public key to certify it. Thus it normally is a *self-signed certificate* in that its own public key is used to certify itself.

Root certificates often are issued by a Certificate Authority, which can act as a Trusted Third Party (TTP) to issue root certificates. A **Certificate Authority** (CA) is an entity such as a business that is trusted to sign (issue) digital certificates for other entities. It is typically assumed that CAs will create only valid and reliable certificates, as they are bound legally to do so. Use of such a certificate implies that one trusts the entity that signed the certificate. In some cases, such as root or top-level CA certificates, the issuer signs its own certificate. Many public CAs are available, for example VeriSign, Inc., but anyone can also run his or her own CA, for example by using one of the readily available commercial server products.

To facilitate interoperability, the international body Comité Consultatif International Téléphonique et Télégraphique (CCITT), which sets international communication standards, created a standard certificate format. This certificate is called *X.509*, the most recent version being X.509 v3. The most widely used format, it is especially popular in Web browsers such as Navigator and IE that support the SSL (secure sockets layer) protocol. SSL is a security protocol that provides privacy and authentication for network traffic and uses certificates to negotiate and establish a secure communication channel between the browser and the Web server. It is defined by the IETF (Internet Engineering Task Force) and is succeeded by the Transport Layer Security (TLS) protocol. X.509 certificates are also used to sign JAR files, in secure e-mail products such as PEM and S/MIME, and in e-commerce protocols such as SET.

All X.509 certificates have the following data, in addition to the signature.

- **Version**. The version of the X.509 standard that applies to this certificate. The version affects what information can be specified in a certificate. So far, three versions are defined.[2]

- **Serial number**. The serial number, assigned by the entity that created the certificate so as to distinguish it from other certificates it issues. This information is used in numerous ways, for example when a certificate is revoked, its serial number is placed in a Certificate Revocation List. A **Certificate Revocation List** (CRL) is a time-stamped list identifying revoked certificates. It is signed by a CA and often made freely available in a public repository.

- **Signature algorithm identifier**. The algorithm used by the CA to sign the certificate.

- **Issuer name**. The X.500 name of the entity that signed the certificate. This is normally a CA.

- **Validity period**. The time period for which the certificate is valid. Each certificate is valid for only a limited amount of time. This period is described by a start date and time and an end date and time and can be as short as a few seconds or almost as long as a century. This is the expected period for which entities can rely on the public value, provided the associated private key has not been compromised. The validity period chosen depends on a number of factors, such as the strength of the private key used to sign the certificate and/or the amount one is willing to pay for a certificate.

- **Subject name**. The name of the entity whose public key the certificate identifies. This name uses the X.500 standard, so it is intended to be unique across the Internet. It is the Distinguished Name (DN) of the entity, for example:

  ```
  CN=Java Duke, OU=Java Software, O=Sun Microsystems, C=US
  ```

  These refer, respectively, to the subject's common name (CN), organizational unit (CU), organization (O), and country (C). Additional fields include `localityName`, the `locality` (city) name such as Palo Alto, and `stateName`, the state or province name, such as California.

- **Subject public key information**. The public key of the entity being named, together with an algorithm identifier that specifies to which public key cryptosystem this key belongs and any associated key parameters.

---

[2] The IETF Public-Key Infrastructure (X.509) working group (PKIX) is in the process of defining standards for the Internet Public Key Infrastructure.

All of the data in a certificate is encoded using two related standards, ASN.1/ DER. Abstract Syntax Notation 1 (ASN.1) describes data. Definite Encoding Rules (DER) describe a single way to store and transfer that data.

Certificates are often stored using the printable encoding format defined by the Internet RFC 1421 standard, instead of their binary encoding. This certificate format, also called *Base64 encoding*, facilitates exporting certificates to other applications (for example, via e-mail). In its Base64 encoding, the encoded certificate is bounded at the beginning and the end by, respectively, by

```
-----BEGIN CERTIFICATE-----
```

and

```
-----END CERTIFICATE-----.
```

Three versions of X.509 are available.

1. X.509 v1, available since 1988, is widely deployed and the most generic.

2. X.509 v2 introduced the concept of subject and issuer unique identifiers to handle the possibility of reuse of subject and/or issuer names. Most certificate profile documents strongly recommend that names not be reused and that certificates not make use of unique identifiers. Version 2 certificates are not widely used.

3. X.509 v3 is the most recent (since 1996) and supports the notion of *extensions*. Anyone may define an extension and include it in the certificate. Some common extensions in use today are

   a. KeyUsage, which limits the use of the keys to particular purposes such as signing only, and

   b. AlternativeNames, which allows other identities to also be associated with this public key, for example, DNS names, e-mail addresses, IP addresses.

Extensions can be marked "critical" to indicate that the extension should be checked and enforced/used. For example, if a certificate has the KeyUsage extension marked critical and set to keyCertSign, then if this certificate is presented during SSL communication, it should be rejected, as the certificate extension indicates that the associated private key should be used only for signing certificates and not for SSL use.

Certificates are available in a number of ways. You can create a self-signed certificate by using the right tools, such as keytool, which is explained later in this chapter. However, some people will accept only certificates signed by a CA. The value a CA provides is that of a neutral and trusted introduction service, based in part on its verification requirements, which are openly published in its Certification Service Practices (CSP).

Or you can request a certificate from a CA. In this case, keytool can assist in generating the request, called a Certificate Signing Request (CSR). Basically, to obtain a certificate from a CA you need a matched pair of public and private keys, which are often generated by a special tool such as keytool or by a browser. You also need to provide information about the entity being certified, such as name and address. You will normally need to provide proof to show the correctness of this information. You then submit the required information in a self-signed certificate so that the CA can verify its integrity.

JDK 1.2 contains a rich set of Java APIs for accessing and managing certificates. The certificate API, found in the java.security.cert package, includes the following classes.

- CertificateFactory. Defines the functionality of a certificate factory, which is used to generate certificates (and associated CRL objects) from their encoding.

- Certificate. An abstract class for managing a variety of certificates. It is an abstraction for certificates that have different formats but important common uses. For example, different types of certificates, such as X.509 certificates and those obtained from the encryption tool Pretty Good Privacy (PGP), share general certificate functionality (such as encoding and verifying) and some types of information (such as the public key).

- CRL. An abstract class for managing a variety of CRLs.

- X509Certificate. An abstract class for X.509 certificates. It provides a standard way to access all of the attributes of an X.509 certificate.

- X509Extension. The interface for X.509 extensions, which are defined for X.509 v3 certificates and X.509 v2 CRLs. These extensions provide mechanisms for associating additional attributes with users or public keys, such as for managing the certification hierarchy and for managing CRL distribution.

◆ X509CRL. An abstract class for an X.509 CRL.

◆ X509CRLEntry. An abstract class for a CRL entry.

The next section describes keytool, which generates, displays, imports, and exports X.509 certificates.

4.4   Helpful Security Tools

To assist developers, JDK 1.2 is delivered with these security tools: keytool, policytool, and jarsigner. These are covered in this section. First, however, it discusses keystore databases.

4.4.1   Keystore Databases

Recall from Section 4.2.4 that a keystore is a protected database that holds private keys and certificates for an enterprise. The default keystore implementation in JDK 1.2 implements the keystore as a file, as depicted in Figure 4.2. Access to a keystore is guarded by a password, which is chosen at the time the keystore is created, normally by the person who creates the keystore. A keystore so protected can be changed only by someone who can provide the current password. In addition, each private key in a keystore can be guarded, for extra security, by its own password.

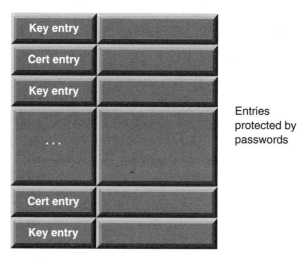

Figure 4.2   Keystore.

Information from a keystore is used by other tools, such as `jarsigner`, to generate or verify digital signatures for JAR files. A JAR file packages class files, images, sounds, and/or other digital data in a single file. `jarsigner` verifies the digital signature of a JAR file, using the certificate that comes with it (it is included in the signature block file of the JAR file). It then checks whether the public key of that certificate is trusted, that is, whether it is contained in the specified keystore.[3]

A keystore contains two types of entries: key entries and a trusted certificate entry. The key entry holds sensitive cryptographic key information and is stored in a protected format to prevent unauthorized access. Typically, a key stored in this type of entry is either a secret key or a private key accompanied by the certificate chain for the corresponding public key. `keytool` and `jarsigner`, as delivered in JDK 1.2, do not handle secret keys.

The trusted certificate entry contains a single public key certificate belonging to an entity. It is called a *trusted certificate* because the keystore owner, by accepting this entry into the keystore, trusts that the public key in the certificate indeed belongs to the identity identified by the subject—that is, the owner—of the certificate. The issuer of the certificate vouches for this by signing the certificate.

All keystore entries (key and trusted certificate entries) are accessed via unique aliases. Aliases are case-insensitive; for example, the aliases "Hugo" and "hugo" refer to the same keystore entry. You specify an alias when you add an entity to the keystore using the –genkey command to generate a key pair (public and private key) or the –import command to add a certificate or certificate chain to the list of trusted certificates. Subsequent `keytool` commands must use this same alias to refer to the entity. For example, suppose you use the alias "duke" to generate a new public/private key pair and wrap the public key in a self-signed certificate via the following command:

```
keytool –genkey –alias duke –keypass dukekeypasswd
```

This command specifies an initial password of dukekeypasswd that will be required by subsequent commands to access the private key associated with the alias "duke." To change the private key password of duke, you use a command like the following, which changes the password from dukekeypasswd to `newpass`:

---

[3]   The `keytool` and `jarsigner` tools replace the `javakey` tool provided in JDK 1.1. These new tools provide more features than `javakey`, including the ability to protect the keystore and private keys with passwords and the ability to verify signatures, in addition to generating them. The new keystore architecture replaces the identity database that `javakey` created and managed. You can import the information from an identity database into a keystore via `keytool`'s –identitydb command.

```
keytool -keypasswd -alias duke -keypass dukekeypasswd -new newpass
```

For better security, a password should not be specified on a command line or in a script unless for testing purposes or you are on a secure system. If you do not specify a required password option on a command line, you will be prompted for one.

Recall that a keystore by default is implemented as a file. Each `keytool` command has an option for specifying the name and location of this persistent keystore file. During keystore creation, if you do not specify a `-keystore` option, the keystore is by default stored in a file named `.keystore` in the user's home directory, as determined by the `user.home` system property. On a Solaris system, `user.home` defaults to the user's home directory. On an MS-Windows system, given username uName, the `user.home` property value defaults as follows.

`C:\Winnt\Profiles\uName`	On multiuser Windows NT systems
`C:\Windows\Profiles\uName`	On multiuser Windows 95 systems
`C:\Windows`	On single-user Windows 95 systems

Thus, if the username is `cathy`, `user.home` defaults to

`C:\Winnt\Profiles\cathy`	On multiuser Windows NT systems
`C:\Windows\Profiles\cathy`	On multiuser Windows 95 systems

The `KeyStore` class provided in the `java.security` package supplies interfaces for accessing and modifying the information in a keystore. Nevertheless, multiple different concrete implementations can be imagined, where each implementation is for a particular type of keystore. Also, keystore implementations are *provider-based*. More specifically, the application interfaces supplied by `KeyStore` are implemented in terms of a *service provider interface* (SPI). A **provider** is a package or a set of packages that supply a concrete implementation of a subset of services that can be accessed from the Java security API. Thus a corresponding abstract `KeystoreSpi` class, also in the `java.security` package, defines the SPI methods that providers must implement. To provide a keystore implementation, the client must implement a provider and supply a `KeystoreSpi` subclass implementation. Chapter 7 describes how to implement a provider.

Applications can choose different types of keystore implementations from different providers, using the `getInstance` method supplied in the `KeyStore` class. A keystore type defines the storage and data format of the keystore information, as well as the algorithms used to protect private keys in the keystore and the integrity of the keystore itself. Keystore implementations of different types need not be compatible in implementation details such as format. The JDK 1.2 default implementation of the keystore uses a proprietary keystore type named "JKS." Types are not case-sensitive; thus "jks" would be considered the same as "JKS."

keytool works on any file-based keystore implementation. It treats the keystore location that is passed to it at the command line as a filename and converts it to a FileInputStream, from which it loads the keystore information. You also can specify a keystore type at the command line. For example, if you have a provider package that supplies a keystore implementation for a keystore type called "pkcs12," you can use the command

```
keystore.type=pkcs12
```

If you do not explicitly specify a keystore type, keytool chooses a keystore implementation based on the value of the keystore.type property specified in the security properties file. The KeyStore class defines a static method, get-DefaultType, that lets applications and applets retrieve the value of the keystore.type property. The following line of code creates an instance of the default keystore type:

```
KeyStore keyStore = KeyStore.getInstance(KeyStore.getDefault-Type());
```

4.4.2   Keytool

keytool can be used to create public/private key pairs and self-signed certificates. These keys and certificates are kept in a keystore, which can be managed also through the use of keytool. For example, you can display, import, and export X.509 v1, v2, and v3 certificates stored as files and to generate new, self-signed v1 certificates.[4]

keytool allows users to specify any key pair generation and signature algorithm supplied by any of the cryptographic service providers that are registered with the Java runtime environment. The default key pair generation algorithm is Digital Signature Algorithm (DSA). The size of a DSA key must be in the range of 512 to 1,024 bits and must be a multiple of 64. The default key size for any algorithm is 1,024 bits. The signature algorithm is derived from the algorithm of the underlying private key. For example, if the underlying private key is of type "DSA," the default signature algorithm is SHA1withDSA, and if the underlying private key is of type "RSA," the default signature algorithm is MD5withRSA.

keytool's default implementation currently handles X.509 certificates. Given a sample DN string

---

[4]   Even though the underlying certificate package supports X.509 v3 format, keytool generates only X.509 v1-formatted certificates due to command-line complexity in dealing with various extensions and options. One can easily imagine extended or customized keytools that take advantage of the v3 format.

```
"CN=Mark Smith, OU=JavaSoft, O=Sun, L=Palo Alto, S=CA, C=US"
```

you can use the following command (which must be typed on a single line) to generate a key for this DN:

```
keytool -genkey -dname "CN=Mark Smith, OU=JavaSoft, O=Sun,
    L=Palo Alto, S=CA, C=US" alias mark
```

Keyword abbreviations are case-insensitive; for example, "CN," "cn," and "Cn" are all treated the same. However, the order of the keywords does matter in that each subcomponent must appear in the designated order CN, OU, O, L, S, C. However, not all subcomponents need be present; subsets are allowed, for example:

```
CN=Mark Smith, OU=JavaSoft, O=Sun, C=US
```

If a DN component string is needed for a command but is not supplied on the command line, the user will be prompted for the string.

keytool can create and manage keystore key entries that each contain a private key and an associated certificate chain. The first certificate in the chain contains the public key corresponding to the private key. When a key is first generated, the chain starts off containing a single element, a self-signed certificate. When a new public/private key pair is generated, the public key is wrapped in a self-signed certificate. Later, after a CSR has been generated and sent to a CA, the response from the CA is imported and the self-signed certificate is replaced by a chain of certificates. At the bottom of the chain is the certificate (reply) issued by the CA that is authenticating the subject's public key.

The next certificate in the chain authenticates the CA's public key. Often, this is a self-signed certificate and also the last certificate in the chain. In other cases, the CA might return a chain of certificates. Here, the bottom certificate in the chain is the same, but the second certificate in the chain is a certificate signed by a different CA, which is authenticating the public key of the CA that received the CSR. The next certificate authenticates the second CA's key, and so on, until a self-signed root certificate is reached. Each certificate in the chain (after the first) thus authenticates the public key of the signer of the previous certificate in the chain.

Many CAs return only the issued certificate, with no supporting chain, especially when the hierarchy is flat, that is, there are no intermediate CAs. In this case, the certificate chain must be established from trusted certificate information already stored in the keystore.

An additional reply format, defined by the PKCS#7 standard, includes the supporting certificate chain in addition to the issued certificate. Both reply formats can be handled by keytool.

The root CA certificate is self-signed. However, the trust aspect of the root's public key does not come from the root certificate itself because anybody could generate a self-signed certificate with the DN. Before you add the root CA certificate to your keystore, you should ensure its authenticity. For example, suppose a certificate is in a file named /tmp/cert. Before you consider adding the certificate to your list of trusted certificates, execute a -printcert command to view its fingerprints, for example:

```
keytool --printcert --file /tmp/cert
Owner: CN=11, OU=11, O=11, L=11, S=11, C=11
Issuer: CN=11, OU=11, O=11, L=11, S=11, C=11
Serial Number: 59092b34
Valid from: Thu Sep 25 18:01:13 PDT 1997 until: Wed Dec 24 17:01:13
    PST 1997
Certificate Fingerprints:
MD5: 11:81:AD:92:C8:E5:0E:A2:01:2E:D4:7A:D7:5F:07:6F
SHA1: 20:B6:17:FA:EF:E5:55:8A:D0:71:1F:E8:D6:9D:C0:37:13:0E:5E:FE
```

In fact, before adding a certificate to the list of trusted certificates in the keystore, keytool prints out the certificate information and prompts you to verify it. You then have the option of aborting the import operation.

keytool can import a certificate from a file using, for example, in response to the following command:

```
keytool --import --alias joe --file jcertfile.cer
```

This command imports the certificates in the file jcertfile.cer and stores it in the keystore entry identified by the alias "joe." Certificates read by the -import and -printcert commands can be either in Base64 or binary-encoded. You can import either a certificate to add it to a list of trusted certificates or a certificate reply received from a CA as the result of submitting a CSR to that CA. Which is imported is indicated by the value of the -alias option. If the alias exists in the database and identifies an entry with a private key, then importing a certificate reply is assumed. keytool checks whether the public key in the certificate reply matches the public key stored with the alias. If the alias identifies an existing certificate entry, the new certificate will not be imported. Otherwise, the alias will be created and associated with the imported certificate.

To export a certificate to a file, use the -export command, as in

```
keytool --export --alias jane --file janecertfile.cer
```

This command exports jane's certificate to the file janecertfile.cer. By default, it outputs a binary-encode certificate, but it also can output a Base64 certificate.

To print the contents of a keystore entry, you use the -list command, as in

```
keytool -list -alias joe
```

If an alias is not specified, the contents of the keystore are printed. The -list command by default prints the MD5 fingerprint of a certificate. If the -verbose option is specified, it prints the certificate in human-readable format.

keytool has built-in default values for the following options:

-alias	"mykey"
-keyalg	"DSA"
-keysize	1024
-validity	90
-keystore	the file named .keystore in the user's home directory
-file	stdin if reading; stdout if writing

Refer to the on-line JDK 1.2 documentation for a detailed explanation of all command options in keytool. The following commands also output help information:

```
keytool
keytool -help
```

Keytool Usage Example

Following is an example to create and manage a keystore that has your public/private key pair and certificates from entities you trust.

First, you need to create a keystore and generate the key pair. You can use the following command, typed on a single line:

```
keytool --genkey --dname "cn=Mark Smith, ou=JavaSoft, o=Sun,
    c=US" --alias business --keypass kpi135 --keystore /working/
    mykeystore --storepass ab987c --validity 180
```

This command creates the keystore mykeystore in the working directory (assuming it does not already exist) and assigns it the password (storepass) ab987c. It generates a public/private key pair for the entity whose DN (dname) has a common name Mark Smith, organizational unit JavaSoft, organization Sun, and two-letter country code US. It uses the default DSA key generation algorithm to create the keys, both 1,024 bits long.

The command creates a self-signed certificate (using the default SHA1withDSA signature algorithm) that includes the public key and the DN information. This certificate will be valid for 180 days, and is associated with the private key in a keystore entry referred to by the alias "business." The private key is assigned the password kpi135.

The command can be significantly shorter if option defaults are accepted, since you are prompted for any required values that are not specified and have no defaults. Thus you could simply type the following:

```
keytool --genkey
```

In this case, a keystore entry with alias "mykey" is created, with a newly generated key pair and a certificate that is valid for 90 days. The rest of the examples in this section assume you executed the -genkey command without options specified and that you responded to the prompts with values equal to those given in the -genkey command used at the beginning of this section.

So far, all you have is a self-signed certificate. A certificate is more likely to be trusted by others if it is signed by a CA. To get such a signature, you first generate a CSR, using the following command:

```
keytool --certreq --file MarkJ.csr
```

This command creates a CSR (for the entity identified by the default alias "mykey") and puts the request in the file named `MarkJ.csr`. You then submit this file to a CA. The CA will authenticate you as the requestor (usually, this is done off-line) and return a certificate, signed by it, authenticating your public key. (In some cases, it will return a chain of certificates.)

You need to replace your self-signed certificate with a certificate chain, where each certificate in the chain authenticates the public key of the signer of the previous certificate in the chain, up to the root CA. Before you import the certificate reply from a CA, you need one or more trusted certificates in your keystore. You determine which one as follows.

1. If the certificate reply is a certificate chain, you need only the top certificate of the chain (that is, the root CA certificate authenticating that CAs public key).

2. If the certificate reply is a single certificate, you need a certificate for the issuing CA (the one that signed it), and if that certificate is not self-signed, you need a certificate for its signer, and so on, up to a self-signed root CA certificate.

The default keystore file in JDK 1.2 ships with five VeriSign root CA certificates, so you probably will not need to import a VeriSign certificate as a trusted certificate in your keystore. But if you request a signed certificate from a different CA and your keystore does not contain a certificate authenticating that CA's public key, you will need to import a trusted certificate from the CA.

A certificate from a CA is usually either self-signed or signed by another CA (in which case you also need a certificate authenticating that CA's public key). Suppose company ABC, Inc., is a CA and you obtain a file named ABCCA.cer that contains purportedly a self-signed certificate from ABC, authenticating that CA's public key. Be very careful to ensure the certificate is valid prior to importing it as a trusted certificate. If you trust that the certificate is valid, then add it to your keystore using the following command:

```
keytool --import --alias abc --file ABCCA.cer
```

This command creates a trusted certificate entry in the keystore, with the data from the file ABCCA.cer, and assigns the alias "abc" to the entry.

Once you have imported a certificate authenticating the public key of the CA to which you submitted your CSR (or there is already such a certificate in the cacerts file), you can import the certificate reply, thereby replacing your self-signed certificate with a certificate chain. This is the chain returned by the CA in response to your CSR (if the CA reply is a chain) or one constructed (if the CA reply is a single certificate) using the certificate reply and trusted certificates that are already available in the keystore in which you imported the reply or in the cacerts keystore file.

For example, suppose you sent your CSR to VeriSign. You can then import the reply by using the following command (assume the returned certificate is named VSMarkJ.cer):

```
keytool --import -trustcacerts --file VSMarkJ.cer
```

Suppose you have used jarsigner to sign a JAR file. Clients who want to use the file will want to authenticate your signature. They can import your public key certificate into their keystore as a trusted entry, or you can export the certificate and supply it to your clients. For example, you can copy your certificate to a file named MJ.cer (assume the entry is aliased by "mykey"):

```
keytool --export --alias mykey --file MJ.cer
```

Using that certificate and the signed JAR file, a client can use jarsigner to authenticate your signature.

Suppose your DN changes, for example because you have changed departments or moved to a different city. You may still use the same public/private key while updating your DN. For example, suppose your name is Susan Miller and you created your initial key entry with the alias "sMiller" and this DN:

```
"cn=Susan Miller, ou=Finance Department, o=BlueSoft, c=us"
```

If you later change from the Finance Department to the Accounting Department, you can still use the previously generated public/private key pair but update your DN by doing the following.

1. Copy (clone) your key entry:

```
keytool --keyclone --alias sMiller --dest sMillerNew
```

This command will prompt for the `storepass` password and for the initial and destination private key passwords, since they are not provided at the command line.

2. Change the certificate chain associated with the copy so that the first certificate in the chain uses your new DN. Start by generating a self-signed certificate with the appropriate name:

```
keytool --selfcert --alias sMillerNew -dname "cn=Susan Miller,
    ou=Accounting Department, o=BlueSoft, c=us"
```

3. Generate a CSR using the information in the new certificate:

```
keytool --certreq -alias sMillerNew
```

and import the CA certificate reply:

```
keytool --import --alias sMillerNew --file VSSMillerNew.cer
```

4. You might want to remove the initial key entry that used your old DN:

```
keytool --delete --alias sMiller
```

MS-Windows also includes a version of the keytool. On-line JDK 1.2 documentation explains its usage, which is essentially the same as the Solaris version used in these examples.

4.4.3 Policy Tool

`policytool` enables you to create new policy files and modify existing ones. Start `policytool` by typing the following at the command line to display the Policy Tool window (Figure 4.3):

```
policytool
```

When you start the policy tool, the Policy Tool window displays, showing policy information for what is sometimes called the *user policy file*. This information includes the policy filename, the keystore URL (if any), and the `codeBase` and

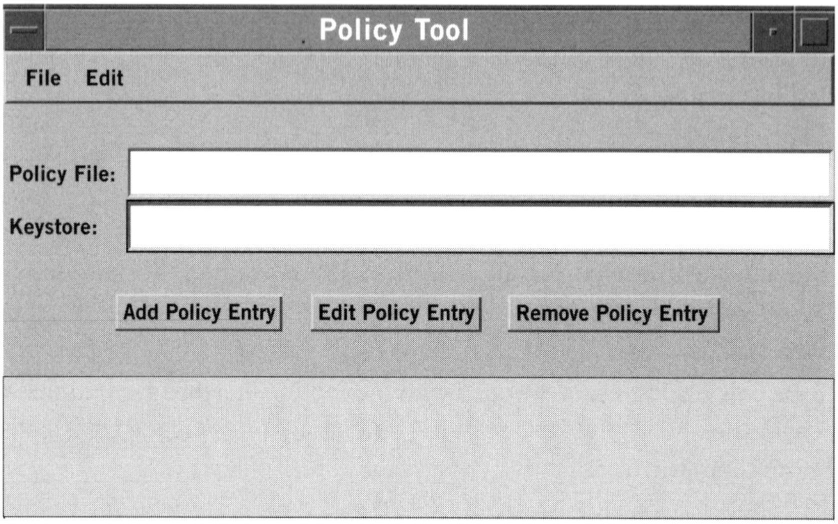

Figure 4.3   `policytool` snapshot.

`signedBy` parts of each policy entry in the policy file. By default, this file is a file named `.java.policy` in your home directory. If `policytool` cannot find this file, it reports that fact and displays a blank Policy Tool window. (The first time you run `policytool`, a user policy file does not exist unless you have created one manually.) You can then either open whatever policy file you want to work on or create a new policy file, by adding policy entries, optionally specifying a keystore, and saving the file.

For example, suppose you want to specify the keystore named "mykeystore" in the `/tests/` directory. On a Solaris system, you would do the following.

1. Type the following URL into the text box labeled New KeyStore URL:

   `file:/tests/mykeystore`

   `policytool` can read a keystore from any location that can be specified using a URL.

2. Specify the keystore type, if needed, by typing the type into the text box New KeyStore Type; for example, "JKS," the proprietary keystore type supported by Sun Microsystems. If you do not explicitly specify a keystore type, `poli-`

cytool chooses a keystore implementation based on the value of the keystore.type property specified in the security properties file.

3. Click OK.

The text box labeled Keystore shows the keystore URL and type.

To add a new policy entry, do the following.

1. Click the Add Policy Entry button in the Policy Tool window to display the Policy Entry dialog box.

2. Using this dialog box, specify an optional codeBase entry indicating the URL location from where the code originates. For example, to indicate code from the local/JavaSoft/TESTS/ directory, type the following into the CodeBase text box:

   file:/JavaSoft/TESTS/

   Also type into the text box the following:

   a. An optional signedBy entry that is the alias name from the keystore used to reference the signer whose private key was used to sign the code. For example, to indicate the alias "duke," type duke into the signedBy text box.

   b. One or more permission entries that indicate which permissions are granted to the code from the source indicated by the codeBase and signedBy values (or to any code if no such values are specified).

   To add a new permission, do the following:

1. Click the Add Permission button in the Policy Entry dialog box to display the Permissions dialog box. Then type or select the following:

   a. **A permission type**. To specify a permission type defined by you or others, type the permission type into the text box. Or double-click one of the built-in types from the drop-down list labeled Permission.

   The complete permission type name appears in the text box to the right of the drop-down list.

   b. **A permission target name**. If you selected a built-in permission type from the Permission drop-down list and permissions of that type have specific target name values, then the drop-down list labeled Target Name contains a list of those values from which you can choose. In the case that the target name possibilities are infinite, but there are some built-in target name specifications that have special meanings, such target names will appear in the drop-down list. For example, the special target name of "<<ALL FILES" will appear in the list for File Permissions.

To specify a target name not available in the drop-down list, type the target name into the text box to the right of the Target Name drop-down list.

c. **One or more actions**, if actions are relevant. Some permissions have only a target name and no actions. For these, leave the text box to the right of the Actions drop-down list blank. (It will automatically be darkened and unavailable for this type of built-in permission.) For permissions requiring action specifications, type the comma-separated list of actions into the text box or select them from the drop-down list. For example, to specify both read and write access to a file specified for a `FilePermission`, first select read (or write—the order does not matter) from the list. The word read appears in the text box. Then select write; the word write will be appended, preceded by a comma and a space.

d. **A `signedBy` alias**. Type the alias into the text box to the right of the Signed By label, if needed. The `signedBy` value for a permission entry is optional. If present, it indicates a signed permission. That is, the `Permission` class itself must be signed by the given alias(es) in order for the permission to be granted.

2. When you have finished specifying the permission information, click OK.

The new permission appears in a line in the Policy Entry dialog box. Add more permissions by following the same sequence of steps.

Once you have finished adding policy entries, click Done in the Policy Entry dialog box. The Policy Tool window displays, containing a line for each new policy entry. The lines contain only the `codeBase` and `signedBy` information (if any). If neither was specified in the Policy Entry dialog box, all that displays is `codeBase <ALL>`. If the policy entry contains any `signedBy` aliases that do not yet exist in your keystore, a warning displays to that effect when you close the policy entry. In this case, click OK and either make a note to create such an alias or edit the policy entry to fix the alias if it was wrong.

You also can edit or remove an existing permission. To edit an existing permission, follow these steps.

1. In the Policy Entry dialog box, click the line for that permission and then click the Edit Permission button. (Alternatively, you can double-click the line for that permission.)

   The Permissions dialog box displays. It looks as it does when you are adding a new permission, except that it is filled with the permission information for the selected permission.

2. To change the information, either make new selections from the drop-down lists or replace the information in the text boxes.

3. When you are done, click OK.

   The Policy Entry dialog box displays the permission with any modifications you made.

To remove an existing permission, select the line for that permission in the Policy Entry dialog box and then click the Remove Permission button.

If `policytool` reports that warnings have been stored in the Warning Log, you can view that log by clicking the View Warning Log command in the Edit menu. For example, if you have a policy file with a keystore URL specifying a keystore that does not yet exist, you will get such a warning at various times, for example when you open the file, that will be stored in the Log. You can continue to work on the policy file even if warnings exist.

MS-Windows includes a version of `policytool` that works essentially in the same way.

4.4.4 Jarsigner

JDK 1.2 introduced a new tool called `jarsigner`. Recall that the JAR enables the packaging of class files, images, sounds, and other data in a single file for faster and easier distribution. A tool named `jar` enables developers to produce JAR files. `jarsigner` can sign JAR files and verify the signatures and integrity of signed JAR files. Attaching digital signatures to a JAR file helps to ensure that its authenticity can be verified by recomputing the signature based on the current JAR content and comparing it with the stored signature. If the two do not match, this means that either the content or the signature in the JAR file was modified. Thus, as long as the private key is kept secret, someone without the private key cannot forge a signed JAR file.

`jarsigner` uses private key and certificate information from a keystore to generate the digital signatures for JAR files. Thus, when using `jarsigner` to sign a JAR file, you first must specify the keystore location as a URL, as well as the alias for the keystore entry containing the private key needed to generate the signature. For example, the following will sign the JAR file named MyJARFile.jar using the private key associated with the alias "duke" in the keystore named "mystore" in the working directory. Since no output file is specified, it overwrites MyJARFile.jar with the signed JAR file.

```
jarsigner -keystore /working/mystore -storepass myspass
-keypass dukekeypasswd MyJARFile.jar duke
```

Because keystores may be of different types, if you do not explicitly specify a keystore type, jarsigner chooses a keystore implementation based on the value of the keystore.type property specified in the security properties file.

Currently, JDK 1.2's default implementation of jarsigner can sign only zip files or JAR files created by the JDK jartool.[5] It signs a JAR file by using either SHA1withDSA or MD5withRSA. A SHA1withDSA algorithm is available from the default SUN provider.

When jarsigner is used to sign a JAR file, the output signed JAR file is exactly the same as the input JAR file, except that it has two additional files placed in the META-INF directory: a signature file with a SF extension and a signature block file with a DSA extension.

A signature file (the SF file) looks similar to the manifest file in that, for each source file included in the JAR file, it contains the filename, the name of the digest algorithm used (SHA), and a SHA digest value, each given on a separate line. In the manifest file, the SHA digest value for each source file is the digest (hash) of the binary data in the source file. In the SF file, however, the digest value for a given source file is the hash of the three lines in the manifest file for the source file. The SF also, by default, includes a header containing a hash of the whole manifest file. The presence of the header enables verification optimization, as described later in the chapter.[6]

The SF file is signed, and the signature is placed in the DSA file. The DSA file also contains, encoded within, the certificate or certificate chain from the keystore that authenticates the public key corresponding to the private key used for signing. jarsigner can use the certificate (chain) to verify the signature.

A successful JAR file verification occurs if the signature(s) are valid and none of the files that were in the JAR file when the signatures were generated were changed since then. JAR file verification involves the following steps.

---

[5]   JAR files are the same as zip files, except they also have a META-INF/MANIFEST.MF file. Such a file will automatically be created when jarsigner signs a zip file.

[6]   The signed header can also be used to assist in sealing a Java software package stored inside a JAR such that no other class can belong to the same package unless the other class is signed by the same signature key.

1. Verify the signature of the SF file itself. The verification ensures that the signature stored in each signature block (DSA) file was in fact generated using the private key corresponding to the public key whose certificate (or certificate chain) also appears in the DSA file. It also ensures that the signature is a valid signature of the corresponding signature (SF) file and thus that the SF file is tamper-free.

2. Verify the digest listed in each entry in the SF file with each corresponding section in the manifest. The SF file may include a header containing a hash of the entire manifest file. When the header is present, then the verification can simply check to see whether the hash in the header indeed matches the hash of the manifest file. If that is the case, verification proceeds to the next step. Otherwise, the hash in each source file information section in the SF file must be checked to determine whether it equals the hash of its corresponding section in the manifest file. The hash of the manifest file that is stored in the SF file header might not equal the hash of the current manifest file, for example when one or more files are added to the JAR file (using the `jartool`) after the signature (and thus the SF file) was generated. When the `jartool` is used to add files, the manifest file is changed (sections are added to it for the new files), but the SF file is not. Given that the interest here is in only those signed files, a verification is still considered successful if signatures and hashes of these files verify.

3. Verify each file that is mentioned in the SF file. `jartool` reads each file in the JAR file that has an entry in the SF file. While reading, it computes the file's digest and then compares the result with the digest for the file in the manifest section. The digests should be the same, or else verification fails. If any security-sensitive verification failures occur during the verification process, the process is stopped and a security exception is thrown that is caught and displayed by `jarsigner`.

A JAR file can be signed by multiple people simply by running `jarsigner` on the file multiple times, specifying the alias for a different person each time, as in the following command sequence:

```
jarsigner myBundle.jar susan
jarsigner myBundle.jar kevin
```

When a JAR file is signed multiple times, the resulting JAR file will contain multiple SF and DSA files, one pair of SF and DSA files for each signature. In the previous example, the output JAR file includes files with the following names:

```
SUSAN.SF
SUSAN.DSA
KEVIN.SF
KEVIN.DSA
```

Refer to the JDK 1.2 on-line documentation for `jarsigner`'s options.

`jarsigner` Compatibility with JDK 1.1

In JDK 1.1, a tool called `javakey` was provided to perform jar signing tasks. The tool was too simplistic for the complicated range of tasks it had to handle and so has been replaced in JDK 1.2 by `keytool` and `jarsigner`. These new tools provide more features than `javakey`, including the abilities to protect the keystore and private keys with passwords and to verify signatures in addition to generating them.

`javakey` generated and managed an identity database that was a mixture (speaking in JDK 1.2 terms) of security policy and keystore. The new keystore architecture replaces the identity database and uses a more standard storage format. To ensure backward compatibility, JDK 1.2 has the following properties.

- Importing the information from an identity database into a keystore is possible, via `keytool`'s -identitydb command. Only trusted identities in the identity database may be imported into a JDK 1.2 keystore.

- `jarsigner` can sign JAR files that were previously signed by using `javakey`.

- `jarsigner` can verify JAR files signed by using `javakey`. Thus it recognizes and can work with signer aliases that are from a JDK 1.1 identity database rather than a JDK 1.2 keystore.

Because the keystore plays a critical role in a security policy, the question arises regarding how to integrate the binary-trust model—codified by `javakey` in JDK 1.1—and the fine-grained trust model in JDK 1.2. More specifically, when the JVM encounters a JAR file in an environment containing a mixture of identity database, keystore, and security policy, what permissions does the JVM grant to the classes inside the JAR file? A number of other questions must be considered when deciding this.

♦ Q1: Is the JAR file signed?

♦ Q2: Is the verified signer present in the identity database? Is the signer trusted?

♦ Q3: Has the verified signer been imported from the identity database into the keystore?

♦ Q4: Does the security policy explicitly grant permissions to the verified signer?

Table 4.1 shows how JAR files that were signed in JDK 1.1.*x* are treated in JDK 1.2. *Default permission* denotes permissions that are granted to all code by default, *Policy permission* denotes the permissions explicitly granted to a particular set of signers, and *All permission* denotes the permission that implies every other permission. An entry containing yes/no means it can be either yes or no.

A few points presented in the table are worth explaining. First, if a signer (identity/alias) is mentioned in the policy file, it must be present in the keystore in order for the policy file to have any effect on the permissions granted. Second, the policy file/keystore combination has precedence over a trusted identity in the identity database in that if such a combination exists, then the trusted signer is not given all permission, as was the case in JDK 1.1. Third, untrusted identities declared in JDK 1.1's identity database are ignored in JDK 1.2. If an untrusted identity is also present in the keystore and mentioned in the policy, then JDK 1.2's policy is in effect and the entry in the identity database is ignored. Otherwise, the JAR file is treated as if it is unsigned. Finally, if a trusted identity is not present in the keystore or is not mentioned in the policy, then the binary-trust model is applied and the signer is given all permissions.

Table 4.1   Permissions Granted when Mixing `javakey` and Keystore

Q1	Q2	Q3	Q4	Permission
No	Yes/no	Yes/no	Yes/no	Default
Yes	No	Yes/no	No	Default
Yes	No	Yes	Yes	Default + policy
Yes	Yes/untrusted	Yes/no	No	Default
Yes	Yes/untrusted	No	Yes	Default
Yes	Yes/untrusted	Yes	Yes	Default + policy
Yes	Yes/trusted	Yes/no	No	All
Yes	Yes/trusted	No	Yes	All
Yes	Yes/trusted	Yes	Yes	Default + policy

4.4.5   Code Signing Example

Here is an example of signing and verifying a JAR file. Suppose you have a JAR
file, bundle.jar, that you want to sign by using the private key of the user whose
keystore alias is "jane" in the keystore named "mystore" in the working directory.
Suppose the keystore password is myspass and the password for jane's private key
is j638klm. You can use the following command (on a single line) to sign the JAR
file and name the signed JAR file sbundle.jar.

```
jarsigner -keystore /working/mystore -storepass myspass
-keypass j638klm -signedjar sbundle.jar bundle.jar JANE
```

The resulting SF and DSA files are JANE.SF and JANE.DSA.

To verify a signed JAR file, use a command such as

```
jarsigner -verify sbundle.jar
```

If the verification is successful, the message "jar verified." displays. Otherwise, an
error message appears. You can get more information about the verification process by using the -verbose option, as follows.

```
jarsigner -verify -verbose sbundle.jar


      198 Fri Sep 26 16:14:06 PDT 1997 META-INF/MANIFEST.MF
      199 Fri Sep 26 16:22:10 PDT 1997 META-INF/JANE.SF
     1013 Fri Sep 26 16:22:10 PDT 1997 META-INF/JANE.DSA
smk  2752 Fri Sep 26 16:12:30 PDT 1997 AclEx.class
smk   849 Fri Sep 26 16:12:46 PDT 1997 test.class


s = signature was verified
m = entry is listed in manifest
k = at least one certificate was found in keystore


jar verified.
```

If, when verifying, you specify the -certs option along with the -verify and
-verbose options, the output includes

- certificate information for each signer of the JAR file, including the certificate
  type,

- the signer's DN information (if, and only if, the certificate is an X.509), and,

- the keystore alias for the signer, in parentheses, if the public key certificate in
  the JAR file matches that in a keystore entry.

Here is an example.

```
jarsigner -keystore mystore -verify -verbose -certs myTest.jar

        198 Fri Sep 26 16:14:06 PDT 1997 META-INF/MANIFEST.MF
        199 Fri Sep 26 16:22:10 PDT 1997 META-INF/JANE.SF
       1013 Fri Sep 26 16:22:10 PDT 1997 META-INF/JANE.DSA
        208 Fri Sep 26 16:23:30 PDT 1997 META-INF/JAVATEST.SF
       1087 Fri Sep 26 16:23:30 PDT 1997 META-INF/JAVATEST.DSA
smk    2752 Fri Sep 26 16:12:30 PDT 1997 Tst.class


X.509, CN=Test Group, OU=Java Software, O=Sun Microsystems, L=CUP,
    S=CA, C=US (javatest)
X.509, CN=Jane Smith, OU=Java Software, O=Sun, L=cup, S=ca, C=us
    (JANE)


s = signature was verified
m = entry is listed in manifest
k = at least one certificate was found in keystore


jar verified.
```

If the certificate for a signer is not an X.509, no DN information is available. In this case, just the certificate type and the alias are shown. For example, if the certificate is a PGP certificate and the alias is "bob," you would get this as output:

```
PGP, (bob)
```

If a JAR file has been signed using the JDK 1.1 javakey tool, and thus the signer is an alias in an identity database, the verification output includes an "i" symbol. If the JAR file has been signed by both an alias in an identity database and an alias in a keystore, the output includes the symbols "i" and "k." When the -certs option is used, any identity database aliases are shown within square brackets (such as "duke" in the following example) rather than within the parentheses used for keystore aliases; for example:

```
jarsigner -keystore mystore -verify -verbose -certs writeFile.jar

        198 Fri Sep 26 16:14:06 PDT 1997 META-INF/MANIFEST.MF
        199 Fri Sep 26 16:22:10 PDT 1997 META-INF/JANE.SF
       1013 Fri Sep 26 16:22:10 PDT 1997 META-INF/JANE.DSA
        199 Fri Sep 27 12:22:30 PDT 1997 META-INF/DUKE.SF
```

```
        1013 Fri Sep 27 12:22:30 PDT 1997 META-INF/DUKE.DSA
smki    2752 Fri Sep 26 16:12:30 PDT 1997 writeFile.html

X.509, CN=Jane Smith, OU=Java Software, O=Sun, L=cup, S=ca, C=us
    (JANE)
X.509, CN=Duke, OU=Java Software, O=Sun, L=cup, S=ca, C=us [duke]

s = signature was verified
m = entry is listed in manifest
k = at least one certificate was found in keystore
i = at least one certificate was found in identity scope

jar verified.
```

MS-Windows includes a version of `jarsigner` that works essentially in the same way.

4.5   Managing Security Policies for Nonexperts

This chapter has discussed the technical details of deploying the JDK 1.2 security architecture, as well as how to configure security policies, create keys and certificates, and sign Java classes. The overall complexity might appear overwhelming to the nonexpert computer user. This complexity is the natural result of JDK 1.2's having a feature-rich security architecture that must cater to a wide range of needs, such as those that arise in programming secure enterprise applications.

Two approaches are useful for the nonexpert when dealing with this complexity. One is to call in professional care and management. In the case of an enterprise environment, system administrators and information resource departments can be made responsible for establishing and deploying security policies on behalf of other corporate employees. Technical details in this and preceding chapters have shown that the Java security architecture design has taken this into account and has introduced a number of ways for the user to defer or delegate security policy decisions to another party. For example, employees can be instructed to configure their browsers to point to a centrally controlled Web page to obtain the current security policy. Or the company might want to customize a version of the browser, which it then distributes to employees.

Developers of enterprise applications can also incorporate security policy management in such a way that the typical user does not have to deal with, or even be aware of, the underlying security management features. In the case of the individual outside of the corporate environment, Internet Service Providers (ISPs) are also a good source for security advice and management. For example, many ISPs already offer limited security mechanisms such as firewalls and junk mail filtering. Thus it is quite reasonable for them to offer security policy management help regarding executable content and mobile code.

The second approach to security management for the nonexpert is to focus on the human interface. Field experience and controlled studies have shown that it is extremely hard for the vast majority of computer and Internet users to understand security issues, which range from terminology to solutions to consequences. Moreover, different users interpret things so differently that it is very difficult to describe security in the same way to a diverse group of people. Thus JDK 1.2 has not attempted to provide a uniform human-computer interface to deal with security policy and management. Instead, it expects that software vendors will integrate such functionalities into their own system environments and customize the contents and presentations to suit the particular set of users of their systems.

For example, computer systems vendors have traditionally shipped security management software with their operation systems. In the near future, many such systems will have Java technology bundled with or integrated into them. In these cases, the accompanying security management software likely will be enhanced with suitable components to manage Java security issues. The benefit of this is that those people who use the management software can continue to use a familiar software with a familiar interface.

Moreover, application developers can choose to embed security solutions in such a way that they are invisible to users. For example, imagine a Java-based application that provides AOL-style Internet access and user experience. Such an application might use many Java features, such as dynamic component upgrading, and provide services such as secure access to e-mail messages. Thus the application will depend on extensive security technology, which calls for security management. In this case, the application can "lock in" the particular security policies that are needed to make it work and not provide any customization capability in this respect. As a result, apart from the initial login process, users do not have to deal with any further security issues, and indeed might not even be aware that complicated security decisions are being made throughout the application.

Security management and user interface remains an under-studied subject, partly because the Internet brought security into the mainstream for the first time, making it an everyday concern, and partly because older technologies have generally not had security as a design goal. As time goes by and extensive security solutions are deployed ubiquitously, developers will gain valuable insight into this important aspect of security technology.

CHAPTER 5

Customizing the Security Architecture

The office of government is not to confer happiness,
but to give men opportunity to work out happiness for themselves.
—William Ellery Channing

Chapter 4 discussed various customization possibilities when deploying the Java security architecture. This chapter goes a step further to investigate some concrete customization examples.

5.1 Creating New Permission Types

Recall that JDK 1.2 introduced a new hierarchy of typed and parameterized access permissions that is rooted by an abstract class, `java.security.Permission`. Other permissions are subclassed either from the `Permission` class or one of its subclasses and generally should belong in packages of their own. For example, the permission representing file system access is located in the Java I/O package, as `java.io.FilePermission`. is `java.io` Other permission classes that are new in JDK 1.2 include

- `java.net.SocketPermission` for access to network resources,

- `java.lang.RuntimePermission` for access to runtime system resources such as properties, and

- `java.awt.AWTPermission` for access to windowing resources.

In other words, access methods and parameters to most of the controlled resources, including access to Java properties and packages, are represented by the new permission classes.

Applications are free to add new categories of permissions. However, it is essential that, apart from official releases, no one extend the permissions that are built into JDK, either by adding new functionality or by introducing additional keywords into a class such as `java.lang.RuntimePermission`. Refraining from doing this maintains consistency. To create a new permission, the following steps are recommended, as shown by an example.

Suppose an application developer from company ABC wants to create a customized permission to "watch TV." The first question is can you use an existing `Permission` object such as the catch-all `RuntimePermission` object or do you need a custom object. Assume that you want to create a new permission class, named `com.abc.Permission`, which extends the abstract class `java.security.Permission` (or one of its subclasses). You also design another new class, `com.abc.TVPermission`, that extends `com.abc.Permission`.[1]

```
public class com.abc.Permission extends java.security.Per-
mission
public class com.abc.TVPermission extends com.abc.Permission
```

You must make sure that the `implies()` method, among other methods, is correctly implemented. If more-elaborate TVPermissions, such as `channel-1:13` or `channel-*`, are allowed, then you might need to implement a `TVPermissionCollection` object that knows how to deal with the semantics of these. Then, you need to include these new permission classes with the application package so that when your application needs them, they can be found by the class loaders.

Next, you want the application's resource management code, when checking to see if a permission should be granted, to call `AccessController`'s `checkPermission` method, using a `com.abc.TVPermission` object as the parameter.

```
public void switchChannel(int channel) {
    com.abc.TVPermission tvperm = new
            com.abc.TVPermission(channel, "watch");
    AccessController.checkPermission(tvperm);
    ...
}
```

---

[1] Class `com.abc.TVPermission` can directly extend `java.security.Permission` as the intermediate `com.abc.Permission` is not always required.

Finally, to grant this permission to applications and applets, you need to enter appropriate entries into the security policy. How to configure the policy was discussed in detail in previous chapters. Basically, you put the string representation of this permission in the policy file so that this permission can be automatically configured for each domain granted the permission. An example of the policy file entry specifying permission to watch channel 5 is as follows, which grants to any code the privilege to watch channel 5.

```
grant {
    permission com.abc.TVPermission "5", "watch";
}
```

When adding a new permission, you should create a new permission class and not add a new method to the security manager. Prior to JDK 1.2, in order to enable checking of a new type of access, you had to add a new method to the `Security-Manager` class. In JDK 1.2, the newly introduced `checkPermission()` method applies to all permission types.

To exercise the built-in access control algorithm, your code should always invoke a permission check by directly calling the `checkPermission()` method of the `AccessController` class. It is not essential that you examine whether there is a class loader or a security manager. On the other hand, if the access control algorithm should be left to the installed `SecurityManager` class, then the method `SecurityManager.checkPermission()` should be invoked instead. Although the default implementation of `SecurityManager.checkPermission()` is to turn around and call `AccessController.checkPermission()`, the `SecurityMan-ager` class can be customized, as shown later in this chapter.

5.2   Composite Permissions

An application might need to be granted many permissions so that it can do its job. Sometimes it is tedious to have to spell out, one by one, the permissions granted. For example, a computer game might need permissions that includes socket permission to connect to the game server, file permission to access a locally stored high-score file, and property permission to look up the player's expert level.

In this case, a "shorthand" that represents all of the said permissions would be very helpful. One way to approach this issue is to create a composite permission, such as a `MyGamePermission`, that implies all of the required permissions. Then the game software can be granted simply a `MyGamePermission`.

A composite permission may be implemented in any of several ways. A `PermissionCollection` class is one example that can imply a range of different types of permissions. Or a new class `CompositePermission` can be defined. In fact, `AllPermission` is just such a composite permission that implies every permission.[2]

However, there is a hidden complication in doing this. When searching a given set of permissions to match a required permission, the default implementation of `AccessController` optimizes the search by looking up the type of the required permission and examining only those given permissions with the appropriate types. For example, when a file access is required, the `AccessController` looks into all given `FilePermissions` and also knows to check if there is an `AllPermission`. When a new type of permission is introduced that can imply a different type of permission, the default `AccessController` does not know this fact in advance. To solve this problem, JDK 1.2's implementation could be changed so that it always compares every given permission with the required permission. This, however, would potentially have resulted in a big performance hit. A better solution is to introduce a new type, say `CompositePermission`, and require that all composite permissions must be of this type. Then the default `AccessController` can be enhanced to look for all given `CompositePermissions`. In this way, performance is affected only when a large number of `CompositePermissions` are granted.

5.3 Customizing Security Policy

The security policy first is processed by the `Policy` class and then is enforced by the `SecurityManager`, so customizing either class would customize the `Policy` implementation. As a first example, suppose you want to allow file access only during office hours, 9 AM to 5 PM. That is, during office hours the security policy decides who can access what files. Outside of office hours, no one can access any file, no matter what the security policy says. To achieve this, you can implement a `TimeOfDaySecurityManager` class, as follows.

```
public class TimeOfDaySecurityManager extends SecurityManager {
    public void checkPermission(Permission perm) {
        if (perm instanceof FilePermission) {
            Date d = new Date();
            int i = d.getHours();
            if ((i >= 9) && (i < 17))
                super.checkPermission(perm);
```

---

[2] We could have implemented a `NoPermission` (or `ZeroPermission`), for completeness, but we did not manage to get this in before code-freeze time.

```
        else
            throw new SecurityException("Out of office hour");
    } else super.checkPermission(perm);
    }
}
```

The TimeOfDaySecurityManager checks to see if the permission to be checked is a FilePermission. If it is, TimeOfDaySecurityManager computes the current time. If the time is inside office hours, it invokes the built-in SecurityManager to check the security policy. Otherwise, it throws a security exception. An application that wishes to enforce the given office hour restriction should install this TimeOfDaySecurityManager in place of the built-in SecurityManager.

The next example concerns the need to keep a record of resource access that was granted or denied, for audit purposes later. Suppose you design a simple AuditingSecurityManager class as follows.

```
public class AuditSecurityManager extends SecurityManager {
    public void checkPermission(Permission perm) {
        Audit.enterRecord(perm);
        super.checkPermission(perm);
    }
}
```

Assume that you also have an Audit class with a method to store an audit record in a safe place. A variation is to enter the audit record after checkPermission and also record the access control result. To do that, you first must catch the potential SecurityException thrown and then rethrow it later.

```
public class AuditSecurityManager extends SecurityManager {
    public void checkPermission(Permission perm) {
        try {
            super.checkPermission(perm);
            Audit.enterRecord(perm, true);
        }catch (SecurityException e) {
            Audit.enterRecord(perm, false);
            throw e;
        }
    }
}
```

To implement complex security policies, you need to spend potentially a lot more effort. For example, if you want to enforce a multilevel security policy, you first must create sensitivity labels for each object.[3] The JVM also has to keep track of interaction between objects and might have to change object labels dynamically (as in a high water-mark model). Then the SecurityManager's checkPermission method will base its decision on the labels of the objects involved in the current thread of execution. As another example, to implement a Chinese Wall (separation of duty) model the JVM must not only monitor object interaction but also keep a history of it. Much research and experimentation is needed in this area.

5.4   Migrating JDK 1.1-Based Security Managers

In JDK 1.1, the java.lang.SecurityManager class was abstract. The default implementations of the SecurityManager's check methods always just threw exceptions. The result was that developers who wanted their applications (such as a browser) to install a security manager had to write their own security manager and provide appropriate concrete implementations of the methods that threw exceptions by default, primarily the check methods.

In JDK 1.2, SecurityManager is concrete so that it can be used as-is as the default security manager in applications. Moreover, its design is also greatly improved. Thus developers who have written their own security manager classes for their applications should consider migrating to JDK 1.2-based security manager classes. In most cases, they should simply use the built-in default implementation.

A number of technical details must be done right in this migration process. This section is devoted to such issues. It begins with a review of JDK 1.1-style security manager classes and then examines JDK 1.2's improvements.

5.4.1   JDK 1.1 Security Manager Classes

In JDK 1.1, local applications and correctly digitally signed applets were trusted to have full access to vital system resources, such as the file system, while unsigned applets were not trusted and could access only limited resources. A security manager was responsible for determining which resource accesses were allowed. In both JDK 1.1 (and therefore in JDK 1.2), the SecurityManager class contains many methods with names that begin with the word "check," sometimes called the check methods. Examples are checkRead and checkConnect. Various methods in the Java libraries call a check method before performing each potentially security-sensitive operation. A security manager routine simply returns if the operation is permitted, but it throws a security exception if the operation is not

---

[3]   This can be done perhaps most conveniently by adding a security-level attribute to the base class, the Object class, but that would be a very significant change.

permitted. The security manager is thereby given an opportunity to prevent completion of the operation by throwing an exception. The only exception to this convention is checkTopLevelWindow, which returns a boolean value instead.

The other methods contained in the SecurityManager class are those related to class loader existence and depth:

```
currentClassLoader
currentLoadedClass
inClassLoader
classLoaderDepth
```

It is important to understand these four methods, as JDK 1.1-style security managers typically base access control decisions on two variables:

1. Whether a class with a class loader (that is, an applet in JDK 1.1) is on the stack

2. The class loader depth, that is, how far down the stack is the most recent occurrence of a method from a class defined using a class loader

For example, a typical JDK 1.1-style security manager has a checkExit method like the following.

```
public void checkExit(int status) {
    if (inClassLoader()) {
        throw new SecurityException();
    }
}
```

Such a method would not allow Runtime.exit to be called when any class defined with a class loader (that is, an applet) is on the stack.

Here is another example.

```
public void checkCreateClassLoader() {
    if (classLoaderDepth() == 2) {
        throw new SecurityException();
    }
}
```

This method says that the class loader depth cannot be 2. That is, the method that called the method that called checkCreateClassLoader must not be in a class defined with a class loader. For example, the constructor for java.lang.Class-Loader calls checkCreateClassLoader, which means the method that calls the constructor for java.lang.ClassLoader must not have a class loader. Thus applets cannot directly create class loaders.

There is a big difference between these two examples, even though both attempt to prevent applets from performing actions. In the first example, check-Exit will throw an exception if an applet is anywhere on the stack. Thus even built-in JDK code cannot exit the JVM if it was called from an applet. In the second example, JDK code is sometimes allowed to create a class loader (for example, when class loader depth is not 2), even if it was called by an applet. That is because the depth of a class with a class loader is used, and not the fact that there is a class loader.

Previous chapters discussed how error-prone these class loader depth methods can be. For the SecurityManager in JDK 1.2, these methods are deprecated and are no longer called by any check methods. They should not be used by any newly written security managers and should be eliminated from existing security managers as well. However, the interfaces are maintained for backward compatibility.

5.4.2   Accommodating JDK 1.1 Security Managers on JDK 1.2

Sometimes an application with an old JDK 1.1 security manager has to be run on the new JDK 1.2 platform. To accommodate this, the implementation of some methods in the SecurityManager class were changed to take into account new features introduced in JDK 1.2.

The four methods mentioned in the previous section have all been modified in three ways:

1. They skip system class loaders.

2. They stop checking after they reach a method on the stack that was marked privileged.

3. They treat the current stack as fully trusted under certain circumstances.

Skip System Class Loaders

A system class loader is defined as a class loader that is equal to the system class loader (as returned by ClassLoader.getSystemClassLoader) or one of its ancestors. Since classes loaded by the system class loader include application classes (loaded off of CLASSPATH), extension classes, and the built-in JDK classes, this modification enables these methods to ignore such code.

This change was made because if you run an application that installs a custom security manager and that security manager is loaded off of CLASSPATH in JDK 1.2, it will have a system class loader associated with it. Recall that application classes did not have a class loader in JDK 1.1. If you called a method such as classLoaderDepth from within the custom security manager and that method was not modified to ignore classes loaded by a system class loader, it would always return 0, which would not be very useful. Similarly, if class loader methods were not changed so that they would skip system classes and a custom security manager was loaded off of CLASSPATH, security holes might develop when the security manager was making decisions based on, for example, disallowing an operation if classLoaderDepth() == 2.

Stop Checking after Reaching a Privileged Method

These four methods stop checking after they reach a method on the stack that was marked privileged (according to JDK 1.2's definition of privileged). This change was needed because, for example, the JDK code need to open files for internal use. Some JDK 1.1-style security managers have a checkRead method that looks like the following.

```
public void checkRead(String file) {
    if (inClassLoader()) {
        throw new SecurityException(..);
    }
}
```

Without the modifications, such a check invoked when running JDK 1.2 would cause a security exception to be thrown when the JDK itself tried to read a file when a class with a nonsystem class loader was on the stack. Under the new security model, all JDK code that tries to perform an operation that its caller might not be allowed to do has a doPrivileged block around it. Modifying inClassLoader just to examine the stack up to and including the frame containing the privileged code results in the inClassLoader method's returning false. This in turn allows the read to occur when the code at the top of the stack is JDK code and is loaded by the system class loader or one of its ancestors.

JDK 1.2 attempts to maintain the stack depth as used in JDK 1.1-style security managers. For example, the constructor for java.security.SecureClassLoader has an explicit call to SecurityManager.checkCreateClassLoader, even though the constructor for its super class (ClassLoader) also does. If the check was not placed in the constructor for SecureClassLoader, then a JDK 1.1-style security manager would allow untrusted code to extend SecureClassLoader and construct class loaders, since the class loader depth would always be greater than 2.

When you are porting an existing JDK 1.1-style security manager, first and foremost you are advised to analyze all of your custom security manager methods before running your security manager under JDK 1.2. Failure to do so could result in a security hole or prevent the proper operation of the JDK. This is due to the fragile nature of JDK 1.1-style security managers. Where possible, you should just use the default implementation of the JDK 1.2 `SecurityManager`. This helps give users and administrators consistent behavior. If this is not possible, you need to take great care when extending the `SecurityManager` class and overriding existing methods.

For example, if you override the `checkRead(String file)` method so that it always throws a security exception, then the JDK itself might fail to operate properly. That is, if some JDK code needs to open a file (to read a properties file or load a JAR file, for example), then throwing a security exception for every read attempt would cause such opens to always fail.

In general, you should override the default methods only if you intend to loosen security, not to make it stronger. To tighten security, you should modify the default policy files and/or install a custom `java.security.Policy` class or object. When overriding security manager methods, you should place a call to the `super.check` method at the point where your overridden check method would throw an exception, as in the following example.

```
public class MySecurityManager extends SecurityManager {
    public void checkRead(String file) {
        if (someCustomSecurityCheckFails()) {
            super.checkRead(file);
        }
    }
}
```

Here, if your custom security check fails, then `super.checkRead` gets called. The default implementation of `checkRead` invokes `checkPermission`, which by default invokes the `AccessController`. This latter invocation enables system code that has done an `AccessController.doPrivileged` before trying to read a file to succeed in reading that file, thereby allowing the JDK itself to function correctly. All other code will be subjected to the current policy in effect, and an access control exception will be thrown if access to that file has not been granted. In other words, your JDK 1.1-style security manager code, by calling `super.check`, will have given the JDK 1.2 built-in `SecurityManager` and `AccessController` a chance to handle situations that are particular to JDK 1.2.

Nevertheless, you should not call `super.check` methods when overriding some of the check methods. This is because the default implementation of these methods might not be as strict as the policy you are implementing in the overridden method. For example, the default `checkAccess(ThreadGroup g)` method protects only the system thread group. If you intend to protect threads in distinct thread groups from each other (for example, applet thread groups), then you do not want to call `super.checkAccess()` at the point you would normally throw a security exception, as doing that would defeat the purpose of your customized check. Instead, you place a call to `super.checkAccess()` as the first statement in your overridden method, as in the following example.

```
public class MySecurityManager extends SecurityManager {
    public void checkAccess(ThreadGroup g) {
        // A call to super will throw an exception if someone
        // is trying to modify the system thread group.
        super.checkAccess(g);
        ...
        // Now perform checks to see if the current caller
        // can modify thread group g, based on to which applet
        // thread group the caller belongs.
        ...
    }
}
```

Treat Current Stack as Fully Trusted

The third change is related to the second and gives these four methods the following behavior. When they encounter a `doPrivileged` stack frame with a `SecurityContext` (or `AccessControlContext`) that was granted `AllPermission`, they treat the current stack as fully trusted, or in JDK 1.1's sense, as if there is no class loader on the stack. This is because a `doPrivileged` frame with `AllPermission` indicates that the caller of this method must be allowed to do anything it wants, regardless of what its callers are. This fully privileged situation is equivalent to when a call to `checkPermission` with `java.security.AllPermission` does not result in a security exception.

5.4.3 Modifying JDK 1.1 Security Managers for JDK 1.2

This section lists the changes made to `java.lang.SecurityManager` methods in JDK 1.2. Also included are suggestions regarding any overrides you might want to make. When modifying your JDK 1.1-style security manager class for JDK 1.2, you really should try to use the built-in JDK 1.2 security manager as is, if at all possible.

To start, as mentioned earlier, the following methods have been deprecated and should not be used:

```
public boolean getInCheck();
protected ClassLoader currentClassLoader();
protected Class currentLoadedClass();
```

```
protected int classDepth(String name);
protected int classLoaderDepth();
protected boolean inClass(String name);
protected boolean inClassLoader();
```

Following are the other methods.

- protected boolean inCheck;

  This field is now deprecated, and any use of it within the JDK has been removed. Instead of using inCheck, you should use checkPermission along with doPrivileged.

- public SecurityManager();

  This constructor was modified to allow multiple SecurityManagers to be created, assuming the caller has RuntimePermission("createSecurity-Manager") permission.

- protected native Class[] getClassContext();

  This method is unchanged. A call to it can be used to emulate the 1.1 behavior of the methods that have been changed in JDK 1.2 (currentClassLoader, currentLoadedClass, classLoaderDepth, and inClassLoader).

- public Object getSecurityContext();

  This method was modified to return a java.security.AccessControlContext object that is created with a call to java.security.AccessController.getContext. In JDK 1.1, it returned null by default.

- public void checkPermission(Permission perm);

  This method is new in JDK 1.2. It calls java.security.AccessController.checkPermission with the given permission. Internally, the JDK always calls SecurityManager.checkPermission instead of calling the AccessController directly. This allows people to override this method to provide additional functionality, such as auditing and graphical user interface (GUI) dialog boxes.

- public void checkPermission(Permission perm, Object context);

  This method is new in JDK 1.2. If context is an instance of Access-ControlContext, then the method AccessControlContext.checkPermission will be invoked on the given context with the specified permission. If context is not an instance of AccessControlContext, then a security exception is thrown.

◆ `public void checkCreateClassLoader();`

This method was modified to call `checkPermission` with the permission `RuntimePermission("createClassLoader")`. If this method is overridden, then a call to `super.checkCreateClassLoader` should be made at the point the overridden method would normally throw an exception, as the second example in Section 5.4.2.2.

◆ `public void checkAccess(Thread t);`

This method was modified. If the thread argument is a system thread—a thread that belongs to the thread group that has a null parent—then this method calls `checkPermission` with the `RuntimePermission("modifyThread")` permission. Applications that want a stricter policy should override this method, where `super.checkAccess` or its equivalent should be called by the first statement in the overridden method. Moreover, the resulting method also should check to see if the calling thread has the `RuntimePermission("modifyThread")` permission, and if it does, return silently. This is to ensure that code granted that permission (such as the JDK itself) is allowed to manipulate any thread.

An example overridden method implementation follows.

```
public class MySecurityManager extends SecurityManager {
    public void checkAccess(Thread t) {
        // A call to super will throw an exception if someone
        // is trying to modify a system thread.
        super.checkAccess(t);
        ...
        if (someCustomSecurityCheckForOtherThreadsFails()) {
            // If the check fails, instead of throwing an
            // exception, call checkPermission, which will
            // throw an exception if needed.
            checkPermission(new
                RuntimePermission("modifyThread"));
        }
        ...
    }
}
```

◆ `public void checkAccess(ThreadGroup g);`

This method was modified. If the thread group argument is the system thread group (that is, it has a null parent), then this method calls `checkPermission` with the RuntimePermission("modifyThreadGroup") permission. Applications that want a stricter policy should override this method, where super.checkAccess or its equivalent should be called by the first statement in the overridden method. Moreover, the resulting method also should check to see if the caller has the RuntimePermission("modifyThreadGroup") permission, and if it does, return silently. This is to ensure that code granted that permission (such as the JDK itself) is allowed to manipulate any thread group.

♦ public void checkExit(int status);

This method was modified to call checkPermission with the Runtime-Permission("exitVM") permission. If this method is overridden, then a call to super.checkExit should be made at the point the overridden method would normally throw an exception.

♦ public void checkExec(String cmd);

This method was modified to call checkPermission with a FilePermission. If cmd is an absolute path, then it is passed as-is as the target for File-Permission. If cmd is not absolute, then the special target <<ALL FILES>> is used. This target is used because it is difficult to determine the actual path of the command that will be executed on an individual platform due to such things as environment variables. If this method is overridden, then a call to super.checkExec should be made at the point the overridden method would normally throw an exception.

♦ public void checkLink(String lib);

This method was modified to call checkPermission with the Runtime-Permission("loadLibrary."+lib) permission. If this method is overridden, then a call to super.checkLink should be made at the point the overridden method would normally throw an exception.

♦ public void checkRead(FileDescriptor fd);

This method was modified to call checkPermission with the Runtime-Permission("readFileDescriptor") permission. If this method is overridden, then a call to super.checkRead should be made at the point the overridden method would normally throw an exception.

♦ public void checkRead(String file);

This method was modified to call checkPermission with the FilePermission(file,"read") permission. If this method is overridden, then a call to super.checkRead should be made at the point the overridden method would normally throw an exception.

♦ public void checkRead(String file, Object context);

This method was modified. If context is an instance of AccessControl-
Context, then the AccessControlContext.checkPermission method will
be invoked on the given context with the FilePermission(file,"read")
permission. If context is not an instance of AccessControlContext, then a
SecurityException is thrown. If this method is overridden, then a call to
super.checkRead should be made at the point the overridden method would
normally throw an exception.

♦ public void checkWrite(FileDescriptor fd);

This method was modified to call checkPermission with the permission
RuntimePermission("writeFileDescriptor"). If this method is overridden, then a call to super.checkWrite should be made at the point the overridden method would normally throw an exception.

♦ public void checkWrite(String file);

This method was modified to call checkPermission with the permission
FilePermission(file,"write"). If this method is overridden, then a call
to super.checkWrite should be made at the point the overridden method
would normally throw an exception.

♦ public void checkDelete(String file);

This method was modified to call checkPermission with the FilePermis-
sion(file,"delete") permission. If this method is overridden, then a call
to super.checkDelete should be made at the point the overridden method
would normally throw an exception.

♦ public void checkConnect(String host, int port);

This method was modified to call the checkPermission method with the permission SocketPermission(host+":"+port,"connect") if the port is not
−1 and with SocketPermission(host,"resolve") otherwise. This behavior is consistent with JDK 1.1, where a port equal to −1 indicates that an IP
address lookup is being performed. If this method is overridden, then a call to
super.checkConnect should be made at the point the overridden method
would normally throw an exception.

♦ public void checkConnect(String host, int port, Object context);

This method was modified. If context is an instance of AccessControl-
Context and if the port is not −1, then this method invokes the method
AccessControlContext.checkPermission on the given context with the

`SocketPermission(host+":"+port,"connect")` permission. If the port is −1, it uses `SocketPermission(host,"resolve")`. If context is not an instance of `AccessControlContext`, then a security exception is thrown. If this method is overridden, then a call to `super.checkConnect` should be made at the point the overridden method would normally throw an exception.

♦ `public void checkListen(int port);`

This method was modified. This method calls `checkPermission` with `SocketPermission("localhost:"+port,"listen")` if the port is not 0 and with `SocketPermission("localhost:1024-","listen")` otherwise. If this method is overridden, a call to `super.checkListen` should be made at the point the overridden method would normally throw an exception.

♦ `public void checkAccept(String host, int port);`

This method was modified to call `checkPermission` with the permission `SocketPermission(host+":"+port,"accept")`. If this method is overridden, then a call to `super.checkAccept` should be made at the point the overridden method would normally throw an exception.

♦ `public void checkMulticast(InetAddress maddr);`

This method was modified to call the `checkPermission` method with the permission `SocketPermission(maddr.getHostAddress(),"accept, connect")`. If this method is overridden, then a call to `super.check-Multicast` should be made at the point the overridden method would normally throw an exception.

♦ `public void checkMulticast(InetAddress maddr, byte ttl);`

This method was modified to call `checkPermission` with the permission `SocketPermission(maddr.getHostAddress(),"accept,connect")`. If this method is overridden, then a call to `super.checkMulticast` should be made at the point the overridden method would normally throw an exception.

♦ `public void checkPropertiesAccess();`

This method was modified to call `checkPermission` with the `PropertyPermission("*", "read,write")` permission. If this method is overridden, then a call to `super.checkPropertiesAccess` should be made at the point the overridden method would normally throw an exception.

♦ `public void checkPropertyAccess(String key);`

This method was modified to call `checkPermission` with the `PropertyPermission(key, "read")` permission. If this method is overridden, then a call to `super.checkPropertyAccess` should be made at the point the overridden method would normally throw an exception.

♦ `public boolean checkTopLevelWindow(Object window);`

This method was modified to call `checkPermission` with the permission `AWTPermission("showWindowWithoutWarningBanner")`. It returns `true` if a `SecurityException` is not thrown and `false` otherwise. If this method is overridden, then a call to `super.checkTopLevelWindow` should be made at the point the overridden method would normally return `false` and the value of `super.checkTopLevelWindow` should be returned. For example:

```
public class MySecurityManager extends SecurityManager {
    public void checkTopLevelWindow(Object window) {
        if (someCustomSecurityCheckFails()) {
            return super.checkTopLevelWindow(window);
        } else return true;
    }
}
```

♦ `public void checkPrintJobAccess();`

This method was modified to call `checkPermission` with the `Runtime-Permission("queuePrintJob")` permission. If this method is overridden, then a call to `super.checkPrintJobAccess` should be made at the point the overridden method would normally throw an exception.

♦ `public void checkSystemClipboardAccess();`

This method was modified to call `checkPermission` with the `AWTPermission("accessClipboard")` permission. If this method is overridden, then a call to `super.checkSystemClipboardAccess` should be made at the point the overridden method would normally throw an exception.

♦ `public void checkAwtEventQueueAccess();`

This method was modified to call `checkPermission` with the `AWTPermission("accessEventQueue")` permission. If this method is overridden, then a call to `super.checkAwtEventQueueAccess` should be made at the point the overridden method would normally throw an exception.

♦ `public void checkPackageAccess(String pkg);`

This method was modified. It first obtains a comma-separated list of restricted packages via a call to `java.security.Security.getProperty("package.access")` and checks to see if `pkg` starts with or equals any of the packages. If it does, then `checkPermission` is called with the `Runtime-Permission("accessClassInPackage."+pkg)` permission. If this method is overridden, then `super.checkPackageAccess` should be called as the first line in the overridden method.

♦ `public void checkPackageDefinition(String pkg);`

This method was modified. It first obtains a comma-separated list of restricted packages via a call to `java.security.Security.getProperty("package.definition")` and checks to see if pkg starts with or equals any of the packages. If it does, then `checkPermission` gets called with the `Runtime-Permission("defineClassInPackage."+pkg)` permission. If this method is overridden, then `super.checkPackageDefinition` should be called as the first line in the overridden method.

♦ `public void checkSetFactory();`

This method was modified to call `checkPermission` with the `Runtime-Permission("setFactory")` permission. If this method is overridden, then a call to `super.checkSetFactory` should be made at the point the overridden method would normally throw an exception.

♦ `public void checkMemberAccess(Class clazz, int which);`

This method was modified. The default policy is to allow access to public members, as well as access to classes that have the same class loader as the caller. In all other cases, it calls `checkPermission` with the `Runtime-Permission("accessDeclaredMembers")` permission. If this method is overridden, then a call to `super.checkMemberAccess` cannot be made, as the default implementation of `checkMemberAccess` relies on the fact that the code being checked is at a location on the stack with depth 4, as in the following.

```
someCaller[3]
java.lang.Class.someReflectionAPI [2]
java.lang.Class.checkMemberAccess [1]
SecurityManager.checkMemberAccess [0]
```

To emulate this behavior, you would need to call `getClassContext` and examine the class loader of the class at index 3, just as the default `checkMemberAccess` method does.

```
if (which != Member.PUBLIC) {
   Class stack[] = getClassContext();
```

```
    if ((stack.length<4) ||
        (stack[3].getClassLoader() != clazz.getClassLoader())) {
        if (checkMemberAccessPermission == null)
            checkMemberAccessPermission =
                new RuntimePermission("accessDeclaredMembers");
            checkPermission(checkMemberAccessPermission);
    }
}
```

This is the only security manager method in JDK 1.2 that is still based on a caller's depth. This is to allow a caller to reflect on classes from the same class loader from which it came.

♦ `public void checkSecurityAccess(String target);`

This method was modified to call `checkPermission` with a `Security-Permission` object for the given target. If this method is overridden, then a call to `super.checkSecurityAccess` should be made at the point the overridden method would normally throw an exception.

♦ `public ThreadGroup getThreadGroup();`

This method is unchanged.

CHAPTER 6

Object Security

If we cannot secure all our rights, let us secure what we can.
—Thomas Jefferson

As you develop applications using the Java language and platform, and especially when you consider security features, you knowingly or unknowingly depend on the underlying object orientation, such as data encapsulation, object name space partition, and type safety. This dependence is also evident in the protection of the runtime's internal state, which is often represented and maintained as Java objects. For example, when using the Java RMI (Remote Method Invocation) package to build distributed Java applications that span across multiple JVMs, you will sometimes find it convenient or even necessary to protect the state of an object for integrity and confidentiality when the state is transported from one machine to another. These security requirements exist when concerned objects are inside a runtime system (for example, in memory), in transit (for example, stored in IP packets), or stored externally (for example, saved on disk).

This means that there is a whole range of object-level security issues that must be correctly dealt with during system development, in addition to code-signing and policy-driven, fine-grained access control mechanisms. This chapter provides a number of techniques for achieving secure programming in Java. It also describes three new interfaces for signing, sealing (encrypting), and guarding Java objects. It begins by discussing some good general practices.

6.1 Security Exceptions

It is not uncommon for a piece of code to catch an exception thrown from lower-level code and then either mask this by translating the exception into a higher-level exception and rethrowing it or do some processing that results basically in its "swallowing" the exception.

For example, suppose you write a class `MyPasswordChecker` that checks a user's password when the user logs in. If the password check fails because the username does not exist, it is bad practice to let the user know that the name has been given wrongly, as doing this would help an attacker to guess available usernames. Instead, a more general error message should be given, such as "login failed."

```
public class MyPasswordChecker {
    public void check(String name, String password)
            throws LoginFailureException {
        try {
        // Call the real password checking routine.
        ...
        } catch (NoSuchUserException e) {
           throw new LoginFailureException():
        }
    }
}
```

However, you should be extremely careful when writing code that masks or swallows security exceptions (such as `AccessControlException` and `SecurityException`) because such an action could potentially mask serious security breaches. Sometimes developers get annoyed by a security exception and take matters into their own hands by substituting their own security policy decision for that of `AccessController` or `SecurityManager`. This attitude of "just-make-the-code-work" is very dangerous, especially if the code being developed might be run as system code and thus be fully trusted. Often, software design can be improved to avoid having to catch and swallow undesirable exceptions.

6.2   Fields and Methods

The Java language provides four access modes, which should be used properly: public, protected, package private, and private. A common example of improper use is the inexperienced programmer who, when writing a time zone class, mistakenly declares fields or variables that are publicly accessible:

```
public TimeZone defaultZone;
```

This design has a number of problems. First, any person or code (including untrusted code) can access this field and directly change the value of the default time zone. Second, because multiple threads can access this field, some synchronization is needed. Following is a better design.

```
private TimeZone defaultZone= null;
public synchronized void setDefault(TimeZone zone) {
    defaultZone = zone;
}
```

Suppose that after product release, you decide that a security check is needed to guard against unauthorized modification to the value of the default time zone, `defaultZone`. You can add a couple lines of security code for the next release of the product, as follows.

```
private TimeZone defaultZone= null;
public synchronized void setDefault(TimeZone zone) {
    AccessController.checkPermission(new
        TimeZonePermission("setDefault"));
    defaultZone = zone;
}
```

A critical point about this product update is that it is done in a way that does not break backward compatibility. That is, a third-party application that runs on the earlier version of the release will still have the same API available when running on the new release. If the `TimeZone` was directly exposed as a public field, as in the first design, a security check (or a synchronization feature) could not be added without changing existing APIs.

To recap, never design public fields or variables that can be accessed directly. Instead, declare these fields as private and provide public accessor methods that mediate access to such fields. Moreover, decide carefully, *for every single public method*, if any such access is sensitive and might require a security check. If a field is intended to be a constant, it can be public but should be made static and final, as discussed in the next section.

Even when methods or fields are protected, as long as the class is not final a subclass can access them. Because an attacker can easily provide a subclass, security can be compromised. Similarly, package private methods and fields can be accessed by any class in the same package. Unless the package is sealed properly, an attacker can easily write a class and declare that class to belong to the package and thus gain access to the package's private methods and fields. Always review all protected and package private methods and fields to see if they should be made private, and if not, whether they should be accessed via accessor methods that perform security checks.

6.3   Static Fields

A **static field** is a per-class field in the sense that its value is shared by all objects instantiated from the same class. Static fields are a mine field that can cause unintended interactions between supposedly independent subsystems. They offer even less protection than do per-object fields. This is because in the latter case, you must have an object's reference in order to access the field, whereas in the former case, anyone can access the field simply by using the class name directly.

As a result, directly exposed, nonfinal public static variables are extremely bad news for security. Never design a class with such variables. Instead, declare them as static private, with appropriate public static accessor methods. You still have to decide carefully if these accessor methods should invoke security checks.

If you have a product already released with such dangerous variables, you should review all nonfinal public static variables and carefully assess the potential damage they can cause. You should eliminate the worst offenders even though doing so breaks backward compatibility. For the rest, if you must keep them for backward compatibility, you can only hope that no one can come up with a way to exploit them.

Another dangerous aspect of static fields is that they can create type safety problems if used casually. For example, a part of the system code might be designed to share a static field internally and have defined a static field Foo. If Foo is typed too loosely, an untrusted applet or application can plant an object of a subtype or a type that is incompatible with what the system programmer intended (for example, when Foo is declared to be of type `java.lang.Object`). This kind of substitution can create very subtle security problems that are difficult to detect and correct.

6.4   Private Object State and Object Immutability

Most objects have private, internal states that should not be randomly modified. Often, other objects need to query the state information. Many programmers implement the query method using a simple `return` statement, as in the following example.

```
public MyClass {
   private boolean status = false;

   public void setStatus(boolean s) {
      status = s;
   }
}
```

```
    public boolean getStatus() {
        return s;
    }
}
```

No problem so far. However, if status is not a simple boolean but rather an array of boolean, serious problems can occur, as here.

```
public MyClass {
    private boolean[] status = null;

    public boolean[] getStatus() {
        return s;
    }
}
```

In this example, once another object obtains reference to status s, it can change the value of s without MyClass's consent. This is because, unlike boolean, an *array* of booleans (or an array of anything) is mutable. Such a consequence might not be what the designer of MyClass intended, since uncontrolled modification to internal state can lead to incorrect or even malicious results.

There is a twist to this problem. In the example with an array of booleans, the simplest way to implement the setStatus method is as follows.

```
public void setStatus(boolean[] s) {
    status = s;
}
```

Again, because s is mutable, even after MyClass has "taken possession of" it, the object that supplied s to MyClass can still change the value of s. Many programmers overlook this possibility.

Thus you should never return a mutable object to potentially malicious code. Further, you should never directly store a mutable object (by assigning the array reference to an internal variable) if the source of the object can be malicious. Because any code can potentially be malicious, the best practice is to clone or copy the objects before returning or storing them.

This discussion brings up the important point of being able to distinguish immutable objects from mutable ones and of the benefit of making objects immutable when possible. For example, array, Vector, and Hashtable are mutable. Even if an array contains only immutable objects (such as String), the array itself is still mutable and anyone with a reference to the array can change entire objects contained in the array.

Figuring out whether an object is immutable is not always easy. This is because immutability depends on what fields and methods are available and whether objects used in those cases are also immutable. This analysis might need to be done recursively, until all loose ends are tracked down and resolved to be immutable.

A final word on immutable objects. Because a password is typically seen as a string of characters, it is common to see Java programs where a String is used to represent a password. Given that a String is immutable, however, there is no way for the application program to erase it when it is no longer needed. Its fate is left entirely with the JVM's garbage collector. For better security, you should use char[ ] to represent passwords and wipe out the content of the array after use.

6.5   Privileged Code

Recall that you can use the PrivilegedAction interface to mark a segment of the code as privileged in the sense that it can then make use of all of its own privileges, independent of its callers' privileges. If a piece of trusted code (such as system code) is privileged, it can load libraries (including native code), read any file, read system properties, and so on. This privileged code segment is a critical region in which mistakes can be made and errors can be costly.

When writing privileged code, always try to keep it as short as possible. This practice not only reduces the chance of making mistakes but also makes auditing the code easier so as to ensure it is accessing only the minimal amount of protected resources.

Also, watch out for the use of *tainted variables*, that is, variables that are set by the caller (that is, passed in as parameters) and thus are not under the control of the privileged code. For example, consider the following privileged code to open a file.

```
public FileInputStream getFileToRead(String filename) {
    FileInputStream fn =
        (FileInputStream) AccessController.doPrivileged(new
                PrivilegedAction() {
            public Object run() {
                return new FileInputStream(filename);
            }
        }
    );
}
```

This code can be used to open a font file when displaying images for applets, even though the original calling applet classes would not have access to the actual font file. However, this example has two flaws. One is that the method is public, so anyone can call it. The other is that there is no sanity check on the filename, so the code blindly opens any file requested by the caller. Either flaw alone can be a problem.[1] Combined, they create the worst possible situation, as now anyone can call this method to open any file desired (assuming the privileged code has the appropriate permissions, which any system code does).

The problem does not stop at public methods. Even if you change `getFile-ToRead` to be nonpublic, another public method can turn around and invoke `getFileToRead`. In this case, once again a tainted variable is used indirectly by privileged code and security could be compromised.

The most conservative way to design such methods is to make them private so that they are not callable from outside of their own class.

6.6   Serialization

Serialization is a feature that allows a class's or object's nontransient state to be serialized, for example for purposes of transporting the class or object to another machine and then deserializing it at the destination. RMI uses serialization extensively, as do other packages. Default implementations of two methods, `write-Object` and `readObject`, are invoked for serialization and deserialization, respectively. You also can write, for a serializable class, `writeObject` and `readObject` methods to customize how serialization and deserialization are done.

Security-conscious implementors should keep in mind that a serializable class's `readObject` method is, in effect, a public constructor that takes as input the values for each of the serialized object's nontransient fields and creates a new object. As the input to `readObject` can be provided by an adversary whose goal is to compromise the object under construction, you cannot safely assume that the input content was generated via the serialization of a properly constructed object of the correct type. As a result, if `readObject` blindly takes its input, various security problems can occur. This is true whether `readObject` is implicit (that is, default provided by the JDK implementation) or explicit (that is, provided by the serializable class in question). In fact, the default implementation of `readObject` does no validity checking whatsoever.

In good defensive programming, if a class has any private or package private fields on which it maintains invariants, an explicit `readObject` method should be

---

[1]   A different set of problems can occur if untrusted code can take advantage of the first problem and cause a large number of arbitrary files to be opened.

provided that checks that these invariants are satisfied, as in the following example.

```
private void readObject(ObjectInputStream s) throws
        IOException, ClassNotFoundException {
    s.defaultReadObject();
    if (<invariants are not satisfied>)
        throw new java.io.StreamCorruptedException();
}
```

Further, if a class has any object reference fields that are private or package private, and the class depends on the fact that these object references are not available outside of the class (or package), the objects referenced by those fields must be defensively copied as part of the deserialization process. That is, the subobjects deserialized from the stream should be treated as untrusted input in that newly created objects, initialized to have the same value as the deserialized subobjects, should be substituted for the subobjects by the readObject method.

For example, suppose an object has a private byte array field, b, that must remain private. Then b should be a clone of the result from readObject, as follows.

```
private void readObject(ObjectInputStream s) throws
        IOException, ClassNotFoundException {
    s.defaultReadObject();
    b = (byte[])b.clone();
    if (<invariants are not satisfied>)
        throw new java.io.StreamCorruptedException();
}
```

Note that calling clone is not always the right way to defensively copy a subobject. If the clone method cannot be counted on to produce an independent copy (and not to "steal" a reference to the copy), for example, when the class of the subobject is not final, an alternative way should be used to produce the copy.

As a conservative alternative to using an explicit readObject method to ensure the integrity of deserialized objects, you can use a readResolve method instead, calling a public constructor from within that method. This absolutely guarantees that the deserialized object is one that could have been produced with a public constructor.

Here are some more points to remember when implementing a Serializable interface. First, use the transient keyword for a field that contain direct handles to system resources and information relative to an address space. Otherwise, if a resource such as a file handle is not declared transient, then while the object is serialized, that part of the state can be altered. This results in the object, after being deserialized, having improper access to resources and thereby causing security breaches or errors. In fact, for correctness reasons, system-specific references should be declared transient, since they make no sense in a different environment in which the object is to be deserialized.

Second, as stated earlier in the section, you should guarantee that a deserialized object does not have state that violates some invariants by having a class define its own deserializing methods. Because deserializing an object is a kind of object creation, if untrusted code has a restriction regarding object creation, then you must ensure that that untrusted code has the same restriction when it deserializes the object. To illustrate the problem, consider the situation when an applet creates a frame. Security requires that a frame always be created to include a warning label "This is an applet window." If the frame is serialized (by anyone, including the applet) and then deserialized by an applet, you must ensure that the frame comes back up with the same warning banner.

Finally, when the state of a serialized object is outside of the JVM, such as when being transported to another machine, the state can potentially be corrupted. Although such corruption cannot be directly prevented by the Java security system, measures can be taken to detect if corruption has occurred. One way is to encrypt the byte stream produced by serialization. Another way is to use `SignedObject` and `SealedObject`, which are covered later in this chapter. However, such measures do not come free, as cryptographic keys must be managed, and this is far from a trivial task.

6.7   Inner Classes

The way *inner class* is currently defined has some security implications. Suppose that class A has a private field that is accessible only from within the class itself. Further suppose that A is rewritten to use inner classes and now encloses an inner class B that requires access to the private field. During compilation, the compiler automatically inserts into the definition of A a (package private) access method to the private field so that B can call this method. A side effect of this design is that any class in the same package as A and B will be able to call the access method and thus access the private field that had been forbidden to it prior to the use of inner classes. Transforming a field from private to package private does not naturally lead to security problems, but you must take care to examine the consequence of such transformations.

The use of inner classes has another design side effect. Suppose that class B is a protected member of class A. After compilation, B's class file defines itself as a public class, but an attribute in the class file correctly records the protection mode bit. Similarly, if B is a private member of A, B's class file defines itself as having package scope with an attribute that declares the true access protection mode. This side effect is not a problem by itself. However, any implementation of the JVM must perform the extra check and honor the true protection attributes.

6.8   Native Methods

Be careful when using native methods. Native methods, by definition, are outside of the Java security system. Neither the security manager nor any other Java security mechanism is designed to control the behavior of native code. Thus errors or security breaches in native code can be a lot more deadly. You should examine native methods for the parameters they take and the values they return. In particular, if a native method does something that effectively bypasses Java security checks, you must be very careful about the access mode of the method. If the mode is public, then anyone can call the method. You must examine the consequences and decide if that method should not be made private.

6.9   Signing Objects

Recall the earlier discussion about the need to protect an object when it is in serialized state and during transit. In fact, quite a few situations exist when the authenticity of an object and its state must be assured. Following are two examples.

♦ An object acting as an authentication or authorization token is passed around internally to any Java runtime as part of the security system functions. Such a token must be unforgeable, and any (innocent or malicious) modification to its state must be detected.

♦ An object is transported across machines (JVMs), and its authenticity still needs to be verified.

♦ An object's state is stored outside of the Java runtime, for example, onto a disk for JVM restarting purposes.

The class `java.security.SignedObject` defines interfaces to sign objects. A series of nested `SignedObjects` can be used to construct a logical sequence of signatures that resemble a chain of authorization and delegation.

A `SignedObject` contains the signed object and its signature. The signed object must be serializable. Informally speaking, a `Serializable` object is an object that implements the `Serializable` interface. In this way, the interface sup-

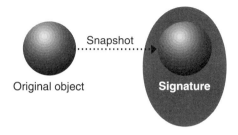

Figure 6.1   Signed objects.

ports `readObject()` and `writeObject()` method calls that convert an object's in-memory representation to and from an "on-the-wire" format that can be transmitted via input and output streams provided on the Java platform.

If the signature is not null, it contains a valid digital signature of the signed object, as depicted in Figure 6.1.

The underlying signing algorithm can be, among others, the NIST standard DSA, using DSA and SHA-1. The algorithm is specified using the same convention for signatures, such as SHA-1withDSA. Sun's JDK always has a built-in implementation of DSAwithSHA-1.

The signed object is a "deep copy" (in serialized form) of an original object. Once the copy is made, further manipulation of the original object has no side effect on the copy. In fact, a `SignedObject` is immutable.

The signature of the `SignedObject` class is as follows. For brevity, exception declarations are not listed.

```
public SignedObject(Serializable object, PrivateKey signingKey,
        Signature signingEngine)
public Object getObject();
public byte[] getSignature();
public String getAlgorithm();
public boolean verify(PublicKey verificationKey,
        Signature verificationEngine);
```

This class is intended to be subclassed in the future so as to allow multiple signatures on the same signed object. In this case, existing method calls in this base class are fully compatible semantically. In particular, any `get` method returns the unique value if there is only one signature and an arbitrary value from the set of signatures if there is more than one signature.

The underlying signing algorithm is designated by a `Signature` parameter to the `sign` and `verify` method calls. A typical usage for signing follows.

```
Signature signingEngine =
    Signature.getInstance(algorithm, provider);
SignedObject so =
    new SignedObject(myobject, privatekey, signingEngine);
```

A typical usage for verification and object retrieval is as follows (having received `SignedObject` so):

```
Signature verificationEngine =
    Signature.getInstance(algorithm, provider);
if (so.verify(publickey, verificationEngine))
  try {
    Object myobj = so.getObject();
  } catch (ClassNotFoundException e) {};
```

Obviously, for verification to succeed, the specified public key must be the public key corresponding to the private key used to generate the signature. Also, the security of `SignedObject` depends on the underlying digital signature algorithm and key management system not having been compromised. The signing or verification engine does not need to be initialized, as it will be reinitialized inside the verify method.

`getObject()` in a sense loses typing information by returning an object of the type `Object`, so the signed objects likely will be used between collaborating parties so that the correct casting can be done. For example, the previous code can be changed as follows.

```
String myobject = new String("Greetings.");
...
if (so.verify(publickey, verificationEngine))
  try {
    String myobj = (String) so.getObject();
  } catch (ClassNotFoundException e) {};
```

In fact, it is probably more common to subclass `SignedObject` so that the correct casting is performed inside the subclass. In this way, static typing information is better preserved.

More importantly, for flexibility reasons, the `verify` method allows customized signature engines, which can implement signature algorithms that are not installed formally as part of a cryptography provider. However, it is crucial that the programmer writing the verifier code be aware what `Signature` engine is being used, as its own implementation of `verify` is invoked to verify a signature. In other words, a malicious `Signature` might choose to always return `true` on verification in an attempt to bypass security checks. For similar reasons, `verify` in the `SignedObject` class is final.

Note that signing objects is different from signing JAR files that contain class files, a feature that first appeared in JDK 1.1.*x*, Navigator 3.*x*, and IE 3.*x*. Signing code facilitates the authentication of static code (bytecode in the case of Java technology, native code in the case of Microsoft's Authenticode), while signing objects deals with objects that might represent a complex transaction application complete with active state information.

6.10   Sealing Objects

The previous section discussed the `SignedObject` class, which provides object authenticity or integrity. The class `SealedObject`, on the other hand, protects an object's confidentiality.[2] These two classes may be combined to provide integrity and confidentiality at the same time.[3] In fact, from a technical design perspective, designing the two classes into one would have been a better choice. In reality, class `SealedObject` is not even in the `java.security` package. Instead, it is included in the `javax.crypto` package as part of the Java Cryptography Extension (JCE) 1.2. This design choice was influenced solely by current U.S. regulations regarding the exporting of encryption software.

Given any `Serializable` object, you can create a `SealedObject` that embeds in its content the original object, in serialized format. Then, a cryptographic algorithm, such as DES, can be applied to the content to protect its confidentiality. The encrypted content can later be decrypted by using the corresponding algorithm with the correct decryption key.

After decryption, the original content can be obtained in object form through deserialization. The content, while encrypted, is not available to anyone who does not possess the correct decryption key, assuming that the cryptosystem is secure.

The signature of the `SealedObject` class is as follows. Exception declarations have been left out.

---

[2]   For those who are interested in researching the history of secure objects, earlier work on secure network objects using Modula-3 and Oblique [78] is related to `SignedObject` and `SealedObject` in that there was the high-level abstraction of secure remote object invocation. However, this abstraction was implemented by establishing a secure communication channel between the two end points and using this channel to send plain object and data. In other words, there was no explicit concept of signing and sealing objects directly.

[3]   Experience in security system design indicates that blindly signing encrypted data is sometimes dangerous. Thus you should create and sign a `SignedObject` first and then use that `SignedObject` to create a `SealedObject`.

```
public SealedObject(Serializable object, Cipher c);
public final Object getObject(Cipher, c);
public final Object getObject(Key, k)
public final Object getObject(Key, k, String provider);
```

A typical usage of this class is illustrated with the following code segments. First, a DES key is generated and the DES cipher is initialized.

```
KeyGenerator keyGen = KeyGenerator.getInstance("DES");
SecretKey desKey = keyGen.generateKey();
Cipher cipher = Cipher.getInstance("DES");
cipher.init(Cipher.ENCRYPT_MODE, desKey);
```

Next, a `SealedObject` is created and encrypted. Note that the `Cipher` object must be fully initialized with the correct algorithm, key, padding scheme, and so on, before being applied to a `SealedObject`.

```
String s = new String("Greetings");
SealedObject so = new SealedObject(s, cipher);
```

Later, the original object is decrypted and retrieved.

```
cipher.init(Cipher.DECRYPT_MODE, desKey);
try {
   String s = (String) so.getObject(cipher);
} catch (ClassNotFoundException e) {};
```

As the case with `SignedObject`, `SealedObject` may be subclassed to provide better static typing information.

6.11   Guarding Objects

Apart from SignedObject that provides object authenticity, JDK 1.2 introduced an interface, `Guard`, and a class, `GuardedObject`, that can be used for object-level access control. A `java.security.GuardedObject` is an object that is used to protect access to another object. Once an object is encapsulated by a `Guarded-Object`, access to that object is controlled by the `getObject` method. This method controls access to the object by invoking the `checkGuard` method on the `java.security.Guard` object that is guarding access. If access is not allowed, a `SecurityException` will be thrown. This is illustrated in Figure 6.2, where solid lines represent method calls and dotted lines represent object references.

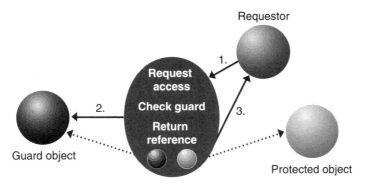

Figure 6.2 Guard and GuardedObject.

Here, when a requestor asks for an object that is guarded by a GuardedObject with a particular Guard, first the Guard is consulted, and then the reference to the desired object is returned to the requestor, if the Guard allows it.

One major motivation for having the GuardedObject class is that often the supplier of a resource is not in the same execution context (such as a thread) as the consumer of that resource. In this case, a security check within the security context of the supplier is often inappropriate because the check should occur within the security context of the consumer.

For example, when a file server thread responds to a request to open a file for reading and this request comes from a different environment, the decision to supply the file must take into account information about the requestor, such as its AccessControlContext. However, sometimes the consumer cannot provide the supplier with such information, for several reasons.

♦ The consumer program does not always know ahead of time what information should be provided (this is quite possible in a dynamically changing environment), and it is undesirable (for example, for performance reasons) to engage in a dialog or negotiation for each request.

♦ The consumer regards information about its execution environment as being too security-sensitive to pass on to another party.

♦ There is too much information or data to pass on.

♦ Information about the execution environment of the consumer cannot be interpreted by the supplier.

To make access control in these situations more uniform and easier to program, GuardedObject was designed so that the supplier of the resource can create an object representing the resource and a GuardedObject containing an embedded resource object and then provide the GuardedObject to the consumer. In creating the GuardedObject, the supplier also specifies a Guard object such that anyone (including the consumer) can obtain the resource object only when certain checks (for example, security checks) inside the Guard are satisfied. Guard is an interface, so any object can choose to become a Guard.

Using GuardedObject has several benefits.

♦ You can correctly embed the protection mechanism together with the protected object so that access to the object is guaranteed to occur in a context in which the protection mechanism will allow it.

♦ You can delay an access control decision from time of request to time of actual access, thus simplifying server programs.

♦ You can replace often used access control lists with object stores and simply store a set of GuardedObjects.

♦ The designer of a class does not need to specify the class's protection semantics, as long as any object instantiated from this class is protected within a GuardedObject and the associated Guard object implements the correct security checks.

♦ The same programming pattern can be used to encapsulate an object's protection mechanisms, which can differ for the object's different method invocations, all inside a Guard.

Note that because the built-in base class java.security.Permission implements the Guard interface, all permissions of this type, including all permissions (on file, network, runtime, and other resources) defined in JDK, are instantly usable as Guard objects.

The interface Guard contains only one method:

```
void checkGuard(Object object);
```

Following is the signature of the GuardedObject class.

```
public GuardedObject(Object object, Guard guard);
public Object getObject();
```

6.11.1 Examples of Using GuardedObject

The following example uses GuardedObject to encapsulate an object's protection semantics completely inside an appropriate Guard object. Note, this is just an example. There is no plan to massively change such classes in JDK to use GuardedObject.

The class java.io.FileInputStream is used as an example, and a stream is created with a given filename, as follows:

```
FileInputStream fis = new FileInputStream("/a/b/c");
```

The implementation of this constructor must be aware that a security check needs to be done, must understand what sort of check is appropriate, and also must sprinkle all constructors with the same (or similar) checks.

This class may be rewritten as follows. First, the class java.security.Permission is made a Guard object by the addition of a new method defined as follows.

```
public abstract Permission implements Guard {
    public void checkGuard() {
        AccessController.checkPermission(this);
    }
}
```

This implementation ensures that a proper access control check takes place within the consumer context, when access to the stream is first requested.

Now the provider side of the code can be simply as follows.

```
FileInputStream fis = new FileInputStream("/a/b/c");
FilePermission p = new FilePermission("/a/b/c", "read");
GuardedObject g = new GuardedObject(fis, p);
```

After object g is passed to the consumer, the following code will recover the FileInputStream, but only if the consumer is permitted to obtain read access to the file "/a/b/c".

```
FileInputStream fis = (FileInputStream) g.getObject();
```

Note that the implementation of FileInputStream itself need not be security-aware (as long as it is always protected by a GuardedObject). This design does not further perform security checks once a FileInputStream is returned to the consumer. This is the same behavior implemented in the FileInputStream class today.

Another potential application of GuardedObject is in the implementation of deferred object requests in the Java IDL (interface definition language) or a similar product. The obvious implementation of this CORBA-style API is to spin a separate thread in the ORB implementation to actually make the (deferred) request. This new thread is created by the ORB implementation, so any information about what code originated the request is lost, thereby making security checking difficult, if not impossible. With GuardedObject, the new thread can simply return a properly guarded object. This forces a security check to occur when the requestor attempts to retrieve the object.

Guard and GuardedObject can be extended (subclassed) to implement arbitrary guarding semantics. For example, the Guard object can check for signature information on class files, thus resulting in a design that is similar to the Gate pattern and the Permit class in the Java Electronic Commerce Framework [20]. In fact, the guard concept in GuardedObject is similar to the well-known guard concept in programming language research. It has been used elsewhere, albeit mostly in specialized forms, for example as a pattern [16]. Its combination with java.security.Permission is a novel feature that makes Guard very powerful for access control on the Java platform.

As another example, hypothetically we can radically rewrite the FileInput-Stream class as follows. For every constructor that does not take a Guard object g as the parameter, a suitable Guard is automatically generated. For every access method (such as read(bytes)), the uniform security check in the form of g.checkGuard() is invoked first.

As with SignedObject, subclassing GuardedObject can better preserve static typing information, where the base classes are intended to be used between cooperating parties so that the receiving party should know what type of object to expect.

CHAPTER 7

Programming Cryptography

Security is the chief pretence of civilization.
—George Bernard Shaw

Earlier chapters briefly covered some of the basic concepts of cryptography, as well as code signing and the use of certificates, which depend on public-key cryptosystems. This chapter goes behind the scenes to look at the Java Cryptography Architecture (JCA) that underlies the APIs and the tools.

JCA first appeared in JDK 1.1. It had fairly limited functionalities that included APIs for digital signatures and message digests. JDK 1.2 significantly extends the JCA into a framework for accessing and developing cryptographic functionality for the Java platform. Loosely speaking, JCA encompasses the parts of the JDK 1.2 security API that is related to cryptography, such as the new certificate management infrastructure that supports X.509 v3 certificates. It also includes a provider architecture that allows for multiple and interoperable cryptography implementations, as well as a set of associated conventions and specifications.

JCA logically covers both the crypto APIs defined in JDK 1.2 and the JCE (Java Cryptography Extension) 1.2, which provides features for encryption, key exchange, MAC (message authentication code), and a number of other encryption-related classes. Thus the JDK and JCE together provide a comprehensive set of platform-independent cryptography APIs. At this time, the JCE is released separately as an extension to the JDK, in accordance with U. S. regulations concerning the export of cryptography. This chapter covers architectural issues that span JDK and JCE but focuses detailed discussion only on those interfaces that are part of JDK.[1]

---

[1] A companion book on JCE 1.2 is planned.

7.1 Design Principles

The design of JCA is guided by two principles:

♦ Algorithm independence and extensibility

♦ Implementation independence and interoperability

The aim of JCA is to let users of the API utilize cryptographic concepts, such as digital signatures and message digests, without concern for the implementations or even the algorithms being used to implement these concepts. At the same time, JCA provides standardized APIs so that developers can request specific algorithms and specific implementations.

Algorithm independence is achieved by defining types of cryptographic services classes, called **service classes**, that provide the functionality of these cryptographic algorithms. Examples include the `MessageDigest`, `Signature`, and `KeyFactory` classes.

Implementation independence is achieved by using a *provider-based architecture*. I discussed the general idea of providers in Chapter 4. A provider in the context of JCA means a **Cryptographic Service Provider** (CSP), a package or set of packages that implement one or more JCA cryptography services, such as digital signature algorithms, message digest algorithms, and key conversion services. An application may simply request a particular type of object (such as a `Signature` object) that implements a particular service (such as the DSA signature algorithm) and receive an implementation from one of the installed providers. If desired, it may instead request an implementation from a specific provider. Providers may be updated transparently to the application, for example when faster or more secure versions are available.

An example is random number generation. JDK 1.1 contains a platform-independent implementation that can be inefficient on some machines. In addition, the implementation is hard-coded and cannot be easily customized. JDK 1.2 enables you to easily configure a customized service that utilizes good random number sources available on a particular platform, such as Linux.

Given the general nature of the API design, implementation interoperability is obtained in the sense that even though various implementations might have different characteristics, they can work with each other, such as using each other's keys or verifying each other's signatures. For example, when the appropriate key factory implementations are installed, for the same algorithm a key generated by one provider would be usable by another and a signature generated by one provider would be verifiable by another. This would apply even though one provider might be implemented in software, while the other is implemented in hardware and one

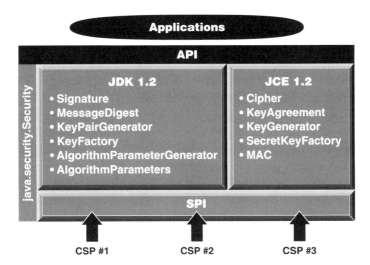

Figure 7.1 JCA architecture.

might be platform-independent, while the other is platform-specific. The interface design is also extensible in that new algorithms that fit in one of the supported service classes can easily be added.

Figure 7.1 depicts the architectural outline of JCA. By following the two design principles given earlier, JCA brings major benefits to the cryptographic software market. On the one hand, application software developers have only one set of APIs (JCA) to worry about, no matter what algorithms they choose to use or what provider packages they install. On the other hand, crypto toolkit or library vendors can compete with each other in intellectual property (for example, patented algorithms and techniques) and performance optimization, while maintaining full interoperability with each other at the level of JCA APIs.

7.2   Cryptographic Services and Service Providers

JCA introduces the notion of the CSP. In JDK 1.1, a provider could, for example, contain an implementation of one or more digital signature algorithms, message digest algorithms, and key generation algorithms. JDK 1.2 adds five services:

♦ Key factories

♦ Keystore creation and key management

♦ Algorithm parameter management

♦ Algorithm parameter generation

♦ Certificate factories

JDK 1.2 also enables a provider to supply a random number generation (RNG) algorithm.

Each JDK installation typically has one or more provider packages installed, and users may add new providers statically or dynamically. Each provider is referred to by a unique name. Users may configure their runtimes with different providers and specify a preference order for each. JCA offers a set of APIs that allow users to query which providers are installed and what services they support. If the application requests a specific provider, only objects from that provider are returned. If no specific provider is given, then a default provider is chosen. When multiple providers are available, a preference order is established. This is the order in which providers are searched for requested services. When a requested service is not provided by the most preferred provider, the next desirable provider is examined, and so on.

For example, suppose you have two providers installed in your JVM, Provider1 and Provider2. Further suppose that Provider1 implements SHA1withDSA and MD5 while Provider2 implements SHA1withDSA, MD5withRSA, and MD5.

If Provider1 has preference order 1 (the highest priority) and Provider2 has preference order 2, then the following behavior will occur.

♦ If you are looking for an MD5 implementation, and both providers supply such an implementation, the Provider1 implementation is returned because Provider1 has the highest priority and thus is searched first.

♦ If you are looking for an MD5withRSA signature algorithm, Provider1 is first searched. No implementation is found, so Provider2 is searched. An implementation is found there and returned.

♦ If you are looking for a SHA1withRSA signature algorithm, neither installed provider implements it, so a `NoSuchAlgorithmException` is raised.

Sun's version of the Java runtime environment comes standard with a default provider, "SUN." Other Java runtime environments might not necessarily supply the "SUN" provider. The "SUN" provider package includes implementation of the following:

- The Digital Signature Algorithm (DSA), described in NIST FIPS 186

- The MD5 (RFC 1321) and SHA-1 (NIST FIPS 180-1) message digest algorithms

- A DSA key pair generator for generating a pair of public and private keys suitable for the DSA algorithm

- A DSA algorithm parameter generator

- A DSA algorithm parameter manager

- A DSA key factory providing bidirectional conversions between (opaque) DSA private and public key objects and their underlying key material

- A proprietary SHA1PRNG pseudorandom number generation algorithm, following the recommendations in the IEEE P1363 standard

- A certificate factory for X.509 certificates and CRLs (Certificate Revocation Lists)

- A keystore for the proprietary keystore type named "JKS"

A service class defines a cryptographic service in an abstract fashion without a concrete implementation. A cryptographic service is always associated with a particular algorithm or type. It either

- provides cryptographic operations (like those for digital signatures and message digests),

- generates or supplies the cryptographic material (keys or parameters) required for cryptographic operations, or

- generates data objects (keystores or certificates) that encapsulate cryptographic keys (which can be used in a cryptographic operation) in a secure fashion.

An example service class is `Signature`. It provides access to the functionality of a DSA. A DSA key factory supplies a DSA private or public key (from its encoding or transparent specification) in a format usable by the `initSign` or `initVerify` methods, respectively, of a DSA `Signature` object.

Programmers can request and utilize instances of the service classes to carry out corresponding operations. The following service classes are defined in JDK 1.2.

♦ `MessageDigest`. Used to calculate the message digest (hash) of specified data.

♦ `Signature`. Used to sign data and verify digital signatures.

♦ `KeyPairGenerator`. Used to generate a pair of public and private keys suitable for a specified algorithm.

♦ `KeyFactory`. Used to convert opaque cryptographic keys of type "Key" into key specifications (transparent representations of the underlying key material), and vice versa.

♦ `CertificateFactory`. Used to create public key certificates and CRLs.

♦ `KeyStore`. Used to create and manage a keystore.

♦ `AlgorithmParameters`. Used to manage the parameters for a particular algorithm, including parameter encoding and decoding.

♦ `AlgorithmParameterGenerator`. Used to generate a set of parameters suitable for a specified algorithm.

♦ `SecureRandom`. Used to generate random or pseudorandom numbers.

A generator and a factory differ within the JCA context in that the former creates objects with new contents, whereas the latter creates objects from existing material (for example, an encoding).

A service class provides the interface to the functionality of a specific type of cryptographic service (independent of a particular cryptographic algorithm). It defines APIs that allow applications to access the specific type of cryptographic service it provides. The actual implementations (from one or more providers) are those for specific algorithms.

The application interfaces supplied by a service class are implemented in terms of a SPI (service provider interface). That is, for each service class, there is a corresponding abstract SPI class that defines the SPI methods that cryptographic service providers must implement.

The `Signature` service class, for example, provides access to the functionality of a DSA. The actual implementation supplied in a `SignatureSpi` subclass would be that for a specific kind of signature algorithm, such as SHA1withDSA, SHA1withRSA, or MD5withRSA.

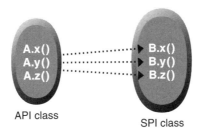

Figure 7.2   API and SPI in a
service class.

An instance of a service class—the `API` object (and of its corresponding `SPI` class)—is created by a call to the `getInstance` method of the service class. The instance encapsulates (as a private field) an instance of the corresponding `SPI` class, the `SPI` object. All `API` methods of an `API` object are declared final, and their implementations invoke the corresponding `SPI` methods of the encapsulated `SPI` object (Figure 7.2).

The name of each `SPI` class is the same as that of the corresponding service class, followed by `Spi`. For example, the `SPI` class corresponding to the `Signature` service class is the `SignatureSpi` class. Each `SPI` class is abstract. To supply the implementation of a particular type of service, for a specific algorithm, a provider must subclass the corresponding `SPI` class and provide implementations for all of the abstract methods.

Another example of a service class is the `MessageDigest` class, which provides access to a message digest algorithm. Its implementations, in `MessageDigestSpi` subclasses, may be those of various message digest algorithms such as SHA-1, MD5, or MD2.

As a final example, the `KeyFactory` service class supports the conversion from opaque keys to transparent key specifications, and vice versa. The actual implementation supplied in a `KeyFactorySpi` subclass is for a specific type of key, for example, DSA public and private keys.

Implementation for various cryptography services are provided by JCA CSPs, such as "SUN." A provider may also implement services that are not generally available, such as one of the RSA-based signature algorithms or the MD2 message digest algorithm.

7.2.1   Installing and Adding a Provider

The basic mechanism for obtaining an appropriate object, for example a `Signature` object, is as follows. Suppose you are a user and you request such an object by calling the `getInstance` method in the `Signature` class, specifying the name of a signature algorithm (such as SHA1withDSA), and, optionally, the name of the provider whose implementation is desired. For example, a government agency might want to use a provider implementation that has received government certification.

Also suppose that the provider you want to use is not installed. When a requested provider is not installed, a NoSuchProviderException is thrown, even if a different installed provider implements the algorithm requested. So you need to install a provider. This involves installing the provider package classes and configuring the provider. There are two ways to install the provider classes:

♦ Place a zip or JAR file containing the classes anywhere on CLASSPATH.

♦ Supply the provider JAR file as an installed or bundled extension.

Next, you need to add the provider to the list of approved providers. You can do this statically or dynamically. To do it statically, edit the Java security properties file. One property you can set there is

```
security.provider.n=masterClassName
```

This declares a provider and specifies its preference order, n. The preference order is the order in which providers are searched for requested algorithms.

masterClassName specifies the provider's *master class*, which is specified in the provider's documentation. This class is always a subclass of the Provider class. Its constructor sets the values of various properties that are required for the JCA APIs to look up the algorithms or other facilities implemented by the provider. Suppose that the master class is COM.abcd.provider.Abcd and that you want to configure Abcd as your third preferred provider. To do so, you add the following line to the security properties file:

```
security.provider.3=COM.abcd.provider.Abcd
```

You also can register a provider dynamically by calling either the addProvider or insertProviderAt method in the Security class. This type of registration is not persistent and can be done only by trusted programs that are granted sufficient permission. For example, the following policy specifies that only code that is loaded from a signed JAR file from beneath the /home/sysadmin/ directory on the local file system can call methods in the Security class to add or remove providers or to set security properties. (The JAR file's signature can be verified using the public key referenced by the alias "sysadmin" in the user's keystore.)

```
grant signedBy "sysadmin", codeBase "file:/home/sysadmin/*" {
    permission java.security.SecurityPermission
                "Security.insertProvider.*";
```

```
        permission java.security.SecurityPermission
                    "Security.removeProvider.*";
        permission java.security.SecurityPermission
                    "Security.setProperty.*";
};
```

7.3   Cryptography Classes

This section describes the design and usage of classes that are central to JCA.

7.3.1   `java.security.Security`

The `Security` class manages installed providers and security-wide properties. It contains only static methods and is never instantiated.

```
public static String getAlgorithmProperty(String algName,
                                          String propName)
public static int insertProviderAt(Provider provider,
                                   int position)
public static int addProvider(Provider provider)
public static void removeProvider(String name)
public static Provider[] getProviders()
public static Provider getProvider(String name)
public static String getProperty(String key)
public static void setProperty(String key, String datum)
```

The `getProviders()` method returns an array containing all of the installed providers (technically, the `Provider` subclass for each package provider). The order of the providers in the array is their preference order. The `addProvider` method adds a provider to the end of the list of installed providers. It returns the preference position at which the provider was added, or –1 if the provider was not added because it was already installed.

The `insertProviderAt` method attempts to add a new provider at a specified position in the preference order in which providers are searched for requested algorithms (if no specific provider is requested). A provider cannot be added again if it is already installed. If the given provider gets installed at the requested position, the provider that used to be at that position, as well as all providers with a position greater than that position, are shifted down, toward the end of the list of installed providers. This method returns the actual preference position at which the provider was added, or –1 if the provider was not added because it was already installed.

The removeProvider method removes the named provider. It returns silently if the Provider is not installed. When the specified provider is removed, all providers located at a position greater than where the specified provider was are shifted up one position, toward the head of the list of installed providers. To change the preference position of an installed provider, you must first remove it and then reinsert it at the new preference position.

7.3.2   java.security.Provider

Each Provider class instance has a name, a version number, and a string description of the provider and its services. You can query the Provider instance for this information by calling the following methods:

```
public String getName()
public double getVersion()
public String getInfo()
```

7.3.3   java.security.MessageDigest

The MessageDigest class is a service class designed to provide the functionality of cryptographically secure message digests such as SHA1 or MD5. A cryptographically secure message digest takes arbitrary-sized input (a byte array) and generates a fixed-size output, called a digest or hash. It should be computationally infeasible to find two messages that hash to the same value, and the digest should not reveal anything about the input that was used to generate it. Thus message digests are sometimes called the "digital fingerprints" of data.

To compute a digest, you first create a message digest instance. As with all service classes, a MessageDigest object for a particular type of message digest algorithm is obtained by calling the getInstance static factory method on the MessageDigest class:

```
public static MessageDigest getInstance(String algorithm)
```

The algorithm name is case-insensitive. For example, all of the following calls are equivalent:

```
MessageDigest.getInstance("SHA")
MessageDigest.getInstance("sha")
MessageDigest.getInstance("sHa")
```

A caller may optionally specify the name of a provider, which will guarantee that the implementation of the algorithm requested is from the named provider:

```
public static MessageDigest getInstance(String algorithm,
                                         String provider)
```

A call to the `getInstance` method returns an initialized message digest object; thus it does not need further initialization.

Next, to calculate the digest of some data, you supply the data to the initialized message digest object. This is done by making one or more calls to one of the update methods:

```
public void update(byte input)
public void update(byte[] input)
public void update(byte[] input, int offset, int len)
```

After the data has been supplied by calls to update methods, the digest is computed using a call to one of the digest methods:

```
public byte[] digest()
public byte[] digest(byte[] input)
public int digest(byte[] buf, int offset, int len)
```

The first two methods return the computed digest. The third stores the computed digest in the provided buffer buf, starting at offset. len is the number of bytes in buf allotted for the digest. The method returns the number of bytes actually stored in buf. A call to the digest method that takes an input byte array argument is equivalent to making a call to `public void update(byte[] input)` with the specified input, followed by a call to the digest method without any arguments.

7.3.4   `java.security.Signature`

The `Signature` class is a service class designed to provide the functionality of a cryptographic digital signature algorithm such as SHA1withDSA and MD5withRSA. A cryptographically secure signature algorithm takes arbitrary-sized input and a private key and generates a relatively short (often fixed-size) string of bytes, called the **signature**. The signature has the following properties.

1. When the public key corresponding to the private key used to generate the signature is provided, it should be possible to verify the authenticity and integrity of the input.

2. The signature and the public key do not reveal anything about the private key.

A `Signature` object can be used to sign data. It can also be used to verify whether an alleged signature is in fact the authentic signature of the data associated with it. Signature objects are modal objects. That is, a Signature object is always in a given state in which it may do only one type of operation. States are represented as final integer constants defined in their respective classes (such as Signature). A Signature object may have three states:

1. UNINITIALIZED

2. SIGN

3. VERIFY

To sign or verify a signature, you create a Signature instance. As with all service classes, a Signature object for a particular type of signature algorithm is obtained by calling the getInstance static factory method on the Signature class.

```
public static Signature getInstance(String algorithm)
public static Signature getInstance(String algorithm,
                                    String provider)
```

A Signature object must be initialized before it can be used. When it is first created, a Signature object is in the UNINITIALIZED state. The Signature class defines two initialization methods, initSign and initVerify, which change the state to SIGN and VERIFY, respectively. The initialization method depends on whether the object is going to be first used for signing or for verification. If for signing, the object must first be initialized with the private key of the entity whose signature is going to be generated. This initialization is done by calling the initSign method:

```
public final void initSign(PrivateKey privateKey)
```

This method puts the Signature object in the SIGN state.

If the Signature object is going to be first used for verification, it must be initialized with the public key of the entity whose signature is going to be verified. This initialization is done by calling the initVerify method:

```
public final void initVerify(PublicKey publicKey)
```

This method puts the Signature object in the VERIFY state.

If the Signature object has been initialized for signing (if it is in the SIGN state), the data to be signed can then be supplied to the object. This is done by making one or more calls to one of the update methods:

```
public final void update(byte b)
public final void update(byte[] data)
public final void update(byte[] data, int off, int len)
```

Calls to the update method(s) should be made until all of the data to be signed has been supplied to the Signature object.

To generate the signature, simply call one of the sign methods:

```
public final byte[] sign()
public final int sign(byte[] outbuf, int offset, int len)
```

The first method returns the signature result in a byte array. The second stores the signature result in the provided buffer outbuf, starting at offset. len is the number of bytes in outbuf allotted for the signature. The method returns the number of bytes actually stored. The signature is encoded as a standard ASN.1 sequence of two integers, r and s.

A call to a sign method resets the Signature object to the state it was in when previously initialized for signing via a call to initSign. That is, the object is reset and available to generate another signature with the same private key, if desired, via new calls to update and sign. Alternatively, a new call can be made to initSign specifying a different private key or to initVerify to initialize the Signature object to verify a signature.

If the Signature object has been initialized for verification (it is in the VERIFY state), it can then verify whether an alleged signature is in fact the authentic signature of the data associated with it. The process begins by supplying the data to be verified (as opposed to the signature itself) to the object. This is done by making one or more calls to one of the update methods:

```
public final void update(byte b)
public final void update(byte[] data)
public final void update(byte[] data, int off, int len)
```

Calls to the update method(s) should be made until all of the data has been supplied to the Signature object.

The signature can then be verified by calling the verify method:

```
public final boolean verify(byte[] encodedSignature)
```

The argument must be a byte array containing the signature encoded as a standard ASN.1 sequence of two integers, r and s. This is an often-used, standard encoding. It is the same as that produced by the sign method. The verify method returns a boolean indicating whether the encoded signature is the authentic signature of the data supplied to the update method(s).

A call to the verify method resets the Signature object to the state it was in when previously initialized for verification via a call to initVerify. That is, the object is reset and available to verify another signature from the identity whose public key was specified in the call to initVerify. Alternatively, a new call can be made either to initVerify specifying a different public key to initialize the

Signature object for verifying a signature from a different entity or to initSign to initialize the Signature object for generating a signature.

7.3.5   Algorithm Parameters

JCA is designed to handle many crypto algorithms. These algorithms can be very different. In particular, each tends to have unique requirements with regard to various parameters, such as key size and defined constant. To organize these parameters, an algorithm parameter specification is defined for each algorithm and all such specifications are divided into a small set of classes.

An algorithm parameter specification is a *transparent* representation of the sets of parameters used with an algorithm. This means that you can access each parameter value in the set individually, through one of the get methods defined in the corresponding specification class (for example, DSAParameterSpec defines getP, getQ, and getG methods, which access p, q, and g, respectively). By contrast, in an *opaque* representation, as supplied by the AlgorithmParameters class, you have no direct access to the parameter fields. Rather, you can get only the name of the algorithm associated with the parameter set (via getAlgorithm) and some kind of encoding for the parameter set (via getEncoded). You can call the getParameterSpec method to convert an AlgorithmParameters object to a transparent specification.

Algorithm Parameter Specification Interfaces and Classes

This section discusses the algorithm parameter specification interfaces and classes in the java.security and java.security.spec packages:

- ◆ AlgorithmParameterSpec
- ◆ DSAParameterSpec
- ◆ AlgorithmParameters
- ◆ AlgorithmParameterGenerator

AlgorithmParameterSpec. This interface is the base interface for the transparent specification of cryptographic parameters. It contains no methods or constants. Its only purpose is to group (and provide type safety for) all parameter specifications. All parameter specifications must implement this interface.

DSAParameterSpec. This class, which implements the AlgorithmParameter-Spec interface, specifies the set of parameters used with the DSA algorithm. It has the following methods:

```
public BigInteger getP()
public BigInteger getQ()
public BigInteger getG()
```

These return the DSA algorithm parameters: the prime p, the subprime q, and the base g.

AlgorithmParameters. This service class provides an opaque representation of cryptographic parameters. As with all service classes, an object of it for a particular type of algorithm is obtained by calling the getInstance static factory method (with a case-insensitive argument) on this class. A caller may optionally specify the name of a provider, thereby guaranteeing that the algorithm parameter implementation requested is from the named provider.

```
public static AlgorithmParameters getInstance(String algorithm)
public static AlgorithmParameters getInstance(String algorithm,
                                              String provider)
```

Once an AlgorithmParameters object is instantiated, it must be initialized via a call to init, using an appropriate parameter specification or parameter encoding.

```
public void init(AlgorithmParameterSpec paramSpec)
public void init(byte[] params)
public void init(byte[] params, String format)
```

params is an array containing the encoded parameters, and format is the name of the decoding format. In the init method with a params argument but no format argument, the primary decoding format for parameters is used. The primary decoding format is ASN.1, if an ASN.1 specification for the parameters exists. Note that AlgorithmParameters objects may be initialized only once and thus are not meant for reuse.

A byte encoding of the parameters represented in an AlgorithmParameters object may be obtained via a call to the getEncoded method:

```
public byte[] getEncoded()
```

This method returns the parameters in their primary encoding format.

To have the parameters returned in a specified encoding format, use this getEncoded method:

```
public byte[] getEncoded(String format)
```

If format is null, the primary encoding format for parameters is used, as in the other getEncoded method.[2]

A transparent parameter specification for the algorithm parameters may be obtained from an AlgorithmParameters object via a call to the getParameter-Spec method:

```
public AlgorithmParameterSpec getParameterSpec(Class paramSpec)
```

paramSpec identifies the specification class in which the parameters should be returned. That class could be, for example, DSAParameterSpec.class to indicate that the parameters should be returned in an instance of DSAParameterSpec (which is in the java.security.spec package).

AlgorithmParameterGenerator. This service class generates a set of parameters suitable for the algorithm that is specified when an AlgorithmParameter-Generator instance is created. To get an AlgorithmParameterGenerator object for a particular type of algorithm, call the getInstance static factory method on the AlgorithmParameterGenerator class.

```
public static AlgorithmParameterGenerator
    getInstance(String algorithm)
public static AlgorithmParameterGenerator
    getInstance(String algorithm, String provider)
```

The AlgorithmParameterGenerator object can be initialized in either of two ways:

♦ Algorithm-independent

♦ Algorithm-specific

The algorithm-independent approach uses the fact that all parameter generators share two concepts, those of a source of randomness and a size. Although the concept of size is universally shared by all algorithm parameters, it is interpreted differently for different algorithms. For example, in the case of parameters for the DSA algorithm, the size is the prime modulus, in bits. When this approach is used, any algorithm-specific parameter generation values default to some standard values.

---

[2] In the default AlgorithmParameters implementation, supplied by the "SUN" provider, the format argument is currently ignored.

An init method takes these two universally shared types of arguments. There is also one that takes just a size argument; it uses a system-provided source of randomness.

```
public void init(int size, SecureRandom random);
public void init(int size)
```

In the algorithm-specific approach, a parameter generator object is initialized using algorithm-specific semantics, which are represented by a set of algorithm-specific parameter generation values supplied in an AlgorithmParameterSpec object.

```
public void init(AlgorithmParameterSpec genParamSpec,
            SecureRandom random)
public void init(AlgorithmParameterSpec genParamSpec)
```

In the generation of the system parameters in, for example, the Diffie-Hellman scheme, the parameter generation values usually consist of the size of the prime modulus and the size of the random exponent, both specified in bits. The Diffie-Hellman algorithm is outside of the scope of JDK and is supplied as part of JCE 1.2.

Once you have created and initialized an AlgorithmParameterGenerator object, you can generate the algorithm parameters using the generateParameters method:

```
public AlgorithmParameters generateParameters()
```

7.3.6 java.security.Key and java.security.spec.KeySpec

This section describes the following interfaces and their subinterfaces:

◆ Key

◆ PublicKey

◆ PrivateKey

◆ KeySpec

Key

Key is the top-level interface for all opaque keys. It defines the functionality shared by all opaque key objects. All opaque keys have three characteristics:

◆ An algorithm—the key algorithm for that key

◆ An encoded form

◆ A format

The key algorithm denotes the algorithm such as DSA or RSA associated with key that will work in combination with related algorithms such as MD5withRSA and SHA1withRSA. The name of the algorithm of a key is obtained using the get method

```
public String getAlgorithm()
```

The encoded form is an external encoded form for the key used when a standard representation of the key is needed outside of the JVM, as when transmitting the key to some other party. The key is encoded according to a standard format (such as X.509 or PKCS#8) and is returned using this get method:

```
public byte[] getEncoded()
```

The format is the format of the encoded key and is returned by this get method:

```
public String getFormat()
```

Keys are generally obtained through key generators, certificates, key specifications (using a KeyFactory), or a KeyStore implementation that accesses a keystore database used to manage keys. Using a KeyFactory, you can parse encoded keys in an algorithm-specific manner. Similarly, you can use Certificate-Factory to parse certificates.

PublicKey and PrivateKey

The PublicKey and PrivateKey interfaces both extend the Key interface. They are methodless interfaces used for type safety and type identification.

A key specification is a transparent representation of the key material that constitutes a key. If the key is stored on a hardware device, its specification may contain information that helps identify the key on the device. A key's being transparent means that you can access each key material value individually, through one of the get methods defined in the corresponding specification class. For example, DSAPrivateKeySpec defines getX, getP, getQ, and getG methods to access the private key x and the DSA algorithm parameters used to calculate the key: the prime p, the subprime q, and the base g.

A key may be specified either in an algorithm-specific way or in an algorithm-independent encoding format such as ASN.1. For example, a DSA private key may be specified by its components x, p, q, and by using its DER encoding.

KeySpec

The KeySpec interface contains no methods or constants. Its only purpose is to group (and provide type safety for) all key specifications. All key specifications must implement this interface.

DSAPrivateKeySpec. This class implements the KeySpec interface, specifying a DSA private key with its associated parameters. It has the following methods that return the private key x and the DSA algorithm parameters used to calculate the key: the prime p, the subprime q, and the base g:

```
public BigInteger getX()
public BigInteger getP()
public BigInteger getQ()
public BigInteger getG()
```

DSAPublicKeySpec. This class implements the KeySpec interface, specifying a DSA public key with its associated parameters. It has the following methods that return the public key y and the DSA algorithm parameters used to calculate the key: the prime p, the subprime q, and the base g:

```
public BigInteger getY()
public BigInteger getP()
public BigInteger getQ()
public BigInteger getG()
```

RSAPrivateKeySpec. This class implements the KeySpec interface, specifying an RSA private key. It has the following methods to return the RSA modulus n and private exponent d values that constitute the RSA private key:

```
public BigInteger getModulus()
public BigInteger getPrivateExponent()
```

RSAPrivateCrtKeySpec. This class extends the RSAPrivateKeySpec class and specifies an RSA private key, as defined in the PKCS#1 standard, using the Chinese Remainder Theorem (CRT) information values. It has the following methods, in addition to the methods inherited from its superclass RSAPrivateKeySpec:

```
public BigInteger getPublicExponent()
public BigInteger getPrimeP()
public BigInteger getPrimeQ()
public BigInteger getPrimeExponentP()
public BigInteger getPrimeExponentQ()
public BigInteger getCrtCoefficient()
```

These methods return the public exponent e and the CRT information integers: the prime factor p of the modulus n, the prime factor q of n, the exponent d mod $(p - 1)$, the exponent d mod $(q - 1)$, and the CRT coefficient (inverse of q) mod p. An RSA private key logically consists of only the modulus and the private exponent. The presence of the CRT values is intended for efficiency.

RSAPublicKeySpec. This class implements the KeySpec interface and specifies an RSA public key. It has the following methods that return the RSA modulus n and public exponent e values that constitute the RSA public key:

```
public BigInteger getModulus()
public BigInteger getPublicExponent()
```

EncodedKeySpec. This abstract class implements the KeySpec interface and represents a public or private key in encoded format. Its getEncoded and get-Format methods return the encoded key and the name of the encoding format, respectively:

```
public abstract byte[] getEncoded();
public abstract String getFormat();
```

PKCS8EncodedKeySpec. This subclass of EncodedKeySpec represents the DER encoding of a private key, according to the format specified in the PKCS#8 standard. Its getEncoded method returns the key bytes, encoded according to the PKCS#8 standard. Its getFormat method returns the string "PKCS8". The X509EncodedKeySpec class, which is a subclass of EncodedKeySpec, represents the DER encoding of a public or private key, according to the format specified in the X.509 standard. Its getEncoded method returns the key bytes, encoded according to the X.509 standard. Its getFormat method returns the string "X.509".

7.3.7   java.security.KeyFactory and java.security.cert.CertificateFactory

This section reviews the factory classes for generating keys and certificates.

KeyFactory

The KeyFactory class is a service class designed to provide conversions between opaque cryptographic keys (of type Key) and key specifications (transparent representations of the underlying key material). Key factories are bidirectional. That is, you can build an opaque Key object from a given key specification (key material) or retrieve the underlying key material of a Key object.

Multiple compatible key specifications may exist for the same key. For example, a DSA public key may be specified by its components *y, p, q,* and *g* or by using its DER encoding according to the X.509 standard. A key factory can be used to translate between compatible key specifications. Key parsing can be achieved through translation between compatible key specifications. For example, when you translate from X509EncodedKeySpec to DSAPublicKeySpec, you basically are parsing the encoded key into its components.

To get a KeyFactory object for a particular type of key algorithm, you call the getInstance static factory method on the KeyFactory class.

```
public static KeyFactory getInstance(String algorithm)
public static KeyFactory getInstance(String algorithm,
    String provider)
```

A caller may optionally specify the name of a provider, which will guarantee that the implementation of the key factory requested is from the named provider of the KeyFactory.

If you have a key specification for a public or private key, you can obtain an opaque PublicKey or PrivateKey object from the specification by using the generatePublic or generatePrivate method, respectively:

```
public PublicKey generatePublic(KeySpec keySpec)
public PrivateKey generatePrivate(KeySpec keySpec)
```

Conversely, if you have a Key object, you can get a corresponding keySpec object by calling the getKeySpec method:

```
public KeySpec getKeySpec(Key key, Class keySpec)
```

KeySpec identifies the specification class in which the key material should be returned. It could be, for example, DSAPublicKeySpec.class to indicate that the key material should be returned in an instance of the DSAPublicKeySpec class.

CertificateFactory

The CertificateFactory class is a service class that defines the functionality of a certificate factory. A certificate factory is used to generate certificate and CRL objects from their encodings. A certificate factory for an X.509 certificate must return certificates and CRLs that are instances of java.security.cert.X509Certificate and java.security.cert.X509CRL, respectively.

♦ To get a `CertificateFactory` object for a particular certificate or CRL type, call the `getInstance` static factory method on the `CertificateFactory` class:

```
public static CertificateFactory getInstance(String type)
```

♦ To specify a provider, use this `getInstance` method:

```
public static CertificateFactory getInstance(String type,
                                  String provider)
```

♦ To generate a certificate object and initialize it with the data read from an input stream, use the `generateCertificate` method:

```
public final Certificate generateCertificate(InputStream is)
```

♦ To return a (possibly empty) collection view of the certificates read from a given input stream, use the `generateCertificates` method:

```
public final Collection generateCertificates(InputStream is)
```

♦ To generate a CRL object and initialize it with the data read from an input stream, use the `generateCRL` method:

```
public final CRL generateCRL(InputStream is)
```

♦ To return a (possibly empty) collection view of the CRLs read from a given input stream, use the `generateCRLs` method:

```
public final Collection generateCRLs(InputStream is)
```

7.3.8   KeyPair and KeyPairGenerator

The `KeyPair` class is a holder for a key pair (a public key and a private key). It has two public methods, one each for returning the private key and public key:

```
public PrivateKey getPrivate()
public PublicKey getPublic()
```

The `KeyPairGenerator` class is a service class used to generate pairs of public and private keys. The generation can be algorithm-independent or algorithm-specific, depending on how the object is initialized.

All key pair generation starts with a `KeyPairGenerator`. A key pair generator for a particular algorithm creates a public/private key pair that can be used with this algorithm. It also associates algorithm-specific parameters with each of the generated keys. To create a KeyPairGenerator, use one of the factory methods:

```
public static KeyPairGenerator getInstance(String algorithm)
public static KeyPairGenerator getInstance(String algorithm,
                                           String provider)
```

A key pair generator needs to be initialized before it can generate keys. In most cases, algorithm-independent initialization is sufficient. All key pair generators share two concepts, those of a source of randomness and a key size. The key size is interpreted differently for different algorithms. For example, in the case of the DSA algorithm, the size is the length of the modulus.

One initialize method takes these two universally shared types of arguments, while another one takes just a key size argument because it uses a system-provided source of randomness:

```
public void initialize(int keysize)
public void initialize(int keysize, SecureRandom random)
```

Since no other parameters are specified when you call the above algorithm-independent initialize methods, the provider must decide what to do about any algorithm-specific parameters to be associated with each key. For example, if the algorithm is DSA and the modulus size (key size) is 512, 768, or 1,024, then the "SUN" provider uses a set of precomputed values for the *p, q,* and *g* parameters. If the modulus size is not one of these values, the "SUN" provider creates a new set of parameters. Other providers might have precomputed parameter sets for more than just the three modulus sizes mentioned here. Still others might not have a list of precomputed parameters at all and instead always create new parameter sets.

In some cases, you need an algorithm-specific initialization, for example when a set of algorithm-specific parameters already exists (as is the case for so-called "community parameters" in DSA). Two initialize methods take an AlgorithmParameterSpec argument. One does not take a SecureRandom argument, in which case its source of randomness is provided by the system.

```
public void initialize(AlgorithmParameterSpec params)
public void initialize(AlgorithmParameterSpec params,
                       SecureRandom random)
```

To generate a key pair, call the following method from KeyPairGenerator:

```
public KeyPair generateKeyPair()
```

Multiple calls to generateKeyPair yield different key pairs.

7.3.9   `java.security.KeyStore`

The `KeyStore` class defines interfaces to access and modify the information in a keystore. Chapter 4 described the keystore, which can be used to manage a repository of keys and certificates, and demonstrated its use by the `keytool` utility. This section discusses `KeyStore`'s API design and implementation.

`KeyStore` is used by `keytool`, `jarsigner`, and `policytool`. It is also used by the default `Policy` implementation when it processes policy files. JDK users can write additional security applications that use or extend `KeyStore`.

Multiple different concrete implementations are possible, where each implementation is for a particular type of keystore. For example, one implementation might provide persistent keystores, while another can use smart cards. Thus keystore implementations of different types are not meant to be compatible.

A `KeyStore` implementation is provider-based. A corresponding abstract `KeystoreSpi` class specifies the SPI interfaces. The `Provider` class typically subclasses from `KeystoreSpi`. JDK contains a default keystore implementation of a proprietary keystore type (format) called "JKS."

`KeyStore` represents an in-memory collection of keys and certificates and manages two types of entries: key entry and trusted certificate entry. To create a `KeyStore` object, call the `getInstance` static factory method on the `KeyStore` class and optionally specify the name of a provider:

```
public static KeyStore getInstance(String type)
public static KeyStore getInstance(String type,
                          String provider)
```

Before a `KeyStore` object can be used, the actual keystore data must be loaded into memory via the `load` method:

```
public final void load(InputStream stream, char[] password)
```

The optional `password` is used to check the integrity of the keystore data. If no password is supplied, no integrity check is performed. If you want to create an empty keystore, pass null as the `InputStream` argument to the `load` method.

Each entry in a keystore is identified by a unique alias string. An enumeration of the alias names present in the keystore can be obtained as follows:

```
public final Enumeration aliases()
```

The following methods determine whether the entry specified by the given alias is a key entry or a trusted certificate entry:

```
public final boolean isKeyEntry(String alias)
public final boolean isCertificateEntry(String alias)
```

The following methods manipulate the content of the keystore:

```
public final void setCertificateEntry(String alias,
                            Certificate cert)
public final void setKeyEntry(String alias, byte[] key,
                            Certificate[] chain)
public final void setKeyEntry(String alias, Key key,
                char[] password, Certificate[] chain)
public final void deleteEntry(String alias)
public final Key getKey(String alias, char[] password)
public final Certificate getCertificate(String alias)
public final Certificate[] getCertificateChain(String alias)
public final String getCertificateAlias(Certificate cert)
public final void store(OutputStream stream, char[] password)
```

7.4   Randomness and Seed Generators

A basic concept of cryptography is random number generation. This is because randomness is the source of security in cryptography and is very useful (and sometimes essential) when generating keys and providing unique identifiers (for example, in challenge-response protocols).

The base class of a random number generator is `java.util.Random`, introduced in JDK 1.0. In the context here, the generator does not actually produce pure random numbers; rather, it produces *pseudorandom* numbers.

Random uses a 48-bit seed, which is modified using a linear congruent formula [37]. Here are its interfaces:

```
public Random()
public Random(long seed)
void setSeed(long seed)
protected int next(int bits)
boolean nextBoolean()
void nextBytes(byte[] bytes)
double nextDouble()
float nextFloat()
double nextGaussian()
int nextInt()
int nextInt(int n)
long nextLong()
```

Basically, you can construct a `Random` object and assign it a seed either in the constructor or via the `setSeed` method. If a seed is not assigned explicitly, it is by default a value based on the time at which the object is created. After the object has been initialized, various `next` methods can be called to obtain the next random number in different forms. The generator is deterministic in that if two instances of `Random` are created with the same seed and if the same sequence of method calls is made for each, both instances will generate and return identical sequences of numbers. Subclasses of `Random` are permitted to use other algorithms.

Security savvy readers will have noticed by now that neither the default seeding scheme nor the subsequent number generation algorithm produces numbers that are as unpredictable as a security application would normally require. This is why `java.security.SecureRandom` is needed—it provides a cryptographically strong pseudorandom number generator (PRNG). This class is discussed next.

7.4.1   `java.security.SecureRandom`

Like other algorithm-based classes in JDK, the `SecureRandom` class provides implementation-independent algorithms, whereby an application requests a particular PRNG algorithm and is handed back a `SecureRandom` object for that algorithm. It can also request a particular algorithm from a specific provider. For example, the default provider "SUN" supports a built-in algorithm named SHA1PRNG.

```
public static SecureRandom getInstance(String algorithm)
public static SecureRandom getInstance(String algorithm,
                                       String provider)
public SecureRandom()
public SecureRandom(byte[] seed)
public void setSeed(byte[] seed)
public void setSeed(long seed)
protected final int next(int numBits)
public static byte[] getSeed(int numBytes)
```

Using `getInstance` is the preferred way to obtain `SecureRandom` objects, even though public constructors can still be called. If these constructors are called, the default provider with the default algorithm is used.

The `SecureRandom` implementation attempts to completely randomize the internal state of the generator itself. However, this seeding process does not happen until the first time that random output is needed, that is, when `nextBytes` is called. Thus the caller can explicitly seed the `SecureRandom` object by calling `setSeed` right after `getInstance`, as in this example.

```
SecureRandom random = SecureRandom.getInstance("SHA1PRNG");
random.setSeed(seed);
```

Once the SecureRandom object has been seeded, it attempts to produce bits as random as the original seeds. At any time, a SecureRandom object might be reseeded using one of the setSeed methods. The newly given seed supplements rather than replaces the existing seed. Thus repeated calls do not reduce randomness. SecureRandom itself can also help with seed generation, for example for another SecureRandom object, via the generateSeed method.

7.5   Code Examples

This section presents several examples to further illustrate how you can use the classes discussed in this chapter.

7.5.1   Example 1: Computing a Message Digest

The first example computes a message digest using the algorithm SHA. Suppose you have a message composed of three byte arrays: i1, i2, and i3. First you create a properly initialized message digest object. Then you run the three byte arrays through the message digest object to calculate the hash, as follows.

```
MessageDigest sha = MessageDigest.getInstance("SHA");
sha.update(i1);
sha.update(i2);
sha.update(i3);
byte[] hash = sha.digest();
```

The call to the method digest signals the end of the input message. It can also take the last segment of the input as a parameter, as in the following.

```
sha.update(i1);
sha.update(i2);
byte[] hash = sha.digest(i3);
```

After the message digest has been calculated, the message digest object is automatically reset and ready to receive new data and calculate its digest. All former state (that is, the data supplied to update calls) is lost.

In some hash implementations, you can obtain intermediate hash values through cloning. Suppose you want to calculate separate hashes for three separate messages of this form:

i1

i1 and i2

i1, i2, and i3

You can perform the computations as follows.

```
/* compute the hash for i1 */
sha.update(i1);
byte[] i1Hash = sha.clone().digest();

/* compute the hash for i1 and i2 */
sha.update(i2);
byte[] i12Hash = sha.clone().digest();

/* compute the hash for i1, i2 and i3 */
sha.update(i3);
byte[] i123hash = sha.digest();
```

This works only if the SHA implementation is cloneable. One way to determine whether cloning is possible is to attempt to clone the MessageDigest object and see if the potential exception is thrown.

7.5.2   Example 2: Generating a Public/Private Key Pair

The second example generates a public/private key pair for the algorithm DSA. Keys are generated with a 1,024-bit modulus, using a user-derived seed, called userSeed. First, you get a KeyPairGenerator object for generating keys for the DSA algorithm. Then, to initialize the KeyPairGenerator, you need a random seed, obtained from a SecureRandom object.

```
KeyPairGenerator keyGen = KeyPairGenerator.getInstance("DSA");
SecureRandom random =
        SecureRandom.getInstance("SHA1PRNG", "SUN");
random.setSeed(userSeed);
keyGen.initialize(1024, random);
```

Suppose you already have a set of DSA-specific parameters—*p*, *q*, and *g*—that you want to use to generate your key pair. Then the key pair generator should be initialized differently, as in the following example.

```
KeyPairGenerator keyGen = KeyPairGenerator.getInstance("DSA");
DSAParameterSpec dsaSpec = new DSAParameterSpec(p, q, g);
SecureRandom random =
        SecureRandom.getInstance("SHA1PRNG", "SUN");
```

```
random.setSeed(userSeed);
keyGen.initialize(dsaSpec, random);
```

Finally, you generate the key pair:

```
KeyPair pair = keyGen.generateKeyPair();
```

7.5.3 Example 3: Generating and Verifying Signatures

This example generates and verifies a signature using the key pair generated in Example 2. First, you create a Signature object. Then, using the key pair generated in Example 2, you initialize the object with the private key and sign a byte array called data.

```
Signature dsa = Signature.getInstance("SHA1withDSA");
/* Initializing the object with a private key */
PrivateKey priv = pair.getPrivate();
dsa.initSign(priv);

/* Update and sign the data */
dsa.update(data);
byte[] sig = dsa.sign();
```

Verifying the signature is straightforward.

```
/* Initializing the object with the public key */
PublicKey pub = pair.getPublic();
dsa.initVerify(pub);

/* Update and verify the data */
dsa.update(data);
boolean verifies = dsa.verify(sig);
System.out.println("signature verifies: " + verifies);
```

Suppose that rather than having a public/private key pair, you have only the components of your DSA private key: x, p, q, and g (the base). Further suppose that you want to use your private key to digitally sign some data, which is in a byte array named someData. Then the following code should be used. This also illustrates how to create a key specification and use a key factory to obtain a PrivateKey from the key specification.

```
DSAPrivateKeySpec dsaPrivKeySpec =
        new DSAPrivateKeySpec(x, p, q, g);
```

```
KeyFactory keyFactory = KeyFactory.getInstance("DSA");
PrivateKey privKey =
        keyFactory.generatePrivate(dsaPrivKey-Spec);

Signature sig = Signature.getInstance("SHA1withDSA");
sig.initSign(privKey);
sig.update(someData);
byte[] signature = sig.sign();
```

Now suppose that your personal attorney, Alice, wants to use the data you signed. For her to do so and so that she can verify your signature, you need to send her three things: the data, the signature, and the public key corresponding to the private key you used to sign the data. You can store the someData bytes in one file and the signature bytes in another and send both files to Alice. For the public key, assume, as in the previous signing example, that you have the components of the DSA public key corresponding to the DSA private key used to sign the data. Then you can create a DSAPublicKeySpec from those components:

```
DSAPublicKeySpec dsaPubKeySpec =
        new DSAPublicKeySpec(y, p, q, g);
```

You still need to extract the key bytes so that you can put them in a file. To do this, you first call the generatePublic method on the DSA key factory already created in Example 2 and then extract the (encoded) key bytes.

```
PublicKey pubKey = keyFactory.generatePublic(dsaPubKeySpec);
byte[] encKey = pubKey.getEncoded();
```

You now can store these bytes in a file and send the file to Alice along with the files containing the data and the signature.

Once Alice receives these files, she copies the data bytes from the data file to a byte array named data, the signature bytes from the signature file to a byte array named signature, and the encoded public key bytes from the public key file to a byte array named encodedPubKey. To verify the signature, she runs the following code, which uses a key factory to instantiate a DSA public key from its encoding.

```
X509EncodedKeySpec pubKeySpec =
        new X509EncodedKeySpec(encodedPubKey);

KeyFactory keyFactory = KeyFactory.getInstance("DSA");
PublicKey pubKey = keyFactory.generatePublic(pubKeySpec);

Signature sig = Signature.getInstance("SHA1withDSA");
sig.initVerify(pubKey);
```

```
sig.update(data);
sig.verify(signature);
```

Alice can also convert PublicKey to a DSAPublicKeySpec in order to access the key components.

```
DSAPublicKeySpec dsaPubKeySpec =
        (DSAPublicKeySpec) keyFactory.getKeySpec(pubKey,
                            DSAPublicKeySpec.class)
BigInteger y = dsaPubKeySpec.getY();
BigInteger p = dsaPubKeySpec.getP();
BigInteger q = dsaPubKeySpec.getQ();
BigInteger g = dsaPubKeySpec.getG();
```

7.5.4   Example 4: Reading a File That Contains Certificates

The final example in this chapter reads a file that contains certificates. In the first, the certificates are Base64-encoded. Such certificates are each bounded at the beginning and the end, respectively, by

```
-----BEGIN CERTIFICATE-----
```

and

```
-----END CERTIFICATE-----.
```

In this process, you convert the FileInputStream, which does not support the mark and reset methods, to a ByteArrayInputStream, which does support those methods. You do this so that each call to generateCertificate consumes only one certificate and the read position of the input stream is positioned to the next certificate in the file.

```
FileInputStream fis = new FileInputStream(filename);
DataInputStream dis = new DataInputStream(fis);
CertificateFactory cf =
    CertificateFactory.getInstance("X.509");
byte[] bytes = new byte[dis.available()];
dis.readFully(bytes);
ByteArrayInputStream bais = new ByteArrayInputStream(bytes);
while (bais.available() > 0) {
   Certificate cert = cf.generateCertificate(bais);
   System.out.println(cert.toString());
}
```

Next, you parse a PKCS#7-formatted certificate reply stored in a file and extract all of the certificates from it.

```
FileInputStream fis = new FileInputStream(filename);
CertificateFactory cf =
    CertificateFactory.getInstance("X.509");
Collection c = cf.generateCertificates(fis);
Iterator i = c.iterator();
while (i.hasNext()) {
    Certificate cert = (Certificate) i.next();
    System.out.println(cert);
}
```

7.6   Standard Names

Whether in Java documentation or code, algorithms, certificates, and keystore types are referred to by specialized names. These names are not chosen randomly, but rather according to adopted standards. This section lists the names used and explains their backgrounds.

7.6.1   Message Digest Algorithms

Message digest algorithm names can be specified when generating an instance of `MessageDigest`.

- **SHA**. The Secure Hash Algorithm as defined in Secure Hash Standard, NIST FIPS 180-1

- **MD2**. The MD2 message digest algorithm as defined in RFC 1319

- **MD5**. The MD5 message digest algorithm as defined in RFC 1321

7.6.2   Key and Parameter Algorithms

Key and parameter algorithm names can be specified when generating an instance of `KeyPairGenerator`, `KeyFactory`, `AlgorithmParameterGenerator`, and `AlgorithmParameters`.

- **RSA**. The RSA encryption algorithm as defined in PKCS#1

- **DSA**. The Digital Signature Algorithm as defined in FIPS PUB 186

7.6.3 Digital Signature Algorithms

The DSA names can be specified when generating an instance of `Signature`.

- **SHA-1withDSA**. The DSA with SHA-1 signature algorithm, which uses the SHA-1 digest algorithm and DSA to create and verify DSA digital signatures as defined in FIPS PUB 186

- **MD2withRSA**. The MD2 with RSA encryption signature algorithm, which uses the MD2 digest algorithm and RSA to create and verify RSA digital signatures as defined in PKCS#1

- **MD5withRSA**. The MD5 with RSA encryption signature algorithm, which uses the MD5 digest algorithm and RSA to create and verify RSA digital signatures as defined in PKCS#1

- **SHA-1withRSA**. The signature algorithm with SHA-1 and the RSA encryption algorithm as defined in the OSI Interoperability Workshop, using the padding conventions described in PKCS#1

7.6.4 Random Number Generation Algorithms

Random number generation algorithm names can be specified when generating an instance of `SecureRandom`.

- **SHA1PRNG**. The name of the PRNG algorithm supplied by the "SUN" provider

  This implementation follows the IEEE P1363 standard (given in its Appendix G.7, "Expansion of source bits") and uses SHA-1 as the foundation of the PRNG. It computes the SHA-1 hash over a true-random seed value concatenated with a 64-bit counter, which is incremented by 1 for each operation. Of the 160-bit SHA-1 output, only 64 bits are used.

7.6.5 Certificate Types

Certificate types can be specified when generating an instance of `Certificate-Factory`.

- **X.509**. The certificate type defined in X.509

7.6.6   Keystore Types

Keystore types can be specified when generating an instance of `KeyStore`.

- **JKS**. The name of the keystore implementation provided by the "SUN" provider

- **PKCS12**. The transfer syntax for personal identity information as defined in PKCS#12

7.7   Algorithm Specifications

When implementing crypto algorithms, a provider should comply with existing standard specifications. Following are some of these specifications and their relationships with JDK implementations. In particular, for each algorithm specification, some or all of the following fields are given.

- **Name**. The name by which the algorithm is known. This is the name passed to the `getInstance` method (when requesting the algorithm) and returned by the `getAlgorithm` method to determine the name of an existing algorithm object. These methods are in the service classes `Signature`, `MessageDigest`, `KeyPairGenerator`, and `AlgorithmParameterGenerator`.

- **Type**. The type of algorithm: `Signature`, `MessageDigest`, `KeyPairGenerator`, or `ParameterGenerator`.

- **Description**. General notes about the algorithm, including any standards implemented by the algorithm, applicable patents, and so on.

- **Key Pair Algorithm** (optional). The keypair algorithm for this algorithm.

- **Key Size** (optional). Legal key sizes for a keyed algorithm or key generation algorithm.

- **Size** (optional). Legal sizes for algorithm parameter generation for an algorithm parameter generation algorithm.

- **Parameter Defaults** (optional). Default parameter values for a key generation algorithm.

- **Signature Format** (optional). The format of the signature for a `Signature` algorithm, that is, the input and output of the `verify` and `sign` methods, respectively.

7.7.1 SHA-1 Message Digest Algorithm

Name: SHA
Type: `MessageDigest`
Description: The message digest algorithm as defined in NIST's FIPS 180-1.
The output of this algorithm is a 160-bit digest.

7.7.2 MD2 Message Digest Algorithm

Name: MD2
Type: `MessageDigest`
Description: The message digest algorithm as defined in RFC 1319. The output of this algorithm is a 128-bit (16-byte) digest.

7.7.3 MD5 Message Digest Algorithm

Name: MD5
Type: `MessageDigest`
Description: The message digest algorithm as defined in RFC 1321. The output of this algorithm is a 128-bit (16-byte) digest.

7.7.4 Digital Signature Algorithm

Name: SHA-1withDSA
Type: `Signature`
Description: The signature algorithm described in NIST FIPS 186, using DSA with the SHA-1 message digest algorithm.
Key Pair Algorithm: DSA
Signature Format: An ASN.1 sequence of two `INTEGER` values r and s, in that order.

```
SEQUENCE ::= { r INTEGER, s INTEGER }
```

7.7.5 RSA-Based Signature Algorithms

Names: MD2withRSA, MD5withRSA, and SHA-1withRSA
Type: `Signature`
Description: The signature algorithms that use the MD2, MD5, and SHA-1 message digest algorithms (respectively) with RSA encryption.
Key Pair Algorithm: RSA

Signature Format: A DER-encoded PKCS#1 block. The data encrypted is the digest of the data signed.

7.7.6   DSA KeyPair Generation Algorithm

Name: DSA

Type: `KeyPairGenerator`

Description: The key pair generation algorithm described in NIST FIPS 186 for DSA.

Key Size: The length, in bits, of the modulus p. This must range from 512 to 1,024 and must be a multiple of 64. The default key size is 1,024.

Parameter Defaults: The following default parameter values are used for key-sizes of 512, 768, and 1,024 bits. The use of the parameter named `counter` is explained in the FIPS document.

For 512-bit key parameters:

```
SEED = b869c82b 35d70e1b 1ff91b28 e37a62ec dc34409b

counter = 123

p = fca682ce 8e12caba 26efccf7 110e526d b078b05e decbcd1e
    b4a208f3 ae1617ae 01f35b91 a47e6df6 3413c5e1 2ed0899b
    cd132acd 50d99151 bdc43ee7 37592e17

q = 962eddcc 369cba8e bb260ee6 b6a126d9 346e38c5

g = 678471b2 7a9cf44e e91a49c5 147db1a9 aaf244f0 5a434d64
    86931d2d 14271b9e 35030b71 fd73da17 9069b32e 2935630e
    1c206235 4d0da20a 6c416e50 be794ca4
```

For 768-bit key parameters:

```
SEED = 77d0f8c4 dad15eb8 c4f2f8d6 726cefd9 6d5bb399

counter = 263

p = e9e64259 9d355f37 c97ffd35 67120b8e 25c9cd43 e927b3a9
    670fbec5 d8901419 22d2c3b3 ad248009 3799869d 1e846aab
    49fab0ad 26d2ce6a 22219d47 0bce7d77 7d4a21fb e9c270b5
    7f607002 f3cef839 3694cf45 ee3688c1 1a8c56ab 127a3daf

q = 9cdbd84c 9f1ac2f3 8d0f80f4 2ab952e7 338bf511

g = 30470ad5 a005fb14 ce2d9dcd 87e38bc7 d1b1c5fa cbaecbe9
    5f190aa7 a31d23c4 dbbcbe06 17454440 1a5b2c02 0965d8c2
    bd2171d3 66844577 1f74ba08 4d2029d8 3c1c1585 47f3a9f1
    a2715be2 3d51ae4d 3e5a1f6a 7064f316 933a346d 3f529252
```

For 1,024-bit key parameters:

```
SEED = 8d515589 4229d5e6 89ee01e6 018a237e 2cae64cd

counter = 92

p = fd7f5381 1d751229 52df4a9c 2eece4e7 f611b752 3cef4400
    c31e3f80 b6512669 455d4022 51fb593d 8d58fabf c5f5ba30
    f6cb9b55 6cd7813b 801d346f f26660b7 6b9950a5 a49f9fe8
    047b1022 c24fbba9 d7feb7c6 1bf83b57 e7c6a8a6 150f04fb
    83f6d3c5 1ec30235 54135a16 9132f675 f3ae2b61 d72aeff2
    2203199d d14801c7

q = 9760508f 15230bcc b292b982 a2eb840b f0581cf5

g = f7e1a085 d69b3dde cbbcab5c 36b857b9 7994afbb fa3aea82
    f9574c0b 3d078267 5159578e bad4594f e6710710 8180b449
    167123e8 4c281613 b7cf0932 8cc8a6e1 3c167a8b 547c8d28
    e0a3aele 2bb3a675 916ea37f 0bfa2135 62f1fb62 7a01243b
    cca4f1be a8519089 a883dfe1 5ae59f06 928b665e 807b5525
    64014c3b fecf492a
```

7.7.7   RSA KeyPair Generation Algorithm

Name: RSA
Type: `KeyPairGenerator`
Description: The key pair generation algorithm described in PKCS#1.
Key Size: Any integer that is a multiple of 8, greater than or equal to 512.

7.7.8   DSA Parameter Generation Algorithm

Name: DSA
Type: `ParameterGenerator`
Description: The parameter generation algorithm described in NIST FIPS 186 for DSA.

Size: The length, in bits, of the modulus p. This must range from 512 to 1,024 and must be a multiple of 64. The default size is 1,024.

CHAPTER 8

Future Directions

*All progress is precarious, and the solution of one problem
brings us face to face with another problem.*
—Martin Luther King, Jr.

With the release of JDK 1.2 and JCE 1.2, Java security has entered an exciting new phase. This is not the beginning of the end, but rather the end of the beginning, as much remains to be done. This chapter touches on some future directions anticipated for Java security technology.

8.1   Security Management

It is accepted wisdom that anything hard to use does not get used in practice. Security is no exception. In JDK 1.2, the Java security development team at Sun Microsystems tried to achieve the goal of simplicity. We designed only the minimum APIs necessary to do a particular job. We distributed functionalities among the classes in such a way that each class is logically self-contained and easy to understand. And we chose simple class and method names while maintaining their accuracy and clarity.

Another feature important to making the security architecture useful in the real world is security management. As said in earlier chapters, JDK itself is not an end-user product, so it might not be the best place to bundle security management software. Instead, system vendors and application builders can create and present the right interfaces (including GUIs) to their respective customers.

Nevertheless, Java Plug-In, a browser plug-in with a Java runtime environment, is increasingly being used directly by end users to upgrade the JVM in their browsers. As a result, the Java Plug-In, as a product directly derived from JDK, can be improved with more management features. For example, it can use the same certificate database that is already present in the browsers, thus eliminating the need to maintain a separate certificate database for it.

Also, when the plug-in encounters previously unknown applets and applications on the Internet, it needs a solution to give the applets their needed privileges in order to run them as they are designed. One approach to this deployment issue is to design a way for the developer to specify the required permissions and a way to help the browser user to understand the meaning and implications of granting those permissions.[1]

Security management is not just for end users. Application developers often do not want to become experts in security simply to write secure applications. They would benefit, for example, from interfaces that they can call to obtain security services without having to know the specifics, such as encryption algorithms, key sizes, and protocol types. Such simple security APIs should greatly increase productivity, as well as the security quality of the resulting applications.

8.2   JDK Feature Enhancement

Several security features, according to customer feedback, are worth investigating for a future version of the JDK. One is resource consumption management. This is relatively easy to implement in some cases, for example when limiting the number of windows an application can pop up at any one time, but a lot more difficult in other cases, for example when limiting memory, CPU, or file system usage in real time and with good performance.

Another feature is the design of class loaders. These are still very delicate in terms of security implications; the current way the `ClassLoader` classes are specified can still be improved. Applets and applications can create class loaders only if the system security policy is configured to allow this to happen, with the only exception of `URLClassLoader`. Such a severe restriction might impede the development of certain applications. Much research is needed on this topic.

A third feature is instant revocation, whereby a granted privilege can be revoked immediately after a change in security policy. Currently, the new policy becomes effective only after its content is refreshed and only for newly started applications or applets. To implement instant revocation might require the privilege system to register itself (as listeners) with the `Policy` object (and perhaps each `Permission` object, if permissions may change their content dynamically). The `Policy` object then would promise to notify the system if it changed its security policy.

---

[1]   For a not-so-good analogy for the specification of required permissions, consider that when you buy shrink-wrapped software, the back of the box typically says things such as "16MB RAM required, 32MB RAM recommended."

Another feature related to security policy is the composition of security policies. Currently, each security manager enforces a particular type of security policy. To enforce a new policy, which might be some combination of two existing policies, you currently need to implement a new `SecurityManager`. Ideally, security policies could be composed without a total rewrite of existing security manager classes.

JDK 1.2 introduced a conservative and robust access control algorithm that can prevent some programming mistakes from turning into security holes. Additional techniques that further this effort are available. For example, recall that the `doPrivileged` primitive in a sense "enables" all permissions granted to a piece of code. In some cases, an application might want to enable only some of its granted permissions. This selective enabling further reduces the security impact of making a programming mistake. We can contemplate enriching the primitive so that it takes an additional parameter, possibly of type `Permission`, `Permission-Collection`, or `Permissions`, that specifies the permissions to be enabled.

Another way to reduce security liabilities is to subdivide the system domain. For convenience, the system domain can be thought of as a single, large collection of all system code. For better protection, however, system code should be run in multiple system domains, where each domain protects a particular type of resource and is given a special set of rights. For example, if file system code and network system code run in separate domains, with the former having no rights to the networking resources and the latter having no rights to the file system resources, the risks and consequences of an error or security flaw in one system domain is more likely to be confined within its boundary.

Moreover, protection domains currently are created transparently as a result of class loading. Providing explicit primitives to create a new domain might be useful. Often, a domain supports inheritance in that a subdomain automatically inherits the parent domain's security attributes, except in certain cases where the parent further restricts or expands the subdomain explicitly.

Finally, a way to consistently handle nonclass content is needed. When applets or applications are run with signed content (classes and other resources), the JAR and `Manifest` specifications on code signing allow a very flexible format. The classes within the same archive can be unsigned, signed with one key, or signed with multiple keys. Other resources within the archive, such as audio clips and graphic images, can also be signed or unsigned. However, it is unclear whether images and audio clips should be required to be signed with the same key if any class in the archive is signed. If images and audio files are signed with different keys, can they be placed in the same `appletviewer` (or browser page) or should they be sent to different viewers? Such questions are not easy to answer. Any response requires consistency across platforms and products in order to be most effective. The current approach is to process all images and audio clips whether or not they are signed. This temporary solution should be improved once a consensus is reached.

8.3   Java Authentication and Authorization Service

When Java technology is used to construct not just a single desktop but a full-fledged distributed system, a whole new range of distributed systems security issues (such as those mentioned in Chapter 1) must be tackled. For example, additional mechanisms are needed to make RMI secure in the presence of hostile network attacks. For Jini, Sun's recently launched connection technology based on Java that enables digital devices to simply connect together, service registration and location must be securely managed if the environment contains coexisting but potentially mutually hostile parties. A full set of higher-level services must be secured, such as transactions for e-commerce. In addition, many lower-level security protocols can be leveraged, such as the network security protocols Kerberos and IPv6. This playing field is too large to speculate about in this short section, but a critical foundation for all of these issues is a facility to authenticate users and to use this information to perform access control.

Recall that JDK 1.2 uses a security policy to decide the granting of individual access permissions to running code and that the decision depends on the code's characteristics, for example where the code is coming from and whether it is digitally signed and if so by whom. Such a code-centric style of access control is unusual. Traditional security measures, most commonly found in sophisticated operating systems, are user-centric, in that they apply control on the basis of who is running an application and not on which application is running. Code-centric access control is justified largely because a user surfing the Web and running executable content it has encountered (for example, mobile code written in Java) retains essentially a constant identity. On the other hand, the user might trust one piece of mobile code more than others and would like to run this code with more privileges. Thus it is natural to control the security of mobile code in a code-centric style.

Nevertheless, Java is becoming widely used in a multiuser environment. For example, a public Internet terminal, an enterprise application (such as the salary tool at Sun Microsystems), or a server handling numerous rental Palm Pilot units all must deal with different users, either concurrently or sequentially, and must grant these users different privileges based on their identities.

The Java Authentication and Authorization Service (JAAS) is designed to provide a standard programming interface for authenticating users and for assigning privileges.[2] Together with JDK 1.2, an application can provide code-centric access control, user-centric access control, or a combination of both. JAAS also

---

[2] The JAAS specification outlined here is under public design review, so the descriptions are
    subject to change.

lays the groundwork to support a general mechanism for cross-protection domain authorization and the "running-on-behalf-of" style delegation.

Authentication has been a topic of security research for decades. However, the Java environment presents unique challenges. The design of JAAS was motivated by the following requirements.

- ◆ **Extensibility**. A need exists for a small but well-grounded set of Java programming interfaces for authentication and authorization that can easily be extended.

- ◆ **Plugability**. Different systems can easily incorporate their new or existing authentication capabilities into the JAAS framework.

- ◆ **Compatibility**. The code-based access control architecture, introduced in JDK 1.2, and the new user-based access control mechanism in JAAS can coexist independently and can also be seamlessly combined to implement sophisticated security policies.

Several existing standards support authentication, including the Generic Security Services Application Programmer's Interface (GSS-API) and Simple Authentication and Security Layer Application Programmer's Interface (SASL). SASL represents a framework that provides authentication support for connection-based protocols. Thus it caters to applications that perform network authentication. Like JAAS, SASL also has a modular architecture. GSS mechanisms such as Kerberos or the Simple Public Key Mechanism (SPKM) may be plugged in under the SASL framework. JAAS, on the other hand, also provides support for authentication in a standalone nonconnection-oriented environment. Thus JAAS and SASL/GSS complement each other to provide both local and network-based support for authentication.

One scenario in which these architectures might coexist involves environments that rely on Kerberos (and possibly other services) for authentication. JAAS login modules could be plugged under the login application to authenticate the user, when initially logging in, to both the underlying operating system as well as to Kerberos (to obtain the user's Kerberos Ticket Granting ticket). By installing a Kerberos login module, the user would not have to perform additional steps, such as execute the command `kinit` at a later time to obtain the ticket. When the user executes client applications that are attempting to authenticate across the network to certain servers that use the Kerberos protocol, those applications could then use SASL, which would presumably have the appropriate Kerberos mechanism plugged in to perform the actual authentication.

8.3.1   Subjects and Principals

Users often depend on computing services to assist them in performing work. To identify its users, a computing service typically relies on usernames. However, users might not have the same name for each service and in fact might even have a different name for each individual service. Furthermore, a service might be a user of other services and subsequently might also have multiple names. JAAS uses the term *subject* to refer to any user of a computing service. Both users and computing services, therefore, represent subjects. The term *principal* represents a name associated with a subject. Since subjects may have multiple names (potentially one for each service with which it interacts), a subject essentially consists of a collection of principals [35, 41].

Principals become associated with a subject only if that subject successfully authenticates to a service. Authentication represents the process by which one verifies the identity of another and must be performed in a secure fashion; otherwise, a perpetrator might impersonate others to gain unrestricted access to a system. Authentication typically involves the subject's demonstrating some form of evidence to prove its identity. Such evidence might be information only the subject would likely know (for example, a password or PIN) or have (for example, a fingerprint or voice pattern).

When a subject attempts to authenticate to a service, it typically provides the proof of its identity along with its name. If the authentication attempt succeeds, the service associates a service-specific principal, using the given name, with the subject. Applications and services can then always determine the identity of the subject simply by referencing the relevant principal associated with that subject.

8.3.2   Credentials

Some services might want to associate other security-related attributes and data with a subject in addition to principal information. JAAS calls such generic security-related attributes *credentials*. A credential might contain information that can be used to authenticate the subject to additional services in the future. A Kerberos ticket [60] represents such a credential. Credentials might also contain or reference data that simply enables the subject to perform certain activities. Cryptographic keys, for example, represent credentials that enable the subject to sign or encrypt data.

Although Kerberos tickets and cryptographic keys exemplify common types of credentials, credentials can represent a wider range of security-related data. Applications running on behalf of users must coordinate with the services upon which they depend so as to agree on the kinds of credentials that are needed and that can be understood or recognized during their interactions. Thus, while some credentials might be standard or well recognized, others might be application- and service-specific. In addition, credential implementations do not necessarily have to contain the actual security-related data; they might simply reference that data. This occurs when the data must physically reside on a separate server or hardware device (for example, private keys on a smart card).

A subject must successfully authenticate to a service to obtain credentials. Upon successful authentication, the service creates the appropriate credential and associates it with the subject. Once a subject has been populated with credentials, applications running on behalf of the subject may (with the proper permissions) then access and use those credentials. JAAS does not impose any restrictions regarding credential delegation to third parties. Rather, it either allows each credential implementation to specify its own delegation protocol (as Kerberos does) or leaves delegation decisions up to the applications.

8.3.3 Pluggable and Stacked Authentication

Conventional services require a subject to provide its name and some form of proof of its identity to authenticate. Depending on the security parameters of the particular service, different kinds of proof may be required. The JAAS authentication framework is based on PAM [71] and thus supports an architecture that allows system administrators to plug in the appropriate authentication services to meet security requirements. The architecture also enables applications to remain independent of the underlying authentication services. Hence, as new authentication services become available or as current services are updated, system administrators can easily plug them in without having to modify or recompile existing applications. The framework is depicted in Figure 8.1.

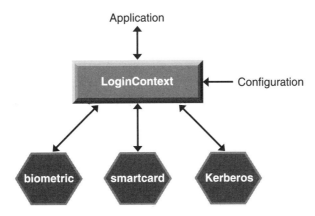

Figure 8.1   Pluggable authentication.

When attempting to authenticate a subject, an application calls into the authentication framework, which JAAS defines as a *login context*. The login context consults a configuration, which determines the authentication service, or *login module*, which gets plugged in under that application. Because the application interfaces only with the login context, it remains completely independent of the configured login module.

Each login module authenticates subjects uniquely. For example, a conventional password-based login module prompts for a username and verifies a password; a smart card login module informs the subject to insert its card into the card reader and verifies a PIN; and a biometric login module prompts for a username and verifies the subject's fingerprint. Depending on the security requirements of the application, a system administrator configures the appropriate login module. In fact, system administrators may also plug multiple login modules under an application. This type of stacked configuration is depicted in Figure 8.2.

A subject authenticates to the login modules in the order specified by the configuration. In general, regardless of whether a login module fails, the subject continues to authenticate to the ensuing login modules on the stack. This helps hide the source of failure from potential attackers. Additional parameters within the configuration allow for exceptions to this rule and also determine which login modules must succeed for the overall authentication to succeed. Details on the login configuration specifics appear on page 238.

The login context reports a successful authentication status back to the calling application only if all of the necessary login modules (as determined by the con-

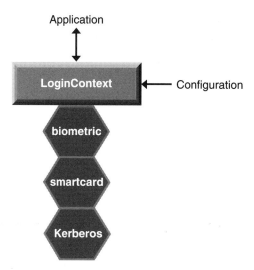

Figure 8.2   Stacked authentication.

figuration) succeed. To guarantee this, the login context performs the authentication steps in two phases. Both phases must complete successfully for the login context to return an overall authentication status noting success.

1. The login context invokes each configured login module and instructs it to verify the identity of the subject only. If all of the necessary login modules successfully pass this phase, the login context then enters the second phase.

2. The login context invokes each configured login module again, instructing it to formally commit the authentication process. During this phase, each login module associates any relevant principals, which hold the authenticated usernames, and credentials with the subject.

Thus, once the overall authentication process has completed, the calling application can traverse through a subject's collection of principals to obtain its various identities and can traverse through a subject's credentials to access supplementary data. Some login modules might associate only credentials (and not principals) with the subject. A smart card module, for example, might authenticate the subject by verifying a provided PIN and upon success simply associate with the subject a credential referencing a cryptographic key on the card. The smart card module in this case does not associate a principal with the subject.

If either the first or second phase fails, the login context invokes each configured login module and instructs them to abort the entire authentication attempt. Each login module then cleans up any relevant state it had associated with the authentication attempt.

During this two-phase process, if a particular login module fails it does not sleep and it does not attempt to retry the authentication. Otherwise, the subject attempting the authentication can detect which login module failed. The calling application owns the responsibility of performing tasks such as retry and may elect to perform them after each complete round (two phases) of authentication.

During the authentication process, login modules have the choice and ability to share information with each other; whether one does depends on its security requirements. One motivation for sharing information is to help achieve single sign-on. For example, stacked login modules may share username and password information, thereby enabling users to enter that information only once but still get authenticated to multiple services. In the case of subjects' having different usernames and passwords for each service, login modules may also coordinate with each other to map such information into the relevant service-specific information. Thus, although the subject enters only a single username and password, that information gets mapped into the respective service-specific usernames and passwords, thereby enabling the subject to again authenticate to multiple services with relative ease.

Configuration

The JAAS login configuration specifies the login modules to be plugged in under a particular application. The configuration syntax is based on that defined by PAM. Following is an example.

```
Login {
    com.sun.security.auth.SampleLoginModule REQUIRED debug=true;
    com.sun.security.auth.SolarisLoginModule REQUIRED;
}
```

Each entry in the configuration is indexed via an application name, `Login` in this example, and contains a list of login modules configured for that application. Authentication proceeds down the list in the exact order listed, with the flag value `REQUIRED` controlling the overall behavior.

Following is a description of the valid flag values.

`REQUIRED`. The login module is required to succeed. Regardless of whether it succeeds or fails, however, authentication still proceeds down the login module list. It must continue, even when faced with failure, because aborting at that point would give potential attackers useful information, such as which module failed and why.

`REQUISITE`. The login module is required to succeed. If it succeeds, authentication continues down the login module list. If it fails, control immediately returns to the application (authentication does not proceed down the login module list).

`SUFFICIENT`. The login module is not required to succeed. If it does succeed, control immediately returns to the application (authentication does not proceed down the login module list). If it fails, authentication continues down the login module list.

`OPTIONAL`. The login module is not required to succeed. If it succeeds or fails, authentication still proceeds down the login module list.

The overall authentication succeeds only if all `REQUIRED` and `REQUISITE` login modules succeed. If no `REQUIRED` or `REQUISITE` login modules are configured for an application, then at least one `SUFFICIENT` or `OPTIONAL` login module must succeed. You can also use a `LoginModule` to define options to support debugging/testing capabilities. To do this, use the key-value pair `debug=true`.

8.3.4 Callbacks

By using the login context, applications remain independent from underlying login modules. However, login modules may be plugged under any type of application. Regardless of the type of application a login module gets plugged under, it must be able to garner information from and display information to subjects via the calling application. For example, a login module that requires username and password information needs the ability to prompt the subject for such information without knowing whether the calling application has a GUI.

The login context solves this problem by allowing applications to specify a *callback* that underlying login modules may use to interact with subjects. Applications provide a callback implementation to the login context, which passes it directly to each login module. Login modules may then invoke the callback to garner or display the relevant information. The callback, implemented by the application, inherently knows whether to construct a graphical window or to simply use a standard output stream. The callback design and usage is depicted in Figure 8.3.

8.3.5 Access Control

The current JDK 1.2 `SecurityManager` class implementation enforces code source-based access controls, controls based on where code came from and who signed it. The JAAS `SecurityManager` implementation augments this security manager with subject-based access controls, controls based on who runs code. Both the code source-based checks and subject-based checks must pass in order for the JAAS `SecurityManager` to grant access to sensitive resources.

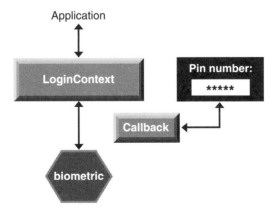

Figure 8.3   Callback design and usage.

Permission Granting

Authentication serves as the basis for authorization [41]. Specifically, once an application knows the exact identity of a subject, it can then specify exactly what set of operations that subject may perform. Since a subject simply represents a nameless container holding relevant information for a user, while principals represent authenticated identities for that subject, the set of permissions granted to a subject depends on the principals associated with that subject and not on the subject itself. In other words, permissions are granted to a subject based on its authenticated principals [41]. The exact set of permissions granted can be configured within an external access control policy.

The policy syntax that JAAS uses is a simple extension of the JDK 1.2 policy syntax specified for code source-based access control, with the addition of a principal entry to the grant statement. Thus the code source-based policy grants permissions to code sources (a URL, together with a signer alias), whereas the JAAS policy grants permissions to principals (identified by the principal classname and the name of the principal itself).

```
grant Principal com.sun.security.auth.SolarisPrincipal "gong" {
    permission java.lang.RuntimePermission "queuePrintJob";
    permission java.io.FilePermission "/home/gong", "read, write";
}
```

Here, any subject with an associated `SolarisPrincipal` principal that has the name "gong" is granted permission to queue print jobs, as well as permission to read and write files from "gong's" home directory.

Enforcing User-Centric Security Policies

In JAAS, applications associate subjects with a thread of operation in order to have access controls enforced on that subject. When that operation executes, the JAAS `SecurityManager` retrieves the associated subject and checks that it has been granted the necessary permissions before permitting sensitive operations to occur and before permitting access to sensitive resources. If the subject has not been granted sufficient permissions, `SecurityManager` throws a `Security-Exception`.

While executing, operations may invoke other operations, thereby creating a sequence of nested operations. When this occurs, each nested operation gets pushed onto a stack. When the JAAS `SecurityManager` must make an access control decision, it investigates the stack and retrieves all of the subjects associated with the operations on the stack. It checks and ensures that every subject on the stack is granted the necessary permissions. If one or more subjects do not have the necessary permissions, `SecurityManager` throws a `SecurityException`. As a result, the overall permissions of the entire stack effectively equals the intersection of permissions granted to the individual subjects on the stack.

In some cases, an operation and associated subject might want to exercise their own permissions and not be dependent, for overall access to be granted, on previous operations on the stack also having the same permissions. This occurs when an executing operation, with an associated subject, queries another operation, with a different associated subject, to perform a certain task on its behalf. While the queried operation certainly has the necessary permissions to perform the requested task, the initial operation typically does not. With the previously described access control model, access would be denied. To overcome this problem, the queried operation, if it has permission, may declare itself privileged. When privileged, the operation does not require its callers or requestors to have been granted the same permissions as itself in order for overall access to a resource to be granted. Only the operation itself, along with its associated subject, needs to have the necessary permission.

Note that if a privileged operation subsequently invokes a nonprivileged operation, then access control decisions again become based on the intersection of permissions granted to both subjects associated with the privileged, and ensuing nonprivileged, operations. The privileged operation in JAAS is modeled after the `doPrivileged` interface in JDK 1.2.

8.3.6 JAAS Implementation

The JAAS implementation consists of approximately 25 classes and interfaces arranged within three packages.

- `javax.security.auth`

    This package contains the fundamental classes required by the JAAS framework, including the `Subject` class and `Credential` interface. Although principals are also a fundamental concept, they do not have a corresponding class or interface in JAAS. Rather, JAAS uses the principal interface already provided by JDK, `java.security.Principal`. The package also includes the basic classes required for authorization. Specifically, it includes a `Security-Manager` class and an access control `Policy` class.

- `javax.security.auth.login`

    This package contains classes that support pluggable authentication. It includes a `LoginContext` class, `LoginModule` interface, `login Configuration` class, and `LoginException` class (to report authentication failures).

♦ `javax.security.auth.callback`

This package contains different callback classes that login modules may use to interact with subjects. This includes a `CallbackHandler` class and `Callback` interface and several callback implementations, such as `NameCallback`, `PasswordCallback`, `TextInputCallback`, and `TextOutputCallback`.

Also included among the packages, but not described here, are various `Permission` classes for proper security checking and `Exception` classes for proper error handling.

8.4 Conclusion

In this book, I took you on a tour inside the Java security architecture. The tour included the various security features that the Java platform provides at multiple layers—at the language level, within the JVM, and throughout core libraries and extensions—as well as the customizations done by applications and applets. You viewed such issues as type safety, object-level security, security policies, fine-grained access control, and security deployment issues. And you visited Java cryptography architecture, which includes support for digital signatures and certificates in JDK and the separately released JCE (Java Cryptography Extension).

The development of the JDK has progressed from the original JDK 1.0, to JDK 1.1, to JDK 1.2. Somewhat parallel to this, separate security extensions also have come into being—first JCE and then JAAS. And the road continues forward.

A few major Java technology trends underlie this development. Understanding these help to see where Java security is headed.

First is that the industrial adoption of Java technology has moved from focusing exclusively on the client side to being deployed also on the server side. Coupled with this new focus is a growing need to handle security issues that are commonplace within an enterprise environment, For example, treating one JVM as owned by a single user is no longer sufficient. Instead, a server application running inside one JVM can represent multiple users. As another example, mission-critical applications must tolerate failure and survive denial-of-service attacks. Thus resource control inside JVMs is becoming more important. As a result, the future holds extensive improvement in security for this application space, with JCE and JAAS being just the start.

The second trend is that the world is getting smaller. Java technology is being deployed on information and Internet appliances such as smart cards, personal digital assistants (PDAs), cell phones, pagers, Internet-capable screen phones, and TV set-top boxes. These devices have unique requirements compared with the typical desktop system to which JDK is targeted. Being smallish in size and memory and relatively underpowered, they often adopt specialized Java platforms, such as PersonalJava and EmbeddedJava. Further, the targeted application environment for these devices have stronger, not weaker, security requirements. For example, a cell phone manufacturer might allow a phone service provider company, as the original equipment manufacturer (OEM) of the phones, to add vendor-specific features, while not wanting any party to be able to change the kernel of the phone.

The situation can be more complicated when, for example, third parties such as a hotel chain start to partner with the phone company to offer loyalty programs. When a new software feature upgrade is dynamically downloaded from the hotel chain to the phone over a wireless connection, it is crucial to ensure the authenticity of the upgrade, the integrity of the wireless connection, and secure isolation between the upgrade (and its sibling application software) and those other software already installed.

To ensure that platforms such as PersonalJava and EmbeddedJava have strong security, one major challenge is to design security features that fit into a small footprint. For example, to meet customer security requirements on set-top boxes and others, the fine-grained access control architecture designed for JDK 1.2 has been ported to PersonalJava.[3] It turns out that the entire security package, including the digital signature infrastructure (and particularly support for digital certificates), is too big; for example, X.509 was obviously not designed for devices currently on the mass market that have small memories. Nevertheless, we managed to achieve the goals because in JDK 1.2 the access control mechanism is related to the signature and certificate infrastructure via a single interface, `java.security.cert.Certificate`. There are no other API dependencies between the two mechanisms. As a result, the crypto features can be made optional, while the access control mechanism can be enhanced to work normally if the crypto features are available and to treat all code as unsigned if they are not.

A related trend is that the world is becoming more connected. This increases the need for secure communication, secure mobile and disconnected operations, secure on-line transactions, and so on.

The last trend is that the hot points surrounding Java technology are no longer just platform and infrastructure issues. More and more, applications coming to market bring new kinds of security design issues that include security user interface and policy management. Traditionally, security technology has focused more on platforms (such as operating systems and networking protocols) and less on

---

[3] A not-yet-publicly-available document describes this porting in more detail. L. Gong, PersonalJava Security Architecture, Draft version 0.1, April 6, 1998.

applications (most of which run as fully trusted). Thus substantial work still remains in this area.

It has taken thirty or so years for computer security to come of age and become a mainstream technology, but still there is a lot to do and many challenges and opportunities to meet. We live in interesting times.

Bibliography

[1] *The Java Extensions Framework*. JDK 1.2 documentation, Sun Microsystems, Inc., 1998. `http://java.sun.com/products/jdk/1.2/docs/guide/extensions`.

[2] K. Arnold and J. Gosling. *The Java Programming Language*, Second Edition. Addison-Wesley, Reading, Mass., 1998.

[3] D. E. Bell and L. J. LaPadula. Secure Computer Systems: A Mathematical Model. *Journal of Computer Security*, 4(2–3):239–263, 1996. A modern reprint of the same titled technical report, ESD-TR-73-278, Vol. 2, The MITRE Corporation, Bedford, Mass., 1973.

[4] S. Bellovin and M. Merritt. Encrypted Key Exchange: Password-Based Protocols Secure Against Dictionary Attacks. *Proceedings of the IEEE Symposium on Research in Security and Privacy*, 72–84, Oakland, Calif., May 1992.

[5] S. Bellovin and M. Merritt. Augmented Encrypted Key Exchange: A Password-Based Protocol Secure Against Dictionary Attacks and Password File Compromise. *Proceedings of the 1st ACM Conference on Computer and Communications Security*, 244–50, Fairfax, Va., November 1993.

[6] S. M. Bellovin and W. R. Cheswick. Network Firewalls. *IEEE Communications*, 50–57, September 1994.

[7] B. N. Bershad, S. Savage, P. Pardyak, E. G. Sirer, M. Fiuchynski, D. Becker, S. Eggers, and C. Chambers. Extensibility, Safety, and Performance in the SPIN Operating System. *Proceedings of the 15th ACM Symposium on Operating Systems Principles*, 251–266, Copper Mountain Resort, Colo., December 1995. Published as *ACM Operating System Review* 29(5):251–266, December 1995.

[8] D. F. C. Brewer and M. J. Nash. The Chinese Wall Security Policy. *Proceedings of the IEEE Symposium on Security and Privacy*, 206–214, Oakland, Calif., April 1989.

[9] M. Burrows, M. Abadi, and R. M. Needham. A Logic for Authentication. *ACM Transactions on Computer Systems*, 8(1):18–36, February 1990.

[10] J. S. Chase, H. M. Levy, M. J. Feeley, and E. D. Lazowska. Sharing and Protection in a Single-Address-Space Operating System. *ACM Transactions on Computer Systems*, 12(4):271–307, November 1994.

[11] D. D. Clark and D. R. Wilson. A Comparison of Commercial and Military Computer Security Policies. *Proceedings of the IEEE Symposium on Security and Privacy*, 184–194, Oakland, Calif., April 1987.

[12] F. Cristian. Understanding Fault-Tolerant Distributed Systems. *Communications of the ACM*, 34(2):57–78, February 1991.

[13] I. B. Damgšard. Design Principles for Hash Functions. *Advances in Cryptology*: Proceedings of Crypto '89, Vol. 435 of Lecture Notes in Computer Science, 416–427. Springer-Verlag, New York, October 1989.

[14] W. Diffie and M. E. Hellman. New Directions in Cryptography. *IEEE Transactions on Information Theory*, IT–22(6):644–65, November 1976.

[15] D. Dolev and A. C. Yao. On the Security of Public Key Protocols. *IEEE Transactions on Information Theory*, IT–29(2):198–208, March 1983.

[16] E. Gamma, R. Helm, R. Johnson, and J. Vlissides. *Design Patterns*. Addison-Wesley, Reading, Mass., 1995.

[17] M. Gasser. *Building a Secure Computer System*. Van Nostrand Reinhold Co., New York, 1988.

[18] J. A. Goguen and J. Meseguer. Security Policies and Security Models. *Proceedings of the IEEE Symposium on Security and Privacy*, 11–20, Oakland, Calif., April 1982.

[19] J. A. Goguen and J. Meseguer. Unwinding and Inference Control. *Proceedings of the IEEE Symposium on Security and Privacy*, Oakland, Calif., April 1984.

[20] T. C. Goldstein. The Gateway Security Model in the Java Electronic Commerce Framework. *Proceedings of Financial Cryptography 97*, 291–304, Anguilla, British Virgin Island, February 1997.

[21] L. Gong, T. M. A. Lomas, R. M. Needham, and J. H. Saltzer. Protecting Poorly Chosen Secrets from Guessing Attacks. *IEEE Journal on Selected Areas in Communications*, 11(5):648–656, June 1993.

[22] L. Gong. Collisionful Keyed Hash Functions with Selectable Collisions. *Information Processing Letters*, 55(3):167–170, August 1995.

[23] L. Gong. Java Security: Present and Near Future. *IEEE Micro*, 17(3):14–19, May/June 1997.

[24] L. Gong, P. Lincoln, and J. Rushby. Byzantine Agreement with Authentication: Observations and Applications in Tolerating Hybrid Faults. *Proceedings of the 5th IFIP Working Conference on Dependable Computing for Critical Applications,* 79–90, Urbana-Champaign, Ill., September 1995.

[25] L. Gong, M. Mueller, H. Prafullchandra, and R. Schemers. Going Beyond the Sandbox: An Overview of the New Security Architecture in the Java Development Kit 1.2. *Proceedings of the USENIX Symposium on Internet Technologies and Systems*, 103–112, Monterey, Calif., December 1997.

[26] L. Gong, R. Needham, and R. Yahalom. Reasoning about Belief in Cryptographic Protocols. *Proceedings of the IEEE Symposium on Research in Security and Privacy*, 234–248, Oakland, Calif., May 1990.

[27] L. Gong and X. Qian. Computational Issues of Secure Interoperation. *IEEE Transactions on Software Engineering*, 22(1):43–52, January 1996.

[28] L. Gong and R. Schemers. Implementing Protection Domains in the Java Development Kit 1.2. *Proceedings of the Internet Society Symposium on Network and Distributed System Security*, 125–134, San Diego, Calif., March 1998.

[29] L. Gong. New Security Architectural Directions for Java (Extended Abstract). *Proceedings of IEEE COMPCON*, 97–102, San Jose, Calif., February 1997.

[30] J. Gosling, Bill Joy, and Guy Steele. *The Java Language Specification*. Addison-Wesley, Reading, Mass., August 1996.

[31] N. Haller, C. Metz, P. Nesser, and M. Straw. A One-Time Password System. Request for Comments (RFC) 2289, Internet Engineering Task Force, February 1998.

[32] M. A. Harrison, W. L. Ruzzo, and J. D. Ullman. Protection in Operating Systems. *Communications of the ACM*, 19(8):461–471, August 1976.

[33] C. Hawblitzel, C-C Chang, G. Czajkowski, D. Hu, and T. von Eicken. Implementing Multiple Protection Domains in Java. *Proceedings of the USENIX Annual Technical Conference*, New Orleans, La., June 1998.

[34] M. P. Herlihy and J. D. Tygar. How to Make Replicated Data Secure. Advances in Cryptology. *Proceedings of Crypto '87*, Vol. 293 of Lecture Notes in Computer Science, 379–391. Springer-Verlag, New York, 1987.

[35] R. Housley, W. Ford, T. Polk, and D. Solo. Internet X.509 Public Key Infrastructure Certificate and CRL Profile. Request for Comments (RFC) 2459, Internet Engineering Task Force, January 1999.

[36] A. K. Jones. *Protection in Programmed Systems*. Ph.D. dissertation, Carnegie-Mellon University, Pittsburgh, Penn., June 1973.

[37] D. E. Knuth. *The Art of Computer Programming, Vol. 2: Seminumerical Algorithms*, Revised Edition. Addison-Wesley, Reading, Mass., 1969.

[38] D. E. Knuth. *The Art of Computer Programming, Vol. 3: Searching and Sorting*. Addison-Wesley, Reading, Mass., 1973.

[39] A. G. Konheim. *Cryptography: A Primer*. John Wiley & Sons, Inc., New York, 1981.

[40] L. Lamport. Password Authentication with Insecure Communication. *Communications of the ACM*, 24(11):770–772, November 1981.

[41] B. Lampson, M. Abadi, M. Burrows, and E. Wobber. Authentication in Distributed Systems: Theory and Practice. *ACM Transactions on Computer Systems*, 10(4):265–310, November 1992.

[42] B. W. Lampson. Protection. *Proceedings of the 5th Princeton Symposium on Information Sciences and Systems*, Princeton University, March 1971. Reprinted in *ACM Operating Systems Review*, 8(1):18–24, January 1974.

[43] B. W. Lampson. A Note on the Confinement Problem. *Communications of the ACM*, 16(10):613–615, October 1973.

[44] C. E. Landwehr. Formal Models for Computer Security. *ACM Computing Survey*, 13(3):247–278, September 1981.

[45] S. Liang and G. Bracha. Dynamic Class Loading in the Java Virtual Machine. *Proceedings of the ACM Conference on Object Oriented Programming Systems, Languages, and Applications*, 36–44, Vancouver, British Columbia, October 1998.

[46] T. Lindholm and F. Yellin. *The Java Virtual Machine Specification*. Addison-Wesley, Reading, Mass., 1997.

[47] T. M. A. Lomas, L. Gong, J. H. Saltzer, and R. M. Needham. Reducing Risks from Poorly Chosen Keys. *Proceedings of the 12th ACM Symposium on Operating System Principles,* Litchfield Park, Ariz. Published in *ACM Operating Systems Review*, 23(5):14–18, December 1989.

[48] D. McCullough. A Hookup Theorem for Multilevel Security. *IEEE Transactions on Software Engineering*, 16(6):563–568, June 1990.

[49] G. McGraw and E. W. Felten. *Java Security: Hostile Applets, Holes, and Antidotes*. John Wiley & Sons, New York, 1997.

[50] C. Meadows. Using Narrowing in the Analysis of Key Management Protocols. *Proceedings of the IEEE Symposium on Security and Privacy*, 138–147, Oakland, Calif., May 1989.

[51] A. J. Menezes, P. C. van Oorschot, and S. A. Vanstone. *Handbook of Applied Cryptography*. CRC Press, New York, 1997.

[52] R. C. Merkle. *Secrecy, Authentication, and Public Key Systems*. PhD thesis, Stanford University, UMI Research Press, Mich., 1982. Revised from 1979 thesis.

[53] R. C. Merkle. A Fast Software One-Way Hash Function. *Journal of Cryptology*, 3(1):43–58, 1990.

[54] C. H. Meyer and M. Schilling. Secure Program Load with Modification Detection Code. *Proceedings of the 5th Worldwide Congress on Computer and Communication Security and Protection–SECURICOM 88*, 111–130, Paris, 1988.

[55] J. K. Millen, S. C. Clark, and S. B. Freedman. The Interrogator: Protocol Security Analysis. *IEEE Transactions on Software Engineering*, SE-13(2):274–288, February 1987.

[56] S. P. Miller, C. Neuman, J. I. Schiller, and J. H. Saltzer. Kerberos Authentication and Authorization System. Project Athena Technical Plan Section E.2.1, Massachusetts Institute of Technology, October 1988.

[57] M. Moriconi, X. Qian, R. A. Riemenschneider, and L. Gong. Secure Software Architectures. *Proceedings of the IEEE Symposium on Security and Privacy*, 84–93, Oakland, Calif., May 1997.

[58] M. Naor and M. Yung. Universal One-Way Hash Functions and Their Cryptographic Applications. *Proceedings of the 21th Annual ACM Symposium on Theory of Computing*, 33–43, Seattle, Washington, May 1989.

[59] R. M. Needham and M. D. Schroeder. Using Encryption for Authentication in Large Networks of Computers. *Communications of the ACM,* 21(12):993–999, December 1978.

[60] B. C. Neuman and T. Ts'o. Kerberos: An Authentication Service for Computer Networks. *IEEE Communications*, 32(9):33–38, September 1994.

[61] P. G. Neumann. *Computer-Related Risks*. Addison-Wesley, Reading, Mass., 1995.

[62] U.S. National Bureau of Standards. *Data Encryption Standard*, January 1977. U.S. Federal Information Processing Standards Publication, FIPS PUB 46.

[63] U.S. General Accounting Office. Information Security: Computer Attacks at Department of Defense Pose Increasing Risks. Technical Report GAO/AIMD-96-84, Washington, D. C., May 1996.

[64] M. O. Rabin. Fingerprinting by Random Polynomials. Technical Report TR-15-81, Center for Research in Computing Technology, Harvard University, Cambridge, MA, 1981.

[65] M. Reiter. Secure Agreement Protocols: Reliable and Atomic Group Multicast in Rampart. *Proceedings of the 2nd ACM Conference on Computer and Communications Security*, 68–80, Fairfax, Va., November 1994.

[66] S. Ritchie. Systems Programming in Java. *IEEE Micro*, 17(3):30–35, May/June 1997.

[67] R. L. Rivest. The MD5 Message-Digest Algorithm. Request for Comments (RFC) 1321, Internet Engineering Task Force, April 1992.

[68] R. L. Rivest, A. Shamir, and L. Adleman. A Method for Obtaining Digital Signatures and Public-Key Cryptosystems. *Communications of the ACM*, 21(2):120–126, February 1978.

[69] J. H. Saltzer. Protection and the Control of Information Sharing in Multics. *Communications of the ACM*, 17(7):388–402, July 1974.

[70] J. H. Saltzer and M. D. Schroeder. The Protection of Information in Computer Systems. *Proceedings of the IEEE*, 63(9):1278–1308, September 1975.

[71] V. Samar and C. Lai. Making Login Services Independent from Authentication Technologies. *Proceedings of the SunSoft Developer's Conference*, March 1996.

[72] R. S. Sandhu. The Typed Access Matrix Model. *Proceedings of the IEEE Symposium on Research in Security and Privacy*, 122–136, Oakland, Calif., May 1992.

[73] F. B. Schneider. Implementing Fault-Tolerant Services Using the State-Machine Approach: A Tutorial. *ACM Computing Surveys*, 22(4):299–319, December 1990.

[74] B. Schneier. *Applied Cryptography*. John Wiley & Sons, New York, 1994.

[75] M. D. Schroeder. *Cooperation of Mutually Suspicious Subsystems in a Computer Utility*. Ph.D. dissertation, Massachusetts Institute of Technology, Cambridge, Mass., September 1972.

[76] M. I. Seltzer, Y. Endo, C. Small, and K. A. Smith. Dealing with Disaster: Surviving Misbehaved Kernel Extensions. *Proceedings of the 2nd USENIX Symposium on Operating Systems Design and Implementation*, 213–227, Seattle, Wash., October 1996. Published as *ACM Operating Systems Review*, 30, special winter issue, 1996.

[77] A. Shamir. How to Share a Secret. *Communications of the ACM*, 22(11):612–613, November 1979.

[78] L. van Doorn, M. Abadi, M. Burrows, and E. Wobber. Secure Network Objects. *Proceedings of the IEEE Symposium in Security and Privacy*, 211–221, Oakland, Calif., May 1996.

[79] D. S. Wallach, D. Balfanz, D. Dean, and E. W. Felten. Extensible Security Architectures for Java. *Proceedings of the 16th ACM Symposium on Operating Systems Principles*, 116–128, Saint-Malo, France, October 1997.

[80] M. V. Wilkes. *Time-Sharing Computer Systems*. MacDonald, London, 1968.

[81] W. A. Wulf, R. Levin, and S. P. Harbison. *HYDRA/C.mmp—An Experimental Computer System*, McGraw-Hill, New York, 1981.

[82] F. Yellin. Low Level Security in Java. *Proceedings of the 4th International World Wide Web Conference*, Boston, Mass., December 1995.

Index

The Addison-Wesley Java™ Series

Ken Arnold · James Gosling

The Java™ Programming Language
Second Edition

ISBN 0-201-31006-6

Mary Campione · Kathy Walrath

The Java™ Tutorial
Second Edition
Object-Oriented Programming for the Internet

ISBN 0-201-31007-4

Campione · Walrath · Huml · Tutorial Team

The Java™ Tutorial Continued
The Rest of the JDK™

ISBN 0-201-48558-3

Patrick Chan

The **Java™ Developers ALMANAC** 1999

ISBN 0-201-43298-6

Patrick Chan · Rosanna Lee

The Java™ Class Libraries
Second Edition, Volume 2
java.applet java.awt java.beans

ISBN 0-201-31003-1

Patrick Chan · Rosanna Lee · Douglas Kramer

The Java™ Class Libraries
Second Edition, Volume 1
java.io java.lang java.math
java.net java.text java.util

ISBN 0-201-31002-3

Patrick Chan · Rosanna Lee · Douglas Kramer

The Java™ Class Libraries
Second Edition, Volume 1
Supplement for the Java 2 Platform
Standard Edition v1.2

ISBN 0-201-48552-4

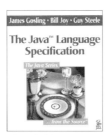

James Gosling · Bill Joy · Guy Steele

The Java™ Language Specification

ISBN 0-201-63451-1

James Gosling · Frank Yellin · The Java Team

The Java™ **Application Programming Interface, Volume 1**
Core Packages

ISBN 0-201-63453-8

James Gosling · Frank Yellin · The Java Team

The Java™ **Application Programming Interface, Volume 2**
Window Toolkit and Applets

ISBN 0-201-63459-7

Li Gong

Inside the Java™ 2 Platform Security Architecture
Cryptography, APIs, and Implementations

ISBN 0-201-31000-7

Jonni Kanerva

The Java™ FAQ

ISBN 0-201-63456-2

Doug Lea

Concurrent Programming in Java™
Design Principles and Patterns

ISBN 0-201-69581-2

Sheng Liang

The Java™ Native Interface
Programmer's Guide and Specification

ISBN 0-201-32577-2

Tim Lindholm · Frank Yellin

The Java™ Virtual Machine Specification
Second Edition

ISBN 0-201-43294-3

Henry Sowizral · Kevin Rushforth · Michael Deering

The Java™ 3D API Specification

ISBN 0-201-32576-4

Kathy Walrath · Mary Campione

The JFC™ Swing Tutorial
A Guide to Constructing GUIs

ISBN 0-201-43321-4

White · Fisher · Cattell · Hamilton · Hapner

JDBC™ API Tutorial and Reference, Second Edition
Universal Data Access for the Java™ 2 Platform

ISBN 0-201-43328-1

Please see our web site (http://www.awl.com/cseng/javaseries)
for more information on these titles.

Addison-Wesley Computer and Engineering Publishing Group

How to Interact with Us

1. Visit our Web site

http://www.awl.com/cseng

When you think you've read enough, there's always more content for you at Addison-Wesley's web site. Our web site contains a directory of complete product information including:

- Chapters
- Exclusive author interviews
- Links to authors' pages
- Tables of contents
- Source code

You can also discover what tradeshows and conferences Addison-Wesley will be attending, read what others are saying about our titles, and find out where and when you can meet our authors and have them sign your book.

2. Subscribe to Our Email Mailing Lists

Subscribe to our electronic mailing lists and be the first to know when new books are publishing. Here's how it works: Sign up for our electronic mailing at **http://www.awl.com/cseng/mailinglists.html**. Just select the subject areas that interest you and you will receive notification via email when we publish a book in that area.

3. Contact Us via Email

cepubprof@awl.com
Ask general questions about our books.
Sign up for our electronic mailing lists.
Submit corrections for our web site.

bexpress@awl.com
Request an Addison-Wesley catalog.
Get answers to questions regarding
your order or our products.

innovations@awl.com
Request a current Innovations Newsletter.

webmaster@awl.com
Send comments about our web site.

mikeh@awl.com
Submit a book proposal.
Send errata for an Addison-Wesley book.

cepubpublicity@awl.com
Request a review copy for a member of the media
interested in reviewing new Addison-Wesley titles.

We encourage you to patronize the many fine retailers who stock Addison-Wesley titles. Visit our online directory to find stores near you or visit our online store: **http://store.awl.com/** or call **800-824-7799**.

Addison Wesley Longman
Computer and Engineering Publishing Group
One Jacob Way, Reading, Massachusetts 01867 USA
TEL 781-944-3700 • FAX 781-942-3076